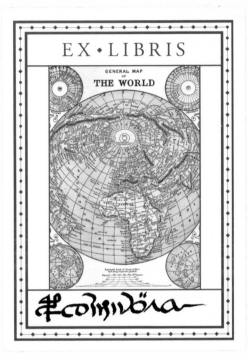

EX · LIBRIS

GENERAL MAP
OF
THE WORLD

Consulting

Consulting

The Complete Guide to a Profitable Career

REVISED EDITION

ROBERT E. KELLEY

CHARLES SCRIBNER'S SONS

NEW YORK

Charles Scribner's Sons
Macmillan Publishing Company
866 Third Avenue, New York, NY 10022
Collier Macmillan Canada, Inc.

Library of Congress Cataloging-in-Publication Data

Kelley, Robert Earl.
    Consulting : the complete guide to a profitable career.
        Revised Edition.

    Includes bibliographical references and index.
    1. Consultants.   I. Title.
HD69.C6K45   1986   658.4'6'02373   86-3912
ISBN 0-684-18617-9

Macmillan books are available at special discounts for bulk purchases for sales promotions, premiums, fund-raising, or educational use. For details, contact:

Special Sales Director
Macmillan Publishing Company
866 Third Avenue
New York, NY 10022

1 2 3 4 5 6 7 8 9 10

Printed in the United States of America

Revised Edition

Designed by Mina Greenstein

Contents

Acknowledgments

Several individuals influenced this book, and I want to thank them publicly.

Caren Mathis, my colleague, interrupted her own writing to discuss, critique, and edit the book. Through her keen observations and her writing skills, she contributed the most to my logic, writing style, and final product.

Drs. Arthur Turner of the Harvard Business School, Jack Hautaluoma of Colorado State University, and Chuck Neidt, acting president, Colorado State University, shaped my interest in and contributed to my thinking about consulting. Each gave freely of his time, experience, and encouragement.

Carol Mann, my agent, and Susanne Kirk, my editor at Scribners, both facilitated the writing through their professional conduct and personal encouragement.

Jonathan Plotkin and Angee Brown helped type and distribute initial drafts and outlines. They both made my getting started easier and funnier. Jonathan made his professional illustrations readily available.

Audrey Leo, my friend and secretary, encouraged me throughout the project. She graciously supervised the production of original drafts.

Dr. Don Parker, dean of Portland State University's School of Business, and Dr. Grover Rodich, chairman of the Management Department, both supported my efforts.

Jeff Timmons, Leonard Smollen, and Alex Dingee gave me permission to adapt material from *New Venture Creation* (Richard D. Irwin, Inc., 1977). I appreciate their courtesy and heartily recommend their book.

I also acknowledge Brian Smith's willingness to allow my adaptation of his material.

LaVerna Green typed the manuscript in final form.

As always, my family deserves unqualified credit for my work.

Finally, I thank all the consultants, consulting firms, consulting associations, and clients who freely provided the information upon which this book is based.

Acknowledgments to Second Edition

Since the release of the first edition, numerous people have contributed directly and indirectly to this current edition.

Pat Kent Chew inspired me to consider a revised edition. She helped me see its value and the improvements it needed. She also provided the time and environment required for a revision. Most important, she has improved my thinking, deepened my empathy for the client's situation, and enabled me to sell better my ideas and recommendations.

Syed Z. Shariq provided material and critiqued portions of the revision. Also, his thinking contributed significantly to the new Chapter 7 on marketing and pricing. Finally, working with him as a consulting colleague has enriched my understanding of the consulting process and broadened my capacity for creative recommendations.

Michelle Wilcox was an integral member of a consulting team (along with Syed Shariq and Ian Wilson) in which we pushed back the limits of creativity and worked on the leading edge of the consulting industry. She contributed to the study mentioned in Chapter 7 regarding the shifts in the consulting profession. She is also living proof that a consultant's true ability can be diminished or heightened by the consulting firm for which one works.

Don Green is one of the most energetic consultants with whom I have had the pleasure of working. He is a quick thinker and a fast learner who is able to cut through the red tape. Unlike many consultants of partner status, Don is always willing to dig in, doing grunt work as well as glamour work. He reinforced my findings that true professionals are intellectually honest with themselves and clients, give more than a day's work for a day's pay, and have fun throughout the project.

Stuart and Ellen Mechlin have constantly supported my work. They supply new ideas and provide real-life examples. They stretch my thinking by being formidable but caring critics. Their home has been a source of both inspiration and refuge on more than one occasion.

SRI International has been a storehouse of colleagues and learning. Steve Waldhorn and Paul Laudicina are role models of how to manage consultants and gold-collar workers. I am indebted to many colleagues for the opportunity to learn from and with them.

Once again, Susanne Kirk, my editor, and Carol Mann, my agent, facilitated this edition through their professional assistance. My lecture agents at the Leigh Bureau have also been very helpful.

Addison-Wesley gave permission to adapt material from my book *The Gold-Collar Worker: Harnessing the Brainpower of the New Work Force* (Reading, Mass: Addison-Wesley, 1985). I appreciate this courtesy.

My family continues to support my work and deserves credit for its inception and continuation.

Finally, my clients in the last five years and my consulting colleagues deserve a round of applause. This book is possible only because they provided information and contributed to my deeper understanding of the profession.

Introduction

The next best thing to knowing something is knowing where to find it.
SAMUEL JOHNSON

The consulting industry, like many industries, is undergoing a change. Traditional large firms have suffered setbacks in the last five to seven years, losing major clients and top-level staff. Their growth has been modest and, in some cases, has dropped significantly. Simultaneously, newer firms have made a big splash in the field, introducing new concepts and approaches. Their growth signifies that consulting remains a lucrative, growth industry for those who are able to innovate for their clients' benefit. Finally, consulting continues to be a productive outlet for thousands of solo practitioners who choose this profession over a nine-to-five job working for someone else. The structure of the industry is evolving, as the larger firms find their dominant position eroding due to increased competition.

One now finds consultants in every field and occupation. Every economic sector is desperately in need of the new ideas and solutions that consultants provide. This demand for consultants is demonstrated in business, education, health care, labor unions, government agencies, and other nonprofit organizations. *Consulting* fills the information void on this influential, multibillion-dollar industry. It is based on a study of the consulting profession and on experience both in consulting and the training of consultants.

The book is addressed primarily to consultants and would-be consultants, and secondarily, to consumers of consulting services. It provides details on consultants, building a consulting practice, and conducting successful consulting projects. Whether consultant or consumer, this book applies to you if you fit one of the following descriptions:

- An experienced executive or technical expert dissatisfied with your job's challenge, pay, or future, you seek consulting for greater financial rewards, to stop feeling underutilized, to be your own boss, or simply to supplement your present income.
- Already a consultant, you need more knowledge to improve your consulting practice.
- You are a part-time consultant—for example, a university professor.
- You find yourself out of work. You see consulting either as a stopgap until you find employment or as a permanent career change.
- You work as an internal consultant strictly for one company. You desire to improve your current services or become an external consultant.
- An executive who frequently uses consultants, you need information to become a "knowledgeable consumer."
- Having used consultants in the past, you now ask yourself, "If they can do it, why can't I?"
- As a student in a business or professional school, you see consulting as an attractive career option.
- As an outsider, you want access to the inner workings of this powerful, high-priced glamour industry.

Consultants exist in every field: business, education, medicine, government, social service, military, and finance. Consulting firms vary in size from one person to over a thousand consultants. Consultants are men, women, and, in some cases, even children. Consultants charge as little as nothing to as much as $3,000–$4,000 a day. Consultants work full-time, part-time, and in-between-times. Some consultants work in many industries. Others consult solely in one industry. Some consultants possess technical knowledge in one particular field; others have acquired a broad range of knowledge across many fields.

This book examines consulting exhaustively. If you are a consultant or would-be consultant, you will find answers to many vital questions: how to set your fees, how to find clients, and how to formulate recommendations. For the consumer, insight is provided into consulting practices. By understanding how consultants work, you will know how to use them and benefit from them.

Consulting is organized to reflect a typical consulting practice. The chapters parallel a consultant's experience from securing a client to managing an office. You will assess your consulting potential in Chapter 2. In Chapters 3 through 8 you will establish your consulting practice. The final chapters, Chapters 9 through 16, teach you how to conduct a consulting assignment. At the end of each chapter, you will find selected references for further study.

Although each chapter can stand alone, each serves as a foundation for the following chapters. If you know little or nothing about consulting, you should read the chapters sequentially to increase your understanding of the consulting process. If you are familiar with consulting, you may want to select chapters of particular interest.

Two approaches are used: task and process. The task approach outlines the specific steps that consultants follow during a project. For example, early in the project the consultant interviews client personnel. The process approach specifies the human and organizational factors that influence the task. For example, how you conduct the interview will influence its outcome. Consequently, you are instructed as to *what* to do and *how* to do it. This knowledge increases your effectiveness and satisfaction as a consultant or client.

Unfortunately, jargon pervades consulting and perpetuates consulting's mystique. In this book jargon has been translated into lay language. For example, consultants refer to client projects as "engagements"; here the term "assignment" or "project" is interchanged.

This book will help both consultants and consumers make the consulting experience more successful and satisfying. Consultants are addressed in the text only as a grammatical convenience. Employers of consultants will obtain the same valuable insights by seeing the consultant's viewpoint.

Consulting

Mapping the Consulting Business

1

If you don't know where you're going, any path will get you there.
ANONYMOUS

The consulting industry has lost some of its mystique but little of its appeal in the last ten years. More and more people enter the field as a means to utilize their valuable brainpower, expertise, and experience. Consulting is now an acceptable career path for individuals at any point in their careers. Between 20 to 25 percent of MBA graduates from the leading schools choose consulting for their first job. Harvard MBAs lead the pack with 31 percent of the 1985 class opting for consulting positions. At the other end of the spectrum, retirees between the ages of 45 (for 20-year government retirees) and 70 are adding to the consulting ranks. After successful industry careers, these consultants contribute their experience and wisdom to the benefit of clients. They also extend their productive working lives via consulting rather than total retirement. In between these two groups are the mid-career consultants. These people choose consulting after obtaining some job and industry experience. They enter the field as a next step in their career development. The field offers them an opportunity to gain experience working in other industries and tackling a wide range of problem situations.

These full-time consultants are joined by hundreds of thousands of part-time consultants who are looking for an alternative outlet for their skills. They work full-time jobs but want the satisfaction and compensation that come from consulting work. Their numbers are often overlooked by researchers and writers of the consulting profession. Yet, they are a vibrant and vital component of the industry.

All these consultants are part of the new breed of worker described in my book *The Gold-Collar Worker.** What they offer to the marketplace is brainpower. They are able to handle complex, unique problems that require expertise and creativity. They know that they can make valuable contributions to their clients. They also know that consulting provides them an opportunity for higher compensation than most other professions. Gold-Collar consultants are not only talented but also hold new attitudes about their talents and careers. They view themselves as their own best investment. As assets, they list their knowledge, training, and work experience. Their goal is to make those assets appreciate rather than depreciate. They see consulting as an opportunity to get the best return on their assets.

With the influx of people into consulting, there is a greater need for information about how to enter and succeed in consulting. Aspiring consultants need to know whether the profession is right for them. If the answer is yes, then they often ask how consultants find clients or whether they need an office or how to charge for their services. These questions are addressed specifically in this book. In this chapter, you will learn about the industry and the reasons consultants are used.

The Consulting Industry Continues to Grow

Consulting as a total industry is difficult to calculate now that it is a part of every field. A U.S. government report estimates that business consulting will exceed $34.6 billion in 1986.† However, its definition of business consulting is rather narrow, only including management and administrative services, public relations, management consulting, economic and sociological research, and unnamed "other" consulting services. This definition does not include the $1.5 billion in management consulting provided by accounting firms; nor does it include engineering consulting, technical computer consult-

* *The Gold-Collar Worker: Harnessing the Brainpower of the New Workforce.* Reading, Mass.: Addison-Wesley, 1985.
 † *1986 U.S. Industrial Outlook,* U.S. Department of Commerce, January 1986.

ing, architectural consulting, or any of the consulting done in all of the other occupations. Nor do these numbers include the enormous amount of part-time consulting that occurs but is not reported to government agencies. It is probably safe to assume that total consulting revenues are at least double that reported for business consulting or approximately $70 billion.

Approximately 550,000 people make a living as business consultants according to the report. If an equal number do consulting outside that definition, the total number of full-time consultants is over 1,000,000—a little less than 1 percent of the workforce. The number of part-time consultants is unknown, although they reportedly equal or double the number of full-time consultants. Thus, it is highly possible that 2 to 3 percent of the working population engages in consulting in one way or another.

Consulting is no longer dominated by a few large firms. Many new firms and solo practitioners have made significant inroads into the large firm's market share. In addition, with almost fourteen million businesses and another one million nonprofit organizations, a tremendous market exists for consulting firms of all sizes.

During the last five years, business consulting has grown between 11.5 and 20 percent annually, marking it as a hot field. The field will continue to grow as more organizations from all sectors utilize the special expertise of these firms. Also, more professionals are expected to seek consulting positions. For example, over 16 percent of all economists are expected to work as consultants in 1990, as compared to 11 percent in 1978.

Critical to the long-term success of consulting is the positive perception that clients hold toward consultants. After struggling through the deepest and darkest recession since the 1929 depression, many executives openly acknowledge that consultants helped keep their businesses afloat. With international competition at a feverish pace and U.S. productivity in the doldrums, consultants are being called in to save the day. They are applying the leading edge thinking of their disciplines to the crucial problems of individual businesses, whole industries, and entire economic sectors. For example, the Public Policy Center of SRI International contributed significantly in helping turn around the fortunes of America's midwestern Rust Bowl in an incisive economic development study.

Consulting services that were once viewed as luxuries are now considered necessities. Public relations, market research, and human resource training are essential to the success of many firms. Services like these enable businesses to maintain their competitive edge in the face of rising competitive pressures. The use of consultants is now a normal part of business for many companies rather than a "once in the while" activity.

In addition to global competition and economic uncertainty, the Information Age has propelled the consulting profession. Increasing information needs have sparked growth opportunities for consultants who either possess or have access to the information. Getting the right information to the right people at the right time is an important role of consultants. Their knowledge and brainpower can command a steep price from an eager and needy buyer.

Technological advances have also spurred demand for consultants. New technology requires advice about its selection, purchase, and use. Prepurchase feasibility studies and postpurchase training and implementation fall to consultants who are more familiar with state-of-the-art technology advances than the average executive. Business people increasingly seek consultants to guide them through the maze of technology.

Businesses use consultants not only for their innovative brain-power but also because it makes economic sense. Consultants are a cost-efficient source of new ideas. Any firm can avoid the cost and time involved in learning a new facet of the industry. Also, in *The Gold-Collar Worker,* I identified a growing trend which I labeled "variable-cost subcontracting." This occurs when an organization does not want to incur the overhead of hiring more full-time people. Instead, they hire consultants on a part-time basis to give them greater flexibility. In this way, the business can staff-up quickly in times of fast growth and cut back if business recedes without the regulatory burdens of laying off full-time employees. For this flexibility, companies are willing to pay consultants a hefty premium.

Another reason for consulting's bright outlook is the rising interest of aspiring consultants. Many individuals who have acquired skills in a particular field are leaving to become entrepreneurs in the consulting business. They want to use their hard-earned expert knowledge in a variety of settings. In addition, they want to gain the financial and psychological rewards of being their own boss.

Social and technological changes continue to ease entry into consulting. Personal computers make it more practical for consultants to work at home. With over fifty thousand computer programs and two thousand computerized data bases to choose from, consultants are better able to stay on top of the information explosion. New and more efficient office tools, such as computer-aided design, help make consultants more productive and less expensive especially for smaller businesses. Computers also put these tools at the disposal of small businesses who could previously not afford them.

The specialization of knowledge and expertise is increasing. The gap between specialist and generalist is widening. This is a boom for consultants since businesses need both specialist consultants to solve specific difficult problems and skilled generalist consultants to help executives understand the totality and complexity of the big picture.

All of these factors combined point to a positive picture for the consulting industry. The previously mentioned U.S. government report indicates that consulting services will continue to outpace total economic growth by a wide margin. Moreover, it will remain one of the fastest growing sectors of the U.S. economy.

Consulting and the Economy

As depicted in Table 1, consulting is almost immune to economic changes. Phil Shay, the former executive director of the Association of Consulting Management Engineers (ACME), described this relationship in his article "Origins of Consulting."* During periods of strong growth and inflation, organizations have money to spend. They seek consultants for two reasons: they can afford the consultants, and consultants can advise them how to spend their money effectively. During a recession, organizations turn to consultants for advice on how to cut costs, save money, and weather the economic storm.

War has always promoted consulting. In wartime, the United

TABLE 1.   The Relationship Between Economy and Consulting

Economy	Consulting
Strong Growth	Fair
Inflation	Good
Recession	Good
War	Good
Depression	Bad
Uncertainty	Great

* Unpublished ms., ACME, 1975, pp. 1–16.

States traditionally turns to its experts for assistance, sparing no expense. Through cost-plus-expense contracts, the government discourages businesses from showing excess profit during wartime. Consequently, businesses use consultants as an added expense that the government pays for either through the contract or by tax deductions. In either case, both consultants and companies benefit.

Depressions negatively affect everyone. Consultants can find sufficient work during depressions, either in salvaging bankrupt businesses or in reconstructing damaged ones; however, obtaining payment becomes a major problem.

In times of economic uncertainty, the outlook for consulting shines. Uncertainty produces anxiety. Anxious people turn to experts to solve their problems and to help them predict the future. Consequently, consultants prosper during these uncertain periods.

Types of Consultants

Consultants come in all shapes, sizes, and industries; however, they usually fall into one of the following eleven classifications.

    1. Large firms employing more than fifty consultants. Arthur D. Little of Cambridge, Massachusetts, heads this group with 1985 sales of $232 million. National and international in scope, these firms usually have four pyramid-like levels of consultants as illustrated in the diagram below.

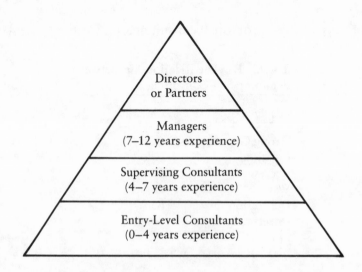

2. Medium-sized firms employing between ten and fifty consultants. Usually regional in scope, these firms have the same staff levels as the larger firms.
3. Small firms employing two to ten consultants. *Venture* estimates that 20–25 percent of all consultants work in firms of this size.
4. Individual practitioners. *Venture* estimates that more than half of all consulting firms are one-person operations.
5. Management advisory divisions of Certified Public Accounting (CPA) firms. CPA firms are major players in the consulting business. The U.S. government estimates that CPA firms produce over $1.5 billion in consulting revenues. Using their ongoing audit and tax relationships, CPA firms have an inside track on many consulting projects. Seven of the "Big Eight" CPA firms place among the top twenty U.S. consulting firms. Twenty years ago, no CPA firms were on the list.
6. Professionals (CPAs, lawyers, engineers, etc.) who also do some consulting. During the course of providing their regular services to clients, these professionals occasionally consult in other areas of expertise.
7. Internal consultants. These consultants, unlike externals who work with many unrelated organizations, work with only one company's divisions, subsidiaries, and new acquisitions. They currently number over 1,000.
8. University-affiliated consultants. These academic specialists usually consult part-time to supplement both their classroom material and their incomes.
9. Research firms, which may be profit or nonprofit, sometimes engage in consulting as a result of their research findings.
10. Public agency consultants, such as the General Accounting Office (GAO) and the Service Corps of Retired Executives (SCORE), provide consulting both to businesses and to other government agencies.
11. Individuals in between jobs.

Carl Sloane, President of Temple, Barker, Sloane and former president of ACME, provides the following breakdown of the management consulting industry.*

* Carl Sloane, "The State of Management Consulting; Retrospective and Prospective," presented to the Institute of Management Consultants, 1985.

Firm Size	Number of Firms
$100 mm +	7
$25 mm +	25
$5 mm +	40–50
$1 mm +	80–100
< $1 mm +	Hundreds
Individuals	Thousands

Sloane lists the seven largest firms with revenues over $100 million as Arthur Anderson; Booz-Allen and Hamilton; McKinsey and Company; Arthur D. Little; Towers, Perrin, Forster, and Crosby; William M. Mercer; and Peat Marwick Mitchell.

Researchers Danielle Nees and Larry Greiner characterize consultants by their orientation rather than their size or origins.* They identify five distinct types of consulting firms. Each has its own characteristics, determined by the staff, the value brought to clients, and the way the firm conducts assignments. These five types are:

1. *Mental adventurers.* These are the "think tank" consultants, like Arthur D. Little, SRI (formerly Stanford Research Institute), Rand Corporation, and Battelle. They enjoy working on complex problems and extending the frontiers of knowledge. Projects are often interdisciplinary in nature with a strong bias toward a rigorous research methodology. The mental adventurers are more interested in substance and quality of thought than organizational politics or slick presentations. They come primarily from scientific and technological backgrounds.

2. *Strategic navigators.* These are the quantitative analysts who help companies understand their marketplace, competition, and future direction. Firms such as the Boston Consulting Group use conceptual models and analytic tools from economics, marketing, and finance to help guide a client's decision about growth, acquisition, and divestment. These companies are heavily populated with young bright M.B.A.s who make up for their lack of business experience with brainpower and hard work.

3. *Management physicians.* Consultants of this type focus on the internal workings of the client's organizational structures, culture,

---

* Danielle B. Nees and Larry E. Greiner, "Seeing Behind the Look-Alike Management Consultants," *Organizational Dynamics,* Winter 1985, pp. 68–79.

systems, and procedures. Unlike the more external focus of the previous two types, management physicians approach client problems
much as an internist would. They work closely with their clients on
a day-to-day basis, which requires interpersonal skills and an interest
in implementation. They have often been referred to as "country
club" consultants because of their approach and the style of their
staff. It is not unusual for firms like McKinsey and Company to have
long-term doctor–patient relationships with their clients.

4. *System architects.*   These consultants pick a narrow systems
problem that requires a specialized technical solution. They might
specialize in computer systems, personnel systems, or transportation
systems. Firms like Booz-Allen and Hamilton or Arthur Anderson
tend to be experts in a single subject, and apply their knowledge by
installing a system that clients can see and use. Very often, they tailor
off-the-shelf systems that they have standardized over hundreds of
projects. These firms tend to attract detail-oriented people who
sometimes lose track of the bigger picture.

5. *Friendly copilots.*   Consultants in this category are the intimate
advisors of presidents and chief executive officers. Generally, they are
older and have considerable business experience. Clients seek them
out because of their judgment and empathy with the client's position.
These consultants most often act as sounding boards for the CEO to
bounce off ideas and sensitive topics. Sometimes referred to as "executive hand-holders," these consultants are generalists. When necessary, they help their clients obtain specialized assistance from the
other four types of consultants.

Nees and Greiner suggest that consultants try to understand what
their characteristics are and how they match the needs of the client.
Rather than trying to be all things to all people, the authors suggest
that consultants work only on projects consistent with their nature.

Who Uses Consultants

Past-President of the Association of Internal Management Consultants Ferdie Setaro has written that clients ask consultants either to
think for them, to help them think, or to help them improve their
thinking processes. Professor Arthur Turner of the Harvard Business

School has made a similar point when describing a consultant's role. Professor Turner distinguishes two types of consultants: those who emphasize their problem-solving ability, and those who emphasize client achievement and client learning of effective performance.

These distinctions help us understand why clients use consultants. When clients hire you because they have neither the time nor the personnel to do the project, then the clients are requesting your problem-solving services. When clients cannot do something because they lack the necessary knowledge, then they are requesting your problem-solving services. My interviews with many consultants and clients indicate that consultants seldom do more than solve problems, although Professor Turner's second category is a desirable outcome of consulting. For efficiency, clients hire consultants' needed expertise rather than learning it themselves.

Given this general backdrop, opportunities for consultants come from the following types of clients:

Clients who need extra help for a period of time.   In essence, consultants help clients do their work by supplementing skills the clients already possess. The size and nature of the personnel system in the United States discourages hiring employees and encourages hiring consultants. Locating good full-time specialists requires six to twelve months. The company absorbs 100 percent of an employee's first-year salary in recruitment and training. Full-time hiring involves approvals, increasing red tape, and growing government regulations. Available and accessible, consultants minimize selection time, orientation and training time, and job-negotiation time. Because the legal standing and role expectations for consultants differ from those of full-time employees, clients can avoid much red tape and government regulation. As a result, clients increasingly turn to consultants as a source of labor.

Clients who need specialized expertise unavailable within the organization.   This category represents the most common type of consultant: the expert hired to solve difficult problems. Small and medium-sized clients offer the greatest opportunities for this brand of consulting. Unlike large organizations, they cannot afford a full-time staff of experts and must rely on consultants.

Clients who cannot or will not find out what to do from an insider.   Clients in large organizations most frequently use consultants for political, organizational, and personal reasons. Politically, clients trying to "save face," by not showing their lack of knowledge to internal colleagues, will turn to an outside consultant. To "snub" inside competitors, clients may resort to outside experts. Clients may want "to keep up with the Joneses" by matching their use of consultants with that of their peers. Clients may have confidential information that they do not want "leaked" inside the organization. For example, premature "leaks" can destroy potential mergers or acquisitions. Consequently, clients may entrust this information to an outside consultant not tied to the internal grapevine.

The structure of large organizations turns a client to outside consultants. In many large and complex businesses, employees do not know if the expertise they need exists internally. An informal survey of chief executive officers (CEOs) substantiates this phenomenon. Many CEOs are unaware of internal consultants working full-time for their organizations. As a result, they turn to outsiders. Large bureaucracies make access to needed expertise difficult. Reluctantly, the client finds it more efficient to work directly with outside consultants. Personal reasons also promote the use of outside consultants. A client may find work easier with an external consultant than an inside expert.

Clients who need an outsider's evaluation of their company's performance, plans, decisions, or internal conflicts.   Consultants provide an "appearance" of objectivity, thoroughness, and competence to the public, the stockholders, or the Securities Exchange Commission. Consultants add credibility to a client's plans and bolster the confidence of the client, bosses, subordinates, and the public. Remember, however, that some clients want the appearance, but not the existence, of objectivity. They seek consultants who will approve their preconceived plans for reorganizations or new capital expenditures.

Clients who need someone to take the "political heat" in sensitive areas.   Some clients hire consultants to do their dirty work, such as firing a subordinate. This maintains the client's "nice guy" image. The consultant makes an easy scapegoat who does not remain after the assignment. In some situations, such as a heated conflict between two top managers, only an external consultant can defuse the potential explosion. Many organizational development consultants earn their living by "taking the heat." Their neutral stance helps clients resolve organizational dilemmas.

Clients who need someone to rescue them from losing their jobs or ruining their careers.   Some clients painfully experience the Peter Principle by rising to the level of their incompetence. Rather than muddle their chances for continued success, these clients call in consultants to help them out of their predicament.

Clients who experience "sudden availability" of funds.   Many government agencies save their budgets until the last half of the fiscal year. Rather than return the excess and experience a budget cut for the next year, they prefer to spend it. Industry sources estimate that 75 percent of the $9.4 million governmental consulting occurs between May and October.

New markets provide another source of funds for clients. One such new market is compliance legislation, for which companies are forced to lay out funds. In fact, business spends over $1 billion annually to comply with more than 55,000 pages of government regulations printed each year. Since many companies are unprepared for compliance, consultants fill this gap.

Another source of new markets results from social and economic changes. The energy crisis spawned a tremendous demand for consultants in transportation efficiency and energy conservation. Watch new trends so that you are ready, able, and available to capitalize on these new opportunities.

Clients who need stimulation or specialized training.   Consultants often serve as catalysts for organizations that need a shot in the arm. Clients will use consultants to revitalize employee thinking, to keep them on the edge of new practices, and to develop their employees' working effectiveness.

Clients who are going bankrupt and have nothing to lose by calling in a consultant.   Many clients know they are failing and can only benefit from using consultants. If the consultant helps them, they save their investment. If they go under, they don't worry about paying the consultant. Needless to say, this is a high-risk position for the consultant.

The Changing Consulting Industry

Since the first edition of this book, I conducted a study to determine how the consulting industry of the 1980s and 1990s differs from the industry during the 1960s and 1970s. As part of this study, chief executive officers (CEOs) of major U.S. service and manufacturing companies that regularly buy consulting services were surveyed to identify their projected needs and expectations over the next two to ten years. A major finding of the study was that clients' expectations had changed dramatically. After 20 years of using consultants, clients had become much more sophisticated about what consultants can do and how to use consultants to the clients' advantage. Although clients with little experience with consultants still favor the generalist, experienced clients want specialists. They look for specialized skills and information to solve specific company problems. As one CEO said, "I don't want a consultant to tell me what my industry will be like in ten years. The consultant should be able to tell me what my company must do in today's market to survive and be competitive ten years from now." Consequently, clients select one consultant over another based on perceived expertise in the specific area of need. These CEOs desire consultants who know their field so well that the consultant represents 90 percent of the solution just by walking in the door. For consultants or firms to succeed in the 1990s, they must be recognized *by clients* as the most expert in their arena.

Clients also seek answers, not methodologies, from consultants. Clients assume that reputable consultants have a good structured process for approaching problems. They are more concerned that the process will lead the consultants to answers that the clients need.

These changed expectations have altered the traditional client–consultant relationship. Clients are moving away from reliance on only one consulting firm. Instead, they are developing a reserve of consultants with different specialties, allowing new specialized consultants to emerge and prosper. Understandably, the number of solo practitioners and small firms grew at an annual rate of 20 percent from 1979 to 1984, while the larger generalist firms held steady or dropped in size during the economic downturn of the early 1980s. As clients' needs become more specialized, as the world becomes more complex, and as clients look to more than one consultant for answers, the opportunities for consultants will continue to grow.

Consulting is a growing, exciting industry that prospers in most economic conditions. The demand for consultants continues to rise, creating new opportunities in every field. You will find employment opportunities in a consulting firm or in your own consulting practice. In any case, consulting offers you career advancement and financial rewards. To evaluate your consulting potential, turn to Chapter 2.

Does Consulting Suit You?

2

*We are told that talent creates its own opportunities. But it sometimes
seems that intense desire creates not only its own opportunities, but its
own talents.*
ERIC HOFFER

In this chapter you will evaluate your potential as a consultant. A
consultant's job is different from most white-collar jobs. It requires
skills applied under difficult working conditions. As a result, consulting is not for everyone. Upon completing this chapter, you will know
if you are suited for consulting.

Self-Assessment Exercises

These exercises will demonstrate whether consulting is right for you.
For maximum benefit, complete the exercises before you read this
chapter. With your results in hand, then read the chapter. Compare
your results with the information provided. From the comparison,
you can judge your consulting potential. You need not complete
every exercise, some of which take a few minutes, while others require a few hours.

Each exercise approaches your consulting potential from a different angle; hence, each exercise produces different information. The

more exercises you try, the better you will be able to judge your potential. For best results, then, complete as many exercises as possible.

The purpose of each exercise is not explained before you do it, in order not to influence your answers. Follow the directions as written and finish the exercise. At the end of the exercise, what the results mean and how to use the information are explained.

Exercise 1

Outline your own autobiography. Use the following guides.

- Think of your entire lifespan: childhood, adolescence, college years, and work years. Include summers, weekends, and holidays.
- If your life were a road, what would the twists and turns be? Point out the hills, valleys, bumps, scenic spots, and rough sections.
- Consider all aspects of your life, not simply work. Include your avocations, family, and so on.
- Focus on what you have done in your jobs as well as their titles.
- Notice what you enjoyed and what you disliked about what you did. How did the activity, the location, the people, and your life circumstances affect your satisfaction?
- Who are the people who affected your life for good or bad? Are they still influencing your life?
- Dwell on the turning points in your life. What options were available at each change point? What are your feelings now concerning the discarded options or the paths not taken?
- For the options you chose, what reasons led you to make the choice you did? List both the "official" or socially acceptable reasons and the "real reasons." Were these reasons yours or other people's?
- What pleasant surprises did you find and what disillusionments did you suffer? Were your expectations met at each turning point? Why or why not? Could you have known the eventual results beforehand?

Project your life into the future.

- Where is it currently headed—personally, socially, spiritually, in terms of family and career?

- What twists and turns can you foresee? What major decisions are on the horizon? What do you expect to be the outcome of these choices? How will they change your life?
- Before you die, what do you want to accomplish and what do you want to happen?
- What future would be ideal? Try to dream up three or four "happy endings" to your life.

Look back over what you have written. Chances are that certain repetitions have occurred. These repetitions represent themes or patterns in your life. Identify these patterns and reflect on them for a while. Are you pleased or displeased with the patterns? While reviewing your autobiography, create two lists:

- Aspects of your past experience you want to include in your future career.
- Aspects of your past experience you want to exclude in your future career.

Now rank each list in order of importance to you. These lists will give you a personal reference point with which to view the remaining exercises in this chapter. As you discover more about yourself and the consulting world, refer to these lists. They will help you determine if consulting is the right job for you.

Exercise 2

DIRECTIONS: Rate how satisfying each of the following qualities is in the work you do.

1 = Satisfying   0 = Neutral   −1 = Dissatisfying

_____ 1) Creating or contributing new ideas.
_____ 2) Communicating in many forms (verbal, written, etc.) with various people.
_____ 3) Advising rather than directing others.
_____ 4) Taking initiative to both start and complete tasks.
_____ 5) Working in new and different locations on a regular basis.
_____ 6) Utilizing positive interpersonal skills to accomplish tasks.

_____ 7) Having little job security.

_____ 8) Inspiring confidence in your judgments.

_____ 9) Not doing the same things all the time.

_____ 10) Managing people, projects, and paperwork on a regular basis.

_____ 11) Being respected by others.

_____ 12) Finding yourself in ambiguous, undefined relationships.

_____ 13) Meeting new people and new situations.

_____ 14) Possessing an expertise in a specific area.

_____ 15) Opportunity for high economic return.

_____ 16) Listening continually and sincerely to others' verbal and nonverbal messages.

_____ 17) Working best without supervision.

_____ 18) Having credibility as a result of expertise, experience, or credentials.

_____ 19) Having to keep solving new problems.

_____ 20) Learning new ideas and applying them.

_____ 21) Constant travel which requires prolonged periods away from home.

_____ 22) Feeling you have helped other people.

_____ 23) Holding strong ethical values concerning the conduct of your work.

_____ 24) Seeing your ideas rejected or not implemented.

_____ 25) Working alone for the most part.

_____ 26) Selling your services to others.

_____ 27) Working long and hard hours until project is completed.

_____ 28) Engaging in self-reflection in order to learn from experience.

_____ 29) Being responsible for the quality and usefulness of your work.

_____ 30) Understanding and utilizing organizational dynamics.

Total your score. A score of 16 to 30 indicates that you fit well with the major requirements of consulting. You might enjoy owning your own firm. 0 to 15 indicates a moderate suitability to consulting. Working for a consulting firm might suit you. -1 to -30 indicates a poor fit with consulting.

*Exercise 3 **

Interview the following people and, if possible, a member of their family:

- a consultant who operates his or her own consulting firm
- a consultant who works for a small consulting firm
- a partner or principal in a large consulting firm
- a consultant who works for a large consulting firm
- a consultant who works for a CPA firm
- an internal consultant
- a consultant employed by a government agency
- someone who tried consulting and did not like it
- clients who use consultants

Each interview will require about one hour. Seek specific information and insights into the consultant's job. You should discuss the consultant's background, the risks, rewards, pitfalls, goals, and personal characteristics. Use the following questions as guides:

- What motivated this person to become a consultant?
- What particular managerial, business, or technical skills does this consultant possess? Give specific examples.
- What activities or things are most important in this consultant's life? Why? Give specific examples.
- If you had to pick one personal characteristic that made the consultant a success, what would it be?
- In what ways did this consultant's family or life situation (e.g., parents, husband, wife, children) influence his or her career decision and ability to become successful?
- What particular conflicts and serious snags did he or she face 1) when becoming a consultant, 2) after one or two years as a consultant, 3) five to six years later? Give specific examples.
- In what ways do these people feel they benefit from a consulting career? What is gained? What is lost or given up?
- Who worked with these consultants in launching their careers? What resources did they utilize (e.g., friends, business associates'

---

* Adapted from *New Venture Creation: A Guide to Small Business Development* by J. Timmons, L. Smollen, and A. Dingee. Homewood, Ill.: Richard D. Irwin, Inc., 1977. Used by permission.

consultants, libraries, professional associations, books, Small Business Administration)?

• How much time does each devote to work each week? Does business or family/social life come first? What about other personal or community activity?

After completing the interviews, compare the various consultants. For each one, list your view of outstanding individual characteristics. Identify their similarities and differences. What general principles can you draw from your observations concerning the demands and requirements of consulting? List these principles in order of importance.

Now examine your list. How do you compare to these consultants? Are you similar or dissimilar? Rate yourself on each element of the list as to how well it describes you.

Now compare your list to the lists derived from your autobiography. Do the demands and opportunities of consulting correspond to the kind of life you desire?

Exercise 4

It is often useful to obtain feedback from others, especially when you are making a major life change. Although others' perceptions of you are not entirely accurate, they provide information that you may overlook or ignore. To insure that you are not victimized by your own good opinion, distribute the lists from Exercises 1, 2, and 3 to at least five people (spouse, parents, friends, colleagues) who know you from a variety of viewpoints. Have them rate you on each list. Then compare their ratings. Are they in agreement with each other? How do you account for the differences? How do they compare with your own ratings? What do you conclude?

At this point, if you have persevered with the exercises, you have an interest in becoming a consultant. You explored data about the field and about yourself. Do not be discouraged if your research shows that consulting is not a good fit. The information gathered through the exercises is limited. You should compare both your research and your conclusions to the information presented in this chapter, since it is based on a wider sample of consultants and is probably more complete than your research. Success in consulting is not totally dependent on how well you fit the consultant mold. History is replete with examples of people who have overcome great odds to achieve success in the field of their choice. You are capable of being one of those outstanding people. The important element is knowing the obstacles and the opportunities you will face in your pursuit.

What Is Required of Successful Consultants?

Consulting is a demanding profession. Consequently, the requirements for success are also demanding. That there is little agreement as to what these actual requirements are, however, is illustrated by the following three examples.

A study by the Association of Management Consultants (AMC), "Personal Qualifications of Management Consultants," found the following attributes essential to successful consultants:

Understanding of people (human relations)
Integrity
Courage
Objectivity
Ambition
Problem-solving ability
Judgment
Ability to communicate
Psychological maturity
Good physical and mental health
Professional etiquette and courtesy
Stability of behavior and action
Self-confidence
Intellectual competence
Creative imagination

It is reasonable to expect that a person with these qualities could succeed in any profession.

A large international consulting firm separates its criteria for selecting consultants into three major categories: basic qualities, basic consulting skills, and essential knowledge. The basic qualities they seek are:

Character
Personableness—favorable appearance and personal impression
Personality—forceful,
Ambition—achiever with a zest for learning
Personal effectiveness—vigor, initiative, drive, capacity to get things done

mature, self-confident,
emotionally stable
Mental equipment—
outstanding analytical,
creative ability

Interpersonal competence—
leadership

This firm believes that with these qualities an individual can learn everything else needed to become an outstanding consultant. In particular, an aspiring consultant with these basic qualities can learn the following basic consulting skills:

Professional approach
Management fundamentals of
business or government
Interviewing and fact-
gathering

Problem-solving approaches
Effective relations with clients
Client communications and
persuasion, both oral and
written

With these basic qualities and skills as a foundation, the firm then looks for the following types of essential knowledge:

Special technical competence
in function, industry,
technique, and general
management
Superior judgment

The firm's managing
philosophy, strategy, and
policies
Caring leadership of firm
personnel
Clientele-building (holding
and attracting clients)

Given evidence of these qualities, skills, and knowledge, this firm believes its consultants will be successful. It is interesting to note, however, that only one of every six consultants hired by this firm reportedly reaches director status.

Jim Kennedy of *Consultants News* boils down the requirements of consulting to "Appearance, Brains, and Charisma." Recognizing that no one element in itself is sufficient, he developed the following formulas:

Brains + either Appearance or Charisma = Success
Brains + Appearance + Charisma = Superstar

Creating a mold for the "effective consultant" is obviously a difficult task. The criteria either end up too platitudinous or too simplistic. Neither situation helps aspiring consultants determine whether they fit consulting.

Over the past several years, I have interviewed consultants and consulting firms across the country, asking what separates successful consultants from unsuccessful consultants. Most respondents prefaced their statements with the caution that no precise formula exists. Instead, successful consultants possess a "critical mass combination" of many skills, characteristics, and information. They emphasize that many combinations lead to success in this unregulated, undefined, and growing profession.

Following this caveat, most respondents easily pinpoint the requirements of successful consultants. The results of my informal survey are summarized in the following seven categories:

1. Consulting process awareness
2. Knowledge needed
3. Skills required
4. Credibility
5. Personality
6. Code of ethics
7. Life-style

The following section explains each category in detail.

Consulting Process Awareness

The first requirement for successful consulting is understanding that consulting is a process with a sequence of stages. These stages are depicted in Table 2. Each stage has a series of tasks that must be performed. This book takes you through each stage of the consulting process. In-depth discussion of each stage will be saved for later chapters.

Important but often overlooked aspects of the consulting process are the effects of human and organizational dynamics on an assignment's outcome. In fact, understanding these dynamics was cited repeatedly as the major factor distinguishing between successful and unsuccessful consultants. Unsuccessful consultants do not understand or utilize these dynamics.

Several dynamics make an impact on consulting assignments. Both the consultant and client affect assignments through their behavior,

TABLE 2. Stages of the Consulting Process

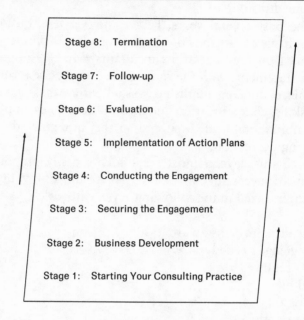

Stage 8: Termination

Stage 7: Follow-up

Stage 6: Evaluation

Stage 5: Implementation of Action Plans

Stage 4: Conducting the Engagement

Stage 3: Securing the Engagement

Stage 2: Business Development

Stage 1: Starting Your Consulting Practice

personalities, attitudes, values, preconceptions, and prior experiences. One consultant might be high-strung and action-oriented, while another might be low-key and patient. Clients who have previously used consulting services act differently from clients who are first-time users.

Groups—such as departments, unions, bowling teams, or top management—exert pressure on consulting assignments. They control or distort important information, they play politics to protect their own vested interests, and they force individual group members to conform to their viewpoint. Moreover, these groups form alliances that either support or resist the consulting project.

The organization affects the assignment through its goals, structure, technology, and communications network. A company with a policy of promoting only from within may need to change in order to obtain necessary expertise from the outside. If it does not, you can imagine the fate of the first person hired from outside the organization. Another consideration is the communications network, particularly the informal one. On my consulting assignments, most of the client's employees know about me and the project long before the top management makes a formal announcement. Depending upon the accuracy and the impact of the transmitted information, the employees greet me with either warmth or hostility. Consequently, I take time at the beginning of all assignments to discuss this phenomenon with my client so that we can utilize the various communications networks.

Environments affect the consulting assignment through changes beyond the control of individuals, groups, and organizations. New environmental demands shift the outcome of many assignments. For example, a motel located near an Air Force base experienced increased demand for accommodations. In response, the owner called in a consultant to devise an expansion plan, including rooms, restaurants, and services. The consultant devised a plan that was implemented successfully during the year. Unfortunately, six months after the expansion, the government decided to close the base.

The problem affects the consulting assignment by shaping the nature of the job. This commonly occurs when the assignment is defined in terms of symptoms or perceived problems rather than the actual problem. However, once the assignment is designed around the wrong problem, it is very difficult to change its course. For example, clients often ask for motivation training programs to counter poor morale. Many morale problems are better corrected through improved employee selection methods or new compensation programs than through motivation seminars. Redefining a goal after starting a project, however, wastes time, energy, and dollars.

Table 3 shows how these process factors affect consulting assignments. The client's problem is filtered through his or her staff. The consultant's assistance is successful only to the extent that the client and the client's staff accept it. As the assistance is filtered from consultant to client to staff, many opportunities for distortion and resistance occur. Furthermore, during this process, the various environments affect the consulting project. Consequently, the consultant must contend with these forces to insure the project's success.

Becoming aware of these forces and their dynamics is no easy task. Successful consultants realize that a client's problem does not exist in a vacuum. Instead, it arises from the client's organization with all its politics and structural levels. For example, every consulting assignment has its supporters and detractors in the client's organization. These forces influence an assignment's success more than the power of the consultant's technical solution. The same holds true for environmental factors beyond a consultant's control. Many of former President Carter's top advisors reported frustration over the influence of his family.

TABLE 3. Factors Affecting Consulting Assignments

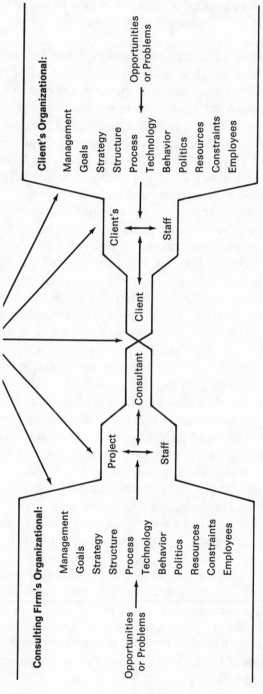

ENVIRONMENTS: Political, Business, Industry, Technical, Professional, Governmental, Cultural, Social, Geographical, Familial

Consulting Firm's Organizational:

Management
Goals
Strategy
Structure
Process
Technology
Behavior
Politics
Resources
Constraints
Employees

Opportunities or Problems → Project ↔ Staff

Consultant

Client

Client's ↔ Staff

Client's Organizational:

Management
Goals
Strategy
Structure
Process
Technology
Behavior
Politics
Resources
Constraints
Employees

→ Opportunities or Problems

The dynamics of environment and personnel not only affect the client's organization, but they also influence consulting projects through the consultant's organization. For example, a Big Eight CPA firm performed a reorganization study for a national firm located in Boise, Idaho. Its advice was to relocate the corporate headquarters to a larger city—preferably Denver—for better transportation and communication facilities. However, the partner in charge of auditing for the Boise office vetoed this recommendation. He had moved to Boise less than a year before to service this major account. If the company moved, he would either have to move again or be stuck in a minor office with no major accounts. Neither option appealed to him.

Understanding these human and organizational dynamics is important for a consultant. Succeeding chapters deal with this challenge.

Knowledge Needed

In order to consult, you must have an expertise in which to consult—the second requirement of successful consultants. As the president of a large Boston-based consulting firm remarked to me, "There are 50,000 Harvard MBAs plus several hundred thousand other MBAs from fine schools who are very intelligent and knowledgeable. The consultant must have something to offer them—something to bring to the party besides a good bedside manner."

A consultant's expertise usually results from an in-depth knowledge of a particular industry, function, or technique. One consultant specializes in the electronics industry, knowing the "ins and outs" and what leads to success in that industry. Another consultant specializes in compensation and benefits. A third consultant specializes in the technique of developing attitude surveys. More often than not, a consultant's expertise combines these three areas, such as a consultant who specializes in developing attitude surveys toward compensation in the electronics industry.

Two distinctions deserve mention here. First, consultants are either generalists or specialists. On the one hand, the specialist provides in-depth, state-of-the-art knowledge that is usually beyond the capability of most companies. For example, most companies cannot keep up with the ever-changing Equal Employment Opportunity Commission (EEOC) requirements. Consequently, EEOC consultants are in strong demand. On the other hand, a generalist provides breadth of experience for a client. A generalist normally has advanced knowledge covering several industries or all major functions and applies this experience to the client's problem. The generalist successfully transfers useful solutions from one industry or field to another. In addition, the generalist helps integrate the ever-increasing specialties. As a result, many consultants earn their living by helping clients coordinate their organizations.

The second distinction involves problem solving vs. teaching. Some consultants use their knowledge strictly to solve client problems; consequently, each time the client has a new or different problem, the consultant is called in. However, some consultants do not see themselves as problem solvers. As mentioned earlier, their specialty is improving client functioning. Their philosophy is characterized by the proverb, "Give me a fish, and I will eat for today; teach me to fish, and I will eat for the rest of my life." Hence, they are specialists of a particular type: specialists in helping clients learn.

Skills Required

As I interviewed and trained consultants across the country, I concluded that consultants seldom need help with their expert knowledge. What they fail to realize is the difference between an expert and a successful consultant. Any college student can list professors who are regarded as national experts but who cannot teach. This discrepancy also occurs in consulting. The successful consultant is one who translates his or her expert knowledge into useful applications for clients. This is the first skill required of consultants.

A second conclusion drawn from my research is that, excluding the skills required by expertise, all the other required skills apply to every type of consulting. In other words, regardless of the type of consulting you perform, the skills needed for success are the same.

These skills fall into four major categories: technical, communications, interpersonal, and administration. Continued consulting success requires competence in all four.

Technical Skills. Technical skills determine whether the consultant has something of value to offer the client, such as, in particular, the ability to apply his or her expertise to the client's problem. In addition, technical skills include the ability to find and solve problems. All too often, we view finding and solving problems as one activity. Researchers at the University of Wisconsin have found that few people are good at both. People who are good problem finders are usually not good problem solvers. Problem finding requires skill in inductive reasoning, whereas problem solving requires deductive reasoning. Few people can successfully use both reasoning processes or switch from one to the other. Consequently, consultants must develop these two reasoning skills to find and to solve their client's problems.

Problem solving leads into another aspect included under technical skills: creativity. We give much lip service to creativity. All too often, we fall into ruts, applying tried-but-tired solutions to new problems.

In his book, *Conceptual Blockbusting,** Professor James Adams of Stanford University points out that creativity requires breaking out of established patterns in order to look at things in a different way. This approach entails both generating new ideas and escaping from old ones. He views the biggest obstacle to creativity as our aversion to problems. Our natural response is to get rid of the problem by finding an answer. Most often we take the first answer that occurs to us and pursue it. We are reluctant to spend the time and mental effort required to conjure up a richer storehouse of alternatives. Unfortunately, the first solution we pursue tends to be a previously tried solution. As a result, we reinforce our own lack of creativity. Therefore, good consultants avoid habits that inhibit creativity and use methods that encourage it. They search for new ways of sensing, thinking, comprehending, learning, and accomplishing for both their own and the client's benefit.

Communication Skills. Communication skills—the ability to convey important information—is another essential requirement. Consultants communicate in a variety of forms: oral, nonverbal, written, and visual. As a matter of routine, most consultants speak with individuals, interview small groups, make audiovisual presentations to large groups, keep informal records, and submit formal written reports. M. Kubr reports in his book, *Management Consulting,* that 70 percent of consulting assignment time is spent in communicating with others. Listening consumes 45 percent of this total

* Third Edition, Reading, Mass.: Addison-Wesley, 1986.

communication time, while speaking (30 percent), reading (16 percent), and writing (9 percent) consume the remaining time. Good communication skills are essential.

The consultant must take into account the client's communication styles as well. Consultants must know the appropriateness of different forms of communication to particular situations. For example, many consulting projects require formal written reports. However, informal, action-oriented organizations may use a series of poster-sized flow charts instead.

Interpersonal Skills.   Interpersonal skills demonstrate the ability to use effectively the behavior of both the consultant and the client during the engagement. These skills include the ability to apply knowledge about the consulting process and about human and organizational dynamics. The relationship between the client and the consultant determines the continuation and potential success of all projects. Consequently, the consultant must possess strong interpersonal skills which not only engender trust and openness, but also set the stage for successful organizational change. The consultant must convey an attitude of helpfulness.

Consultants make a major mistake by relying too heavily on their roles as consultants. They forget that the client is first a human being, second a businessperson, and third a consultee. The client has needs, predispositions, and feelings that the consultant must acknowledge. Beware of becoming self-important: you'll lose clients.

Administrative Skills.   Consultants are business people. They must possess the administrative skills required for business success and for managing projects, people, and paperwork on a regular basis. Consultants who own or manage an entire consulting firm must know how to operate the many facets of an enterprise. Establishing the business, marketing, pricing, fee collections, and new business development are essential. Since many excellent consultants fail to establish a continuing practice, these skills are discussed more fully in Chapters 3–8.

As Table 4 indicates, the skill requirements change during a consultant's career. New consultants are usually hired on the basis of technical expertise. They may possess only minimally acceptable skills in the other three areas. When the consultant moves into a supervisory position, more emphasis is placed on communication

TABLE 4.   Skill Requirement Changes During a Consultant's Career

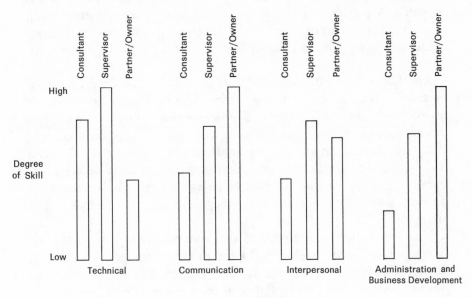

Type of Skills

and administration skills. Moreover, since supervisors have the most contact with the client, they must use interpersonal skills adroitly. By the time a consultant becomes a partner/owner, he or she performs two main functions. The first is securing clients for the continuation of the business, which requires a heavy marketing emphasis. The second function is administration—that is, management of the firm. Whereas the supervisor's administrative skills are oriented toward project management, the partner/owner must operate the entire business. The partner/owner's focus is on short- and long-term profitability, as well as development of the firm's potential.

Credibility

Consultants must establish credibility—the fourth ingredient of successful consulting. Clients want someone they can trust; before they trust you, they want proof of your trustworthiness.

You establish credibility best with knowledge, skills, and work or consulting experience. Consultants with ten years' experience at an international consulting firm usually have no credibility problems when they open their own firm. The top-selling real estate salesperson has established his or her credibility. A former employer's retaining you as a consultant is a positive sign of your experience credibility. It provides a clear indication of your value to prospective clients.

Another way to build credibility is through education credentials, especially from prestigious institutions. The business world respects people with graduate degrees; clients recognize the hard work and determination required for graduate work. Other important credentials are state licenses, professional memberships, and advanced training seminars. All these demonstrate that you are a professional intent upon establishing yourself as an expert. Although credentials do not ensure your performance, they help relieve a client's initial anxiety.

Your reputation and references also help establish your credibility. A consultant must quickly build a reputation for good judgment, objectivity, character, and performance. References and past accomplishments indicate good performance. Former clients, employers, professors, and colleagues can serve as a reinforcing network for your consulting practice. Secure written recommendations from such people along with their permission to use them as references. Most professional associations consider it unethical to reveal client identities without their permission. Thus, considering client confidences and your own best interest, obtain permission in writing, if possible. Most satisfied clients are willing to serve as references, and, in some cases, will actively promote your reputation.

Personality

The fifth requirement of a good consultant is certain personality characteristics. Psychological testing has shown that individuals attracted to the same profession tend to share common interests and to have similar personalities. Through my interviews, although not substantiated by rigorous psychological testing, I have reached the same conclusion about consultants. When consultants describe their personalities, certain characteristics repeatedly emerge.

Consultants are self-starters. They need little outside motivation or direction because they take the initiative to start and complete tasks. Self-starters usually have high energy levels. They can work long and hard hours on a regular basis. This internally directed energy enables them to work under pressure and to meet multiple deadlines—a common experience for most consultants.

Self-confidence is another trait of consultants. To build client confidence, they must first believe in themselves and in their abilities. They acknowledge the truth in the maxim, "If you do not believe in yourself, very few other people will." Since consultants often ask clients to take considerable risks, they need self-confidence to overcome a client's hesitation. Self-confidence closely relates to another necessary personality trait: the ability to deal with rejection and failure. Consultants often lose proposal bids, make mistakes, and see their recommendations rejected. Like a good lawyer or salesperson, the consultant moves on to the next project.

Consultants also possess a high tolerance for ambiguity. Frequently, their roles are not well defined in the client's organization. A skilled consultant can jump into problem situations and remain unruffled. Consultants need to be level-headed.

Finally, curiosity and creativity play important parts in a consultant's personality makeup. Good consultants enjoy learning about new people, new organizations, new ideas, and new problems. The challenge and change of pace of consulting stimulate them. Moreover, they enjoy the creativity that facing new problems demands. They see problems not as constraints but as opportunities for growth and change. Many consultants find it difficult to turn off their curiosity or creativity. One consultant confessed that when in restaurants, hotels, and service stations, she probes the employees for information about their firm's activities. Then she devises new ways to make the operation more efficient or beneficial.

Networking

To survive as a consultant, you must create personal and professional networks. These networks serve several major functions. First, they provide a source of emotional support. While you are developing your consulting practice, you will feel lonely. Days may pass when your phone remains silent unless you initiate the calls. You will experience self-doubt about your decision to become a consultant. The long days and unending activities necessary to get your new business off the ground will drain you emotionally. Or, when a project takes you away from home for several days or weeks at a time, your emotional strength may ebb. At these points, your networks are very helpful. They can buoy your spirits and reaffirm your career goals. Your experienced professional colleagues can commiserate with you about their own feelings as they built their practices. They can help you put everything in perspective.

Your networks are essential if you are to build an ongoing consulting practice. As we will discuss in Chapters 6 through 8, projects seldom come in the door looking for you. Your ability to attract projects depends to a great extent on the quality and skillful use of your network. If you have an extensive network of potential clients, or colleagues who know potential clients, you are in a good position to market your services. If your network is small or spotty, you will be forced to make a high number of low-probability cold calls. A warm referral beats a cold call any day. You won't stay in business long if your network does not produce referrals.

Finally, your network is helpful when you bid on projects and when you conduct them. You will encounter some potential projects that require multiple skills or expertise that you do not possess *in toto*. Rather than decline the project (or worse yet, accept it when you are not fully qualified), you can contact qualified colleagues to join you in bidding for the project. Your network allows you to build a project team that can meet the client's needs. You may also find yourself in a solo project when you encounter something outside your expertise. Having competent colleagues you can call will save you anxiety, headaches, and lost time. If you are still learning the consulting process, having another, experienced consultant in your network can be very useful in teaching you the basics.

Your networking ability is critical for your success. An effective network connects you to people, diverse expertise, potential clients, and to professional, as well as emotional, support. Good networks produce ongoing two-way communication. Leads are passed along and favors are exchanged. In good networks, everyone benefits.

Code of Ethics

Consultants, like other professionals, hold strong values concerning the conduct of their work. Since a consultant's most valuable asset is his or her reputation, successful consultants have a strong sense of ethics. Most of the professional consulting associations listed in the appendix have developed codes of ethics for their members. Since consulting is currently unregulated, these codes offer some protection to the public. They also help differentiate the true professionals from the hucksters.

Most codes outline the consultant's responsibilities to the client and the public. As a general rule, consultants are expected to place the client's interest ahead of their own. This includes keeping client information confidential, working within your scope of competence, and monitoring your own performance. Conflicts of interest are to be avoided. Consultants should not have financial interest in their clients' companies, hold directorship or controlling interest in the client's competitors without disclosure, nor have any relationships or interests that might compromise the consultant's judgment. The consultant keeps in mind the distinction between actual conflict of interest and the appearance of such conflict. Although the appearance of conflict may in fact be harmless, it places the consultant in the awkward position of self-defense. When in doubt, ask your colleagues or contact your professional association. Above all, discuss the situation fully, perhaps even in writing, with your clients.

Good consultants believe in regular self-examination of their consulting practices. During and after engagements, established consultants reflect on what has transpired in order to learn from the experience. They consider both the positive and negative aspects of the engagement. Based on this reflection, they draw out principles that apply to future projects. Many consultants compile a list of these "principles" throughout their careers. They review these principles before starting new projects. A written code serves as a useful source to a consultant who desires to write professionally. Consultants will draw upon these experiences and share them through articles and books. Much of the knowledge about consulting is gathered and transmitted in this manner.

Many consultants regularly review their attitudes about people, organizations, change, business, and consulting. Although some consultants hold similar assumptions on these topics (for instance, that change is constant), the actual assumptions are not at issue here. Rather, it is important to know your assumptions and to review them on a periodic basis. Have your learning and experience over time altered or challenged your assumptions? For example, do you think that people are basically self-motivated, or do you think they require heavy external pressure to perform? Is problem solver or teacher the better dominant role as a consultant? Do organizations need formal structure or loose designs? It is important to answer these questions at specific points in time and to review them throughout your career.

As a consultant, you must know what motivates you. Is it internal drive, personal dreams, feelings of insecurity, money, family, status, recognition, colleagues, or some combination of the above? Have the motivations in your life changed over time? How do they influence your desire to be a consultant and your ability to act as one? Again, although the answers to these questions are important, the primary challenge is to monitor your answers in light of your experience and ambition.

Life-Style

The life-styles of most consultants differ from the average business person's. Consulting is envisioned as a glamour industry: high fees, first-class travel, and hobnobbing with top executives. This image presents only the positive side. Actual working conditions belie this glamorous veneer. For example, although most consultants set their own hours, the hours are long. Problems demand immediate and sustained attention. The consultant gets absorbed in the project, spending many days until the situation is resolved. The effort becomes especially draining if you are working on several projects simultaneously, as most consultants do. So, even if you are consulting in your favorite city, you have little chance to enjoy its pleasures when working from 7:00 A.M. till 8:00 or 9:00 P.M.

Travel is constantly required for many consultants. Major consulting firms caution new employees to expect to spend 20–60 percent of their time traveling. Consultants spend weeks at a time away from home. If you are a solo practitioner, you may have greater control over your travel. However, if you are successful, then sooner or later an out-of-town client will seek your services. At that time, you will face expanding your reputation and clientele at the expense of traveling.

Consulting on the road imposes extraordinary personal demands. To be at a client's office by 9:00 A.M., you either leave on a 6:00 A.M. flight or arrive the night before. It requires living from a suitcase and eating hotel meals. Often, the consultant travels alone without the social or emotional support of family and friends and without the business support of colleagues or office workers. Add to this long hours, intense pressure, and uncertain living conditions, and a tremendous amount of stress results.

Many road trips involve seeing several clients either interspersed in the same city or sequentially from city to city. What consultants remember of each city is the airport, the hotel, and the client. Consultants claim that both cities and clients begin to blur if they spend too much time traveling. One consultant carried several briefcases with him when traveling—one for each client. This was his method for keeping his clients separate.

Consulting does have rewards that compensate for this life-style. Autonomy is one. Ideally, consultants shape their working conditions to match their desired life-style. They can limit their travel and their clientele as they see fit. Solo practitioners often report that the opportunity to shape their jobs and control their futures was the most compelling reason for becoming consultants.

Another reward is the chance to help and influence clients. Consultants obtain satisfaction from making a positive contribution to both clients and society. Like other professionals, consultants know the special feeling that comes from helping other people, especially those in trouble.

A final set of rewards involves high earnings, status, and respect. Consulting offers the opportunity for higher earnings than are available in white-collar jobs. Your status is usually higher among both your peers and the community. Respect for consultants is growing, since consultants are playing an influential role in society. Society respects individuals who establish their own independent business and make it flourish.

Consulting, then, is a trade-off. The rewards can be great, but the price is high. For this reason, the previously mentioned self-examination is important. To avoid burning out, you must continually bear in mind that the rewards outweigh the negatives.

Consulting As Your Career

Table 5 depicts career path opportunities for the average white-collar worker in our society. Many options face us as we pursue our careers. These options fall under the four basic roles that make up our business world: worker, manager, owner/entrepreneur, and consul-

TABLE 5.   Career Options as You Progress Through Your Career

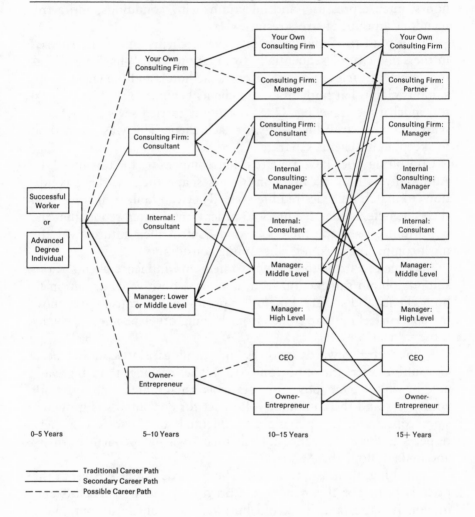

0–5 Years   5–10 Years   10–15 Years   15+ Years

———————— Traditional Career Path
———————— Secondary Career Path
– – – – – – Possible Career Path

tant. The traditional and most common path moves us from the worker role to the manager role; then we work our way up the management ladder.

However, recent evidence indicates that this pattern is changing. For example, the Harvard Business School, the traditional bastion of training future managers, has seen over 25 percent of its graduates enter consulting since 1977. Student interest in small-business ownership has spawned numerous entrepreneurship courses and programs in business schools across the country. Pat Chew, a recognized career counselor and author of *MBA: Preparing and Applying for Graduate Study in Management,** identifies both consulting and small-business ownership as major career paths in the 1980s. Society is recognizing the need for alternative options early in one's career.

Career alternatives always exist, although most people tend to contract their options rather than expand them in order to lessen the number of choices they face and reduce the corresponding anxiety. This situation need not occur, especially for individuals interested in consulting. Many career options exist for those with the skills, talents, and personalities previously described in this chapter. Securing another career option involves recognizing where the demand is and how to meet it. Many books on this topic exist; some are listed at the end of this chapter.

As mentioned earlier, consultants are Gold-Collar Workers.† They hold new and different attitudes about themselves and their careers. Because they think for a living, they are less content to stay in one job or one rut for very long. They are less likely to put up with the rigidness and absurdities of bureaucratic management in traditional companies. Instead, they choose among career options on the basis of which option will enable their assets—their knowledge, experience, and training—to appreciate, not depreciate. Thus, they do not feel confined to follow traditional career paths.

Gold-collar consultants are also able to follow their own paths because of their relative affluence. Consulting, like most gold-collar occupations, pays well. Often their spouses are also gold-collar workers, which increases their income base. With multiple income streams and a great deal of career mobility, gold-collar consultants are choice-driven rather than need-driven. They can act on their values without worrying about economic repercussions. In effect, they can approach their careers as if they were consumers. If they like the opportunities and benefits of one option, they will select it in much the same way they would shop for any other major purchase. They are internally driven to meet their own goals and expectations rather than externally driven to please other people.

A word of explanation is needed here concerning the difference between consultants and managers. Much is made of this distinction in the popular press. Managers are described as doers, implementers, and decision makers who accept responsibility. Consultants are pic-

---

* New York: Harper & Row, 1981.
† R. E. Kelley, *The Gold-Collar Worker: Harnessing the Brainpower of the New Workforce.* Reading, Mass.: Addison-Wesley, 1985.

tured as thinkers, advisors, and conceptualizers who are shy about taking on responsibility. It is said that people who make good managers do not make good consultants and vice versa, but this maxim is true only if these people fail to recognize and utilize the necessary role change. For those capable of the transition, little problem exists.

What you must keep in mind is that each of us can handle more than one role. Although some people feel more comfortable in certain roles, it is unlikely that they will or should confine themselves to only those roles.

As you progress through your consulting career, you are required to play multiple roles. For example, those of us who own our own consulting firms are owners, managers of our workers, and consultants to our clients. The consultants in our firms are workers in the sense that they produce the services of our firms, as well as being consultants to clients. Hence, we must continually distinguish which occupations require us to play what particular role and when to avoid the trap of labeling ourselves and our careers in ways that interfere with our effective functioning and limit our career options.

Additional Sources of Help

Those interested in more in-depth material on career self-assessment and job hunting may refer to the following sources:

Common Body of Knowledge for Management Consultants. New York: Association of Consulting Management Engineers, 1957.

Making the Most of Management Consulting Services. J. H. Fuchs. New York: Amacom, 1975.

Manager's Guide to Successful Job Hunting. K. Traxel. New York: McGraw-Hill, 1978.

New Venture Creation: A Guide to Small Business Development. J. Timmons, L. Smollen, and A. Dingee. Homewood, Ill.: Richard D. Irwin, Inc., 1977.

Self Assessment and Career Development. J. Kotter, V. Faux, and C. McArthur. Englewood Cliffs, N.J.: Prentice-Hall, 1978.

What Color Is Your Parachute? R. Bolles. Berkeley, Calif.: Ten Speed Press, 1986.

Where Do I Go from Here with My Life? J. Crystal and R. Bolles. New York: Seabury Press, 1974.

Starting Your Own Practice

3

To open a business, very easy; to keep it open, very difficult.
CHINESE FORTUNE COOKIE

If you are reading this chapter, you have decided to open your own consulting practice. You are combining two of America's fastest growing dreams: to start your own business and to be a consultant. Both are major undertakings, but the combined rewards make them worthwhile.

The major focus in this chapter is the business side of starting your own business. The characteristics of entrepreneurs are explored and essential business principles are reviewed. Preplanning is extremely important. To aid your planning efforts, a typical business plan is applied to consulting firms. This chapter will help you develop your own business plan. You will shape your consulting dream into an actual consulting business.

Self-Assessment Exercises*

Please complete the exercises that begin on page 44 before reading the remaining text. Place an "X" in the appropriate column as you

* Adapted from *New Venture Creation: A Guide to Small Business Development.* Used with permission.

compare yourself with consultants, entrepreneurs, and other business people. Make an honest, accurate, and realistic assessment of how you measure in each dimension.

Entrepreneurs, venture capitalists, and psychologists believe these twenty-two criteria are important for entrepreneurial success. No one is exceptionally strong or weak in all these characteristics. The goal is to identify your strengths and weaknesses before you begin your consulting firm. As a result, you can prepare yourself for expected problems by making plans to overcome your weak points. This chapter will help you with this process.

Consulting as a Business

Operating a consulting business is just like operating any other business. You must never lose sight of that fact. Too many consultants ignore the business aspect of consulting. This unfortunate occurrence has two causes. First, many professionals disdain business; in fact, they became professionals so they would not have to "work in business." Second, the consulting industry has played down the business aspect of consulting. It has developed euphemisms for business terms. Hence, consultants do not market their services; they "develop business." They do not set a price on their services; they charge a "fee." They do not go on sales calls; they arrange an "initial diagnostic interview." Traditionally, the consulting industry promoted an image that placed it on a higher plane than ordinary businesses. Only recently have consulting firms advertised and developed marketing strategies. As competition grows, consulting firms are forced to attend to the business nature of their industry.

In its simplest form, business has two components: revenues and expenses. Revenues are normally generated through sales. Consultants must sell just like everyone else. In consulting, you sell your time and your expertise rather than a product. You place a dollar value (your fee) on each. How you do this will be discussed in Chapter 5. Once paid for your time and expertise, you have completed a sale. This sale is similar to selling anything from cars to computers.

Expenses are what it costs you to sell and provide your services. Renting an office, developing proposals, and hiring staff are typical expenses. Expenses are generally of two types: unavoidable and extravagant. For example, most consultants have an unavoidable typing expense. However, having a full-time secretary with a $10,000 word processor is likely to be extravagant. Expenses are also described as fixed and variable. Fixed expenses stay at the same dollar amount regardless of how much revenue you generate. For instance, your rent stays the same if you generate $3,000 worth of business one month and $30,000 the next. However, if you use subcontractors when needed, then your subcontracting expense depends on how often you use them. This, in turn, depends on your sales revenues.

Your revenues must exceed your expenses for you to make a profit. Profit generally means expending considerable effort to generate revenues by selling and providing services while controlling fixed and variable costs. If you cannot perform these tasks, you will not stay in business. This holds true even if you work in someone else's consulting firm. If the expenses the firm incurs on your behalf (salary, benefits, training) exceed the revenues you generate for it, then you will be fired. Your success in your own firm or in anyone else's depends upon your generating new sales and billing out to clients at a rate that exceeds the expenses you create.

Establishing a profitable business is explored in the remainder of this chapter. To begin properly, you must know what business you are in, and this is the topic of the next section.

Define Your Services and Capabilities

Most people begin with a vague notion that they want to be consultants. It is very important to become specific. The public wants to know that your business is clear in your mind before they pay for your services. The longer it takes you to explain your type of consulting, the less interested they become. Many consultants make two mistakes in this regard. First, they explain what they do in vague, long sentences, which bore and confuse the client. Second, they want to be a jack of all trades; they do not want to be tied down to any particular area. The public cannot distinguish between these two types. Instead, potential clients write off both types as amateurs. All consultants should learn from Sam Goldwyn, the movie producer. People constantly hounded him to invest his money in their latest money-making scheme. He soon tired of listening to long, confused stories as they explained their plans. To save time and effort, he handed out his business card and then said, "Write your idea on the back of it. If you can't, then it is not clear enough in your own mind."

Exercise 1. Entrepreneurial Characteristics

	Top p1%	Top 5%	Rest of Top Third	Middle Third	Lower Third
Drive and energy level. What is your personal energy level—that is, your ability to work actively for long hours with less than normal sleep?	___	___	___	___	___
Self-confidence. What is your self-confidence level—that is, your belief in yourself and your ability to achieve your goals and a sense that events in your life are self-determined?	___	___	___	___	___
Long-term involvement. What is your commitment to long-term, future projects and to goals that may be quite distant?	___	___	___	___	___
Money as a measure. Do you view money (salary, profits, or capital gains) as the scorecard of what you have accomplished rather than the procurement of luxuries or the achievement of power?	___	___	___	___	___
Persistent problem solving. Do you have an intense and determined desire to complete tasks and solve problems?	___	___	___	___	___
Goal setting. What is your ability and commitment to set clear and challenging goals that are also realistic and attainable?	___	___	___	___	___
Moderate risk taking. What is your preference for taking moderate, calculated risks, where the chances of winning are not so small as to be a "gamble," nor so large as to be a "sure thing," but provide a reasonable and challenging chance of success?	___	___	___	___	___

Dealing with failure. What is your ability to use failures as learning experiences and to better understand your role in causing the failure in order to avoid similar problems in the future?

_____

Use of feedback. What is your demonstrated capacity to seek and use feedback on your performance in order to take corrective action and to improve?

_____

Taking initiative and seeking personal responsibility. What is the level of your desire to seek and take initiative and to put yourself in situations where you are personally responsible for the success or failure of the operation—in other words, are you a doer?

_____

Use of resources. To what extent do you seek to identify and obtain expertise and assistance that is needed in the accomplishment of your goals, rather than allow your personal achievement to prevent people from helping you?

_____

Competing against self-imposed standards. What is your tendency to establish your own high but realistic standards of performance and to compete with yourself?

_____

Internal locus of control. Do you believe that one's accomplishments as well as failures lie within one's personal control and influence, rather than being determined by luck or other external, personally uncontrollable events and circumstances?

_____

Tolerance of ambiguity. To what extent can you tolerate and live with modest to high levels of ambiguity and uncertainty concerning job/career security and work-related events on a continuous basis?

_____

Exercise 2. *Entrepreneurial Role Requirements*

	Top p1%	Top 5%	Rest of Top Third	Middle Third	Lower Third
Accommodation to the venture. To what extent are your entrepreneur's career and venture treated as the number one priority—above family, community, etc.?	___	___	___	___	___
Total immersion. What is your ability to totally immerse and commit yourself to the building of the business? Are you willing to invest life savings, reduce income by as much as one-half in starting up and early years, and to view the business as a way of life?	___	___	___	___	___
Creativity and innovation. To what extent do you place value on creative, innovative work and derive personal satisfaction from it, rather than doing the routine or merely doing a difficult task better?	___	___	___	___	___
Knowledge of the business one wants to start. To what extent do you have a thorough and proven operating knowledge of the business to be started?	___	___	___	___	___

People and team building. To what extent have you demonstrated the capacity to attract, motivate, and build a high-quality team whose capable management skills, know-how, and personal styles meet the needs of the venture?

_____   _____   _____   _____

Economic values. To what extent do you believe in and are you committed to the conventional economic and financial values of the American system of free enterprise, such as profits, capital gains, private ownership, earnings per share, etc.?

_____   _____   _____   _____

Ethics. To what extent does your business conduct tend to be defined by and adaptive to the demands and needs of each situation rather than by a rigid code of conduct applied uniformly regardless of different conditions and circumstances?

_____   _____   _____   _____

Integrity and reliability. To what extent are you respected for dependability, reliability, and honest dealing?

_____   _____   _____   _____

Here is an example of a cogent presentation of function. A consultant in the field of industrial psychology explains his job: "I help manufacturing organizations obtain better performance from their employees. I design selection procedures, job descriptions, reward systems, and training programs to improve the worker-organization 'fit' and to increase the productivity of both." In two sentences, he conveys the essence of his business. Clients can quickly identify how he is able to assist in solving their problems.

To help you specify your consulting practice, learn to use the reporter's best friends: *who* does *what* to *whom, how, why, where, when,* and at *what expense.* Think of what you have to offer a client in a language that the client understands. Once you have answered these questions, you have made a good start on the next essential component of starting your business: the business plan. Before you go on to the next section, write a short description of your present or future consulting practice. Answer the questions raised in the preceding sections. Then summarize your description in one or two simple, nonjargon sentences.

Develop a Business Plan

Most of you probably want to be consultants first and business owners second. Ownership may simply be a means of becoming a consultant. To ensure that your major efforts are spent consulting, you need a business plan with which to operate your business.

A business plan is to a business executive what a blueprint is to a builder. The business plan performs three major functions. The plan's first and primary function forces you to think through each aspect of your business. Most aspiring entrepreneurs think initially of their potential service/product and the market. The business plan, however, has a wider scope, as indicated later in the sample outline.

You will face numerous decisions during your first months of operation. Many of these decisions are best made before you open your doors. For instance, how should you approach potential customers? How much revenue do you need to make a profit? Do you need a partner? These are crucial questions that affect your firm's success. Prior to your opening you can fully explore the alternatives, since you will not have daily business matters competing for your time, attention, and energy. Your business plan helps you anticipate these important decisions and give them the proper attention they deserve.

The business plan's second function is to allow a "dry run" before you actually perform your first consulting engagement. It exposes you to potential sales, financing requirements, personnel, profits, and problems. It simulates what you can expect in the early months and years of operations. A well-formulated plan prepares you for the expected and frees your energy to handle the unexpected.

The business plan's third function is as a sales tool for both you and potential investors. It inspires confidence. If you are familiar with every aspect of your business, you will possess the accompanying self-confidence of knowing what to expect. This self-confidence is essential if you need to persuade others to invest their money in you. Armed with a realistic, comprehensive, and well-documented plan, you will go a long way in convincing investors. Since they are investing in you as well as your business, they look for signs that you are confident enough to lead, rational enough to plan realistically, and orderly enough to present your plan properly. Your business plan should display evidence of these qualities.

Business plans vary in length and nature. Presented below is a summary of topics normally included in formal business plans. For in-depth discussion of business plans, two excellent books are listed in the reference section at the end of this chapter: *New Venture Creation* and *Up Your Own Organization*.

Typical Business Plan*

Cover Page. Name of company; address; phone; date

Introductory Summary. One- or two-page explanation of proposal's major features

Table of Contents. List of major topics and page numbers

Your Company. The business you are in; the services you provide

The Industry. History; current status; future prospects

Market Research. Competition; market size; trends

Market Analysis. Your customers; estimated market share and sales

---

* This material is adapted from *New Venture Creation* by J. Timmons, L. Smollen, and A. Dingee. Used by permission.

Marketing Plan. Your strategy; pricing; sales approach; advertising; promotion; service policies

Management Team. Organization chart; duties of key management personnel; capsule resumes of key management personnel; management compensation and ownership; board of directors

Supporting Professional Assistance. Lawyer; accountant; banker; insurance agent

Operations Plan. Geographical location; facilities and improvements; operations strategy

Research and Development Program. Product/service improvements; process improvements; development of new products; costs and risks

Overall Schedule. Timing and interrelationship of all major events important to starting and developing your business

Critical Risks and Problems. Potential competitive responses; unfavorable industry trends; costs of delays and over-runs; failure to achieve sales projections; etc.

Financial Plan. Profit and loss forecasts; pro forma cash flow analysis; pro forma balance sheets; break-even charts

Proposed Financing of Company. Desired financing; use of funds

Legal Structure of Firm. Sole proprietorship; partnership; corporation

Appendixes. Sales forecast and market surveys; resumes of key management personnel; personal financial statements of professional owners; publications by key personnel; letters of reference; newspapers, magazines, or books related to the business or the industry

Introductory Summary. This one- or two-page introduction summarizes the important information included in your business plan. A well-written summary is important, especially if you want to attract investors. Since investors read it first, make it appealing, convincing, readable, and produced in clean type on good paper stock. Write the summary after you have written the entire plan. Include one or two main sentences from each section. Describe the company, the owners, the services you are offering, the market opportunities, your sales and profit projection, and your financing needs and capabilities.

Table of Contents.   The table of contents enables the reader to know what is included in your business plan and to refer to each part quickly. Since different readers (and investors) are interested in different aspects of the business, the table of contents saves them time by pinpointing where to turn.

Your Company.   In this section, use the results from the previously completed exercise under "Define Your Services and Capabilities" (p. 43). Describe what business you are in, what services you offer, and your principal customers. Mention when your business began (or will begin), its previous performance, and the founders/owners of the firm. When describing your services, show how they differ from competitors'. Include the potential for developing and offering related services in the future.

The Industry.   Give a short history of both the consulting industry and the industries in which you plan to consult. Include major developments that shaped both. Then describe the current status of the industry, such as products, markets, and dominant firms. Finally, concentrate on trends in the industry. These trends can be internal (such as new product developments, new markets and customers, or new companies) or external (such as the effects of new government regulations, developments in other industries, new customer demands, fads, social/demographic changes, or national/international changes). Identify the sources upon which these trends are based.

Market Research.   Market research is a crucial section of your business plan. Many new consultants do not focus on the market in which they will operate. Enamored of their "good idea," they fail to learn whether the market exists for it. Since it is important to estimate sales, you must know the size of your market, the trends, and your competitors to determine your eventual sales capability.

Determine the size of the current total market for your consulting service. If you plan to consult only in New York, then use that as your total market. If you will only consult to real estate companies with over $100 million in sales, then use that as your total market. Describe the total market's size in both number of potential clients and potential sales dollars. Indicate the sources of data and methods used to establish this current market size, such as government reports, trade associations, marketing research firms, or published material.

After determining the current size of the market, identify the trends in your market. Project market growth over the next three to five years. Specify any major internal or external factors that will affect market growth, such as new companies, government regulations, and population changes. Again, indicate the sources and methods used to make the projections.

Your potential and actual competitors have a major effect on your survival. Fortunately, consulting is a growing, new industry. As a result, you can find areas in which you will have no competition. However, it is important to assess realistically the strengths and weaknesses of competitors, if they exist. Identify their size, what services they offer, what customers they service, their performance, their prices, their profitability, and their growth rate. If possible, determine how well they are meeting their customers' needs. What competitors have dropped out of the market and why? Who are the two or three major competitors? What is the current market share of each? In what way can you capitalize on their weaknesses? Will it be easy or difficult to compete with them? Which part of their market do you want and how do you plan to capture it? How do you think they will respond to you?

Market Analysis.   In your market analysis, identify your expected major clients, estimate your potential annual sales to each, and assess your potential market share. These, of course, depend on the results of your market research.

Who are the major clients you want to attract? Can you group them according to common, identifiable characteristics, such as geographic location, industry, or needs? Have any of them expressed an interest in you as a consultant or in your type of consulting? Who in the client's organization makes the decision to engage a consultant? On what basis is the decision made, especially when choosing among different consultants (quality, price, personal contacts, or political pressure)? By answering the above questions, you will have a head start in developing your marketing campaign to attract these clients.

After identifying your potential client base, estimate your potential sales to each client. Indicate clients who will make commitments now and why they are willing to do so. When do you expect to make sales to the others? You will find it useful to estimate your sales in dollars and number of consulting hours for each quarter during the next three years. Note the growth pattern and assumptions you used when making these estimates. Are these assumptions realistic? For example, can a $1-million company afford to pay you $30,000 a year in consulting fees? Probably not.

Finally, estimate your market share for each quarter during the next three years. Take into account the total market size, its trends and growth rate, the competition and its growth rate, and your own sales estimates. Based on these factors, where will you stand in the marketplace—first? last? the only? Will your market share and position improve over time? If so, how?

Keep in mind that most markets profitably support only the top three competitors. If you are not one of the top three competitors, what can you realistically do to become one? If you cannot become one, how can you redefine either your business or your target market so that you are one of the top three competitors? This will be discussed at more length in Chapter 6, "Marketing Your Services."

Marketing Plan. To reach your estimated sales projection, you must develop a strategy that describes what is to be done in marketing, how it will be done, and who will do it. You will target specific clients with particular sales approaches. Determine which aspects of your firm's services—quality, price, or industry experience—you will stress in your marketing efforts. How do you plan to bring your services to the attention of prospective clients? Do you plan to advertise, make phone calls, send out brochures, or attend trade conventions? How much will these efforts cost and when will you incur these costs? How long can you absorb these costs before you generate revenues? In addition, determine who will be responsible for sales and how you will evaluate his or her efforts. Methods to approach your marketing plan are more fully developed in Chapter 6, "Marketing Your Services."

Management Team. The management team is responsible for making your business successful. If you are a solo practitioner, then you are the management team. You perform all the major tasks of planning, marketing, accounting, financing, organizing, and consulting. However, research on small-business success indicates that teams have a higher success rate than individuals. The most successful teams are those in which the team members complement each other's skills. Rather than have three managers whose skills are identical to yours, create a proper balance of technical, managerial, and business skills.

This diverse but balanced team is often required if you are seeking outside investors. These investors expect growth businesses to insure a return on their investment. Experienced investors know that one individual usually is not skilled in every facet of the business, nor will he or she have the time to perform each facet if the business is growing. On the other hand, if you want to limit yourself to a small individual consulting practice, you can perform the necessary tasks. If not, you might rely on assistance from outside professionals, an approach that will be discussed later.

An organizational chart visually represents the key management roles in the company and who will fill each position. The organizational chart also indicates the relationship between the various management personnel—who supervises whom. Include this chart in your business plan.

The organizational chart pictorially represents the duties and responsibilities of each manager. The next step is to specify in writing what these duties and responsibilities are. Written job descriptions at the start promote a clear understanding of each job function. New management teams mistakenly assume that everyone knows what needs to be done *and* will do it. Unfortunately, each manager assumes the other person will do it, and important duties are neglected.

To supplement the organizational chart and job descriptions, you should provide capsule resumes of each key manager. Include name, age, education, recent employment history, and accomplishments to date. Stress the training, experience, and accomplishments of each manager relative to the duties he or she will perform in your business. Be concrete in your description of accomplishments; include sales or profit improvements, technical achievements, and ability to manage personnel. Keep these descriptions brief. Put more detailed resumes in the appendixes of your plan.

In light of each manager's responsibilities and experience, you will determine compensation and ownership privileges. Base salaries on those received at the most recent independent jobs. Ownership privileges are usually dependent on equity investment or on significant performance contributions to the firm. Clarify these money issues at the outset so that each manager knows the monetary rewards of his or her efforts.

Filling each management position with a highly qualified individual can overburden your business with high overhead, which might exceed your sales forecast. Three options are available to you. You may trade company ownership for salary. Managers who are committed to the business and who believe in its growth potential often sacrifice current salary for future profits. A second alternative is to compose a board of directors that complements the skills of your management team. A properly selected board can fill the gaps in your team. The board can offer objective advice when you cannot afford a large staff of specialists. Unfortunately, many small-business owners overload their boards with relatives simply to comply with state laws. An effective board must have seasoned business people and knowledgeable professionals with continuing interest in your firm's progress. This reduces your overhead and increases your chances for success. A third alternative is to rely on supporting professional services, which is the next major section of your business plan.

Supporting Professional Assistance. Consulting firms should quickly establish relationships with necessary professionals such as a lawyer, an accountant, a banker, and an insurance agent. Capable professionals provide significant part-time assistance when you cannot afford a full-time, high-priced staff member. Seek out professionals who are familiar with consulting firms and with your potential clients' types of businesses. These professionals also help build your referral network. Their contacts in the business community lead you to clients who need your type of consulting. When obtaining these outside professionals, ask yourself what they will add to your firm in both skills and marketing efforts. For example, choose a lawyer who has a different set of business contacts than does your accountant. In essence, view these professionals as an extension of your management team.

Operations Plan. Your operations plan describes how you will carry out the major function of your business, consulting. It specifies your personnel, office, and equipment requirements. View your current and future personnel needs in light of personnel availability and cost. Regarding office location, discuss the relative advantages and disadvantages of each possible location. For instance, a major advantage of working at home is lower overhead. Disadvantages are the possibility of family interruptions and lack of "status." In addition, consider how and when to expand your office space and equipment.

Project the cost and timing of such expansion over a three-year period. More information concerning office and equipment needs is
presented in Chapter 4, "Outfitting Your Office."

Every business needs an operations plan that specifies how the
work will get done. It outlines the chain of events required to produce your service or product. Chapters 5–16 of this book represent
a complete operations plan for a consulting business. You will modify these chapters to your own particular consulting business. The
important point is that you outline the work flow required to sell
and complete your consulting engagements. Show how the steps in
the process are related to each other, the timing required, who will
complete each step, and what the projected costs are. These efforts
enable you to schedule your engagements, to estimate your costs,
and to set your fees. In addition, they give you a sense of control over
your operations.

Research and Development Program.   Consulting firms perform
research and development in the same way any other business does.
Research and development appears in many forms and has costs attached to it. As you determine how you will perform your first consulting project, you are, in essence, doing research and development.
You are developing your service so that it is saleable to the public.
Reading this book is research and development. Both the cost of the
book and the time you spend reading it are research and development expenditures. This holds true for other continuing education
expenses. This form of research and development is known as service
or product improvement.

Another form of research and development is process improvement, or efficiency in providing service. For example, consider the
consultant in business expansion feasibility studies. The first feasibility study performed will take longer and therefore cost more than
the tenth study because the consultant learns with experience and
becomes more efficient. More than likely, the consultant will charge
the same for the first and tenth studies. This process improvement,
then, allows the consultant to improve scheduling, to reduce cost in
providing the service, and to increase profits.

At some point, you may want to expand your business by offering
new services. These new services are essential to survival and growth
because the services you provide today will be outdated at some future point. Demand for your current services will diminish, while

new services will take over the market. For instance, organization studies were a mainstay at major management consulting firms in the 1960s. In the 1970s, they were replaced by strategic planning studies. Technology studies have proliferated in the 1980s.

Future-oriented firms prepare for this situation. To obtain maximum mileage from old services, they try to find new markets for them. In this way, they maximize their investment in those services. For example, the previously mentioned management consulting firms sold organization studies mainly to large businesses. During the 1970s they turned to the medium-sized and smaller businesses as a market for those studies. In the 1980s, they have gone to Europe and Asia as potential markets for those studies.

A second approach continually develops new services to meet current market needs. You can develop new services in a variety of ways, each of which has its own particular costs. You can hire someone capable of providing the new services. This saves you training costs but also increases your salary overhead, particularly while the new employee is creating the market for the service. You take the risk that the market cannot support this new service. Another alternative is to let other consultants or universities develop the new service. You can wait to see if the market demand develops. If so, you then learn and develop the new service as quickly as possible to cash in on the demand. This is called the "follower" or "me, too" strategy, since you let someone else assume the costs and risks of development. However, you sacrifice market share because the innovator has a time lead on you.

A final alternative is to be the innovator. You can develop the new service and create the market. This involves heavy start-up costs both in research and development and in marketing. However, if your efforts are successful and you can limit your competitor's ability to be a "follower," then the rewards of market dominance are substantial.

Regardless of which strategy you choose, you must give thought to future services. Stay closely attuned to your clients and anticipate the trends within your own field. Estimate when your services will peak in demand and when you must begin your research and development efforts to maintain a steady flow of business.

Research and development costs money. Every hour you spend on research and development is usually an hour not billable to a client. Develop a research and development budget, including both the costs and time spent for your various efforts. Research and development efforts are often underestimated. This influences both your project scheduling and your cash flow projections. To offset this discrepancy, include a 25–30 percent cost and time contingency.

Since research and development is a cost, you must carefully control it. If possible, try to incorporate your research and development efforts within the context of client engagements. For instance, it is costly and risky to develop a new service without specific client input. You bear all the expenses and you run the risk of market rejection. Instead, find a client whose situation requires the new service. In the course of the engagement, you develop the new service, which meets the client's needs and which can be offered to other clients. You minimize both your costs and your market exposure. For example, a computer consulting firm realized that government agencies would soon computerize their accounting departments. These agencies would need computer programs to perform these functions. Rather than develop these programs in isolation, they found a city that hired them to develop the program. They now sell that same program to government agencies across the country at a large profit.

Overall Schedule. Your schedule pinpoints the timing and interrelationship of all the major events important to starting and developing your business. Some people use flow charts. Other people use Program Evaluation and Review Technique (PERT) diagrams to help visualize the process of starting, operating, and planning for a growing business. You should specify your goals in terms of opening your office, beginning your sales campaign, receiving your first consulting engagements, completing your first engagements, receipt of first payments, research and development, and so forth. Then prepare a month-by-month schedule showing the sequence and timing of all the steps required to reach your goals. Include sufficient detail of all the activities required to complete each step. Create deadlines for each activity. Indicate which steps can be completed independently rather than sequentially, thus saving time. However, keep in mind that even though five tasks can theoretically be performed in one time period, you (or your staff) may not have the time to devote to all of them.

Be aware of what might disrupt your schedule and the potential effects of the disruption. In addition, everyone underestimates the time it takes to do things. Be realistic about your schedule by allowing a 50–100 percent contingency of additional time. Remember that this schedule is your major tool once you open your business.

Critical Risks and Problems.   A seasoned businessperson realizes that every venture entails certain risks. What are the possibilities of competitive responses to your actions? Are there possible unfavorable trends in the industry? What are the impacts of schedule delays or over-runnning your budget? What will happen if you fail to meet your sales projections? There may be other risks peculiar to your own situation, such as the effects of a family member becoming sick. Specify which potential risks and problems are most critical to your consulting firm. Then, describe your plans for coping with and minimizing the impact of each. In essence, draw up contingency plans before you need them, not later. This will also indicate which potential risks are in your control and which are beyond your control.

Financial Plan.   Your financial plan identifies the sources and uses of money in your business. Translate all your previously made goals and plans into dollars and cents. You show your financial standing through four basic documents: profit and loss forecasts, cash flow projections, pro forma balance sheets, and break-even charts. To gain an in-depth understanding of these items, meet with your accountant. You might also refer to the books mentioned at the end of this chapter.

To begin, "pro forma" refers to how things might be during some future period. It is a projection into the future based on current information and assumptions.

Profit and Loss Statement.   Your profit and loss statement is also known as the income statement. In your pro forma profit and loss statement, you plan the profits of your business. Utilizing your previously developed sales forecast, you then budget the costs outlined in your operations plan. Your costs will include sales, marketing, salaries, rent, equipment, utilities, and so on. As indicated earlier, these costs are divided into fixed and variable costs. From your projected sales revenues you subtract your costs to arrive at your profitability. Prepare your profit and loss projection monthly for the first year of operation and quarterly for the following two years.

Be realistic in these estimates of profit and loss. It is not unreasonable for consulting firms to show a loss during the first months of operation. Rather than hide this fact, incorporate it into your planning. Remember to question your assumptions in order to make an assessment of their impact. For instance, if your bad debt rate is higher than expected, how will it affect your profits? By examining such issues on paper, you avoid financial disasters later.

Pro Forma Cash Flow Analysis.   The pro forma cash flow analysis explains the amount and timing of expected cash inflows and outflows. The cash flow statement is usually divided into two parts: the sources of company funds and the uses to which these funds are put. Sources of funds normally include sales revenue, owner investment, loans, and outside equity investment. Uses of funds typically are expenditures for rent, salaries, equipment, taxes, interest on loans, and other costs. The purpose of the cash flow analysis is to determine if you will have enough incoming sources of funds to meet your required outgoing uses. This balance is known as liquidity.

Sometimes, especially during your first few months, you will not have enough sales revenue to finance your short-term costs. This usually occurs for one of three reasons: 1) your sales are below projection, 2) your costs rise unexpectedly, or 3) you have not yet been paid for consulting work already performed. This latter reason is labeled "overdue accounts receivable." Most professionals experience accounts receivable problems during their early months of operation because people tend to pay professionals *after* they have paid other outstanding bills. Your cash flow analysis prepares you for this situation and enables you to plan your cash needs.

Make cash flow projections for each month of your first year and quarterly thereafter. Utilize your projections for sales, costs, and accounts receivable collection rate to pinpoint financing needs. Insure sufficient working capital to bridge any gaps between the outpouring of costs and incoming revenues. This gap, if any, is normally overcome through owner investment, outside equity investment, long-term bank loans, or short-term lines of credit. You must decide how to obtain the additional financing, on what terms, and how to repay it. The repayment, then, becomes an item under uses of funds.

A detailed cash flow analysis avoids a common pitfall of new businesses: "going broke while making a profit." You may consult every hour of every day, making a large profit on paper. However, if you are not paid on a timely basis, then you cannot meet your costs. Before long, your creditors will foreclose on you, regardless of the tremendous profit you are waiting to collect. By anticipating your cash flow requirements ahead of time, you can direct your attention to operating problems without the distractions of periodic cash crises.

Pro Forma Balance Sheets.   The pro forma balance sheets summarize the assets and liabilities of the firm. You determine your firm's net worth by subtracting the liabilities from the assets. Your balance sheet will indicate how your investment has grown over a period of time. Outside investors typically examine pro forma balance sheets to determine if the company is within acceptable assets-to-liabilities limits.

Break-even Chart.   A break-even chart visualizes the amount of sales revenue needed to cover all costs. The point at which this occurs is your break-even level. The difference between your projected sales and your break-even sales represents your profit. The larger the difference, the greater your cushion if your projections fall short. Discuss how you can lower your break-even point in case you fall short of your sales projections.

Proposed Financing of Company.   After determining how much money you need, you must figure out where it will come from. Most consultants suggest that you secure enough financing to cover your costs for at least six months and sometimes up to two years because of the cash flow problems mentioned earlier. It takes a while to establish your practice and even longer to get paid. Consequently, you must secure financing to tide you over until your operation is running smoothly.

Most consultants provide their own financing at the outset. They live off savings, cash in insurance policies, or consult part-time while holding down another job. A working spouse can provide the necessary financial support.

If you need to turn to outside financing, consider which type is most appropriate for your needs. Loans require collateral and interest payments but not control of your business. Outside investors typically desire control and profit share in return for investment. Discuss these alternatives with your accountant, lawyer, and banker. Indicate how much money is needed and how the money will be spent, such as on marketing or research and development.

Legal Structure of Firm.   As Donald Dible states in his book *Up Your Own Organization,* "The three most common legal structures for a business are the sole proprietorship, the partnership, and the corporation. The differences among these three legal structures involve the personal financial risk to which the participants are vulnerable, the requirements of federal, state, and local tax regulations, and those arrangements necessary to make investment in the enterprise attractive to investors." The information below is only an introduction. You should discuss this matter in depth with both your accountant and your lawyer before you make your decision.

Sole Proprietorship.   Between 70 and 80 percent of the 13.9-million businesses in this country are sole proprietorships. Although no accurate count exists, the vast majority of consulting firms also fall in this category. The reason for these large numbers is that sole proprietorships are the easiest and simplest legal structures to form. Under this arrangement, you and your business are one and the same for the most part. In most states, if you use your name as the business name, you do not have to file under the "assumed business name" statutes. Your firm's net income is taxable as your personal income. You have an unlimited liability for the debts of your firm. On the other hand, you are the only person who receives any share of your firm's profits. Finally, the legal life of the business ends with your death.

Partnership.   There are two types of partners: general and limited. General partners control the day-to-day operations of the firm. General partners usually have unlimited liability for the firm's debts and are responsible for the acts of each and every other general partner. Limited partners, also known as silent partners, exercise no control over daily operations. They typically invest money or other assets, except services, in return for a share of the firm's profits or assets. Their liability is limited to the amount of their investment. The relationship between the general and limited partners is specified in the Limited Partnership Agreement.

Partnerships have both advantages and disadvantages. Partnerships allow you to pool the resources and skills of several people. Consequently, you can divide the labor and responsibilities. This team approach increases the probability of success. On the negative side, difficult impasses develop when partners become incompatible. In addition, the death of any general partner usually terminates the partnership's life. Both these situations can interfere with your firm's continued functioning.

Corporations.   Corporations are legal entities, separate and distinct from you as an individual. Most major businesses are corporations. Corporations have several advantages. They offer permanence, continuing despite the death of individual shareholders. Your personal liability for the firm's debt is limited to the amount you invest in stock. Depending on your tax bracket, you may achieve tax advantages by incorporating. Finally, for attracting additional outside equity investment, the corporation is the most attractive.

Corporations also have several disadvantages. They are typically subject to higher taxes and fees. For example, it can cost between $300 and $1,000 to incorporate. The procedures, reports, and statements required by the government become cumbersome. Your powers are limited to those stated in the charter. You may have difficulty doing business in another state due to laws governing corporations. Corporations have difficulty overcoming the "impersonal" image created by societal stereotypes and government regulations. Finally, the other stockholders may not have your devotion to the firm.

In summary, firms become more legally and financially complex as they move from sole proprietorship to partnership to corporation. For most consulting firms, the sole proprietorship will be the simplest and offer the greatest tax incentives. It depends primarily on the amount of liability you want to risk. However, discuss the pros and cons of each structure with your attorney and accountant.

Appendixes. If you seek outside financing, attach specific additional information as appendixes. The appendixes include your complete sales forecast and any market surveys you have performed or used. Also, provide information concerning the owners and key management personnel. Include in-depth resumes of these personnel, specifying their educational and employment backgrounds. Outside investors also want to know the financial condition of the owners. Therefore, present personal financial statements of each owner. If your key personnel have published material, especially related to your firm's activities, attach copies as an appendix. Also, substantial letters of reference can make an impact on potential investors. The content of these letters should enhance the image of your firm. Choose references whose opinions make a difference in the business world, such as bankers, well-known business people, professionals, etc. Finally, include any newspaper articles, magazine articles, books, or annual reports related to your business, the industry, or your competitors. This allows the investors to acquaint themselves with your situation; it also demonstrates your familiarity with the endeavor you propose.

At this point, you know how to complete a business plan. By completing each section of the plan, you will command the success requirements for your consulting practice. More than likely, you have already faced and resolved many major problems. By performing this task before you open your doors, you will increase the likelihood of success. With your business plan as a guide, you can focus your major energies on consulting rather than on operating your business. You are now ready to put your plan into action. Your next step is to establish your office—the topic of Chapter 4.

Additional Sources of Help

Business Plans that Win Dollars. S. Rich and D. Gumpert. New York: Harper & Row, 1985.

Entrepreneuring in Established Companies. S. Brandt. New York: Dow-Jones–Irwin, 1985.

Entrepreneuring: The Ten Commandments. S. Brandt. Reading, Mass.: Addison-Wesley, 1982.

How to Organize and Operate a Small Business. C. Baumback, K. Lawyer, and P. Kelley. Englewood Cliffs, N.J.: Prentice-Hall, 1973.

Managing Your Accounting and Consulting Practice. M. A. Altman and R. Well. New York: Matthew Bender & Co., 1978.

New Venture Creation: A Guide to Small Business Development. J. Timmons, L. Smollen, and A. Dingee. Homewood, Ill.: Richard D. Irwin, Inc., 1977.

Ownership. T. E. Hughes and D. Klein. New York: Charles Scribner's Sons, 1984.

SBA Publications: Free Management Aids; SBA Publications: For-Sale Booklets; SBA Publications: Checklist for Going into Business. U.S. Small Business Administration. Washington, D.C.: U.S. Government Printing Office.

Up Your Own Organization: A Handbook to Start and Finance a New Business. D. Dible. Santa Clara, Calif.: The Entrepreneur Press, 1976.

Request information concerning taxes, permits, and laws from the department of commerce in your particular state.

Outfitting Your Office

If the journey is long, take only necessities. This leaves room to acquire luxuries along the way.
ANONYMOUS

You must do three things before you can open your doors to the public: 1) establish your office with necessary government permits, supplies, equipment, and personnel; 2) determine your fees; and 3) design your marketing plan. These three activities are related to the earlier discussion of expenses and revenues. The start-up costs of establishing and maintaining your office will constitute your initial expenses. By knowing your expenses, you can determine the fees you must charge in order to break even and to make a profit. With knowledge of your expenses and fees, you can design your marketing plan to generate sufficient revenues. The remainder of this chapter will discuss how to establish your office while controlling your expenses. Chapters 5 and 6 are devoted to fee structures and marketing.

It is relatively easy and inexpensive to open a consulting practice; however, an important factor in the success of any new business is the owner's ability to control expenses.

Office

Consultants debate the advantages of different office locations. The debate is twofold. First, is it professional to work out of your home? Second, if you work in an office building, where should it be located? No hard-and-fast rules or research indicate higher success for different locations. As a general practice, many consultants begin by working from their homes. As their practice grows, they move into office space.

Consultants traditionally work from their homes for one reason: money. It reduces a major expense. However, do not fool yourself by thinking you have no rent when you work at home. You either pay rent or a mortgage on your home. The percentage of floor space devoted to your office is the percentage applied to your home payments to determine your office rent. This rent should be incorporated into your fees and deducted from your income taxes if the space you use for an office is a separate room in which no personal activities take place. The use of half your living room is not deductible.

Consultants are now working at home for other reasons. Some want to be closer to their families. Others want to avoid commuting and gas consumption. Still others find they can perform most of their work at home, so there is little need for an office. Whatever the reason, some important factors deserve consideration. First, before you set up a home office, make sure you can control both your time and your concentration. Realistically evaluate if you can work for long periods undisturbed by family matters. Will the ringing door bell, or the washing machine, or the children playing interfere with your work? Can you establish guidelines with family members as to when you can be disturbed and what they can expect from you? Answers to these questions are crucial to your success.

Second, do you expect to receive visitors, especially clients, at your office? Although most consultants go to the client's location, occasionally the reverse is true. Are both your home and your office presentable for such occasions? Do you have a separate, private entrance into your office or will your visitor walk through your home to reach your office? What impression will both your home and your office make on your visitor? If it is difficult for you to evaluate this, ask a friend or colleague. Remember, your professional image is important. You don't want anyone to think you are running a backyard operation.

Third, if you have children, you should have a separate phone in-

stalled to make it easier for clients to reach you. Either buy a recording device or retain an answering service to answer calls when you
are busy or away from the office.

Most large consulting firms argue that professionals should shun
the marginal image produced by offices located in homes. They prefer office space with a prestigious address. When moving into office
space, you should consider four factors: expense, image, proximity
to clients, and referral potential. Expense and image are self-
explanatory. Proximity to clients involves reducing time spent traveling between your office and your client's work place. Proximity
also enables the client to visit you. The last important aspect is the
building's referral potential. Does the building also house other
professionals (such as lawyers) who might make referrals to you?
Does it contain businesses that could be prospective clients? Rather
than locate in a building with a veterinarian, a photographer, and a
hairdresser, get extra mileage from your location by surrounding
yourself with complementary professionals and business clients.

To reduce the initial cost of office space, you should follow the
advice that has been given by numerous consultants. First, rent a
small office. Rarely do you need an entire suite of offices at the beginning. Discuss your future expansion needs with your potential land-
lord. Most landlords are happy to accommodate growing firms in
order to insure long-term rental income. Second, share an office or
suite of offices with other professionals. Often, several professionals
will rent a suite of offices. Each person gets his or her own office,
while they share a common waiting area. In addition, they might
share a receptionist/secretary who is located in the waiting area. The
receptionist/secretary's salary, like other expenses, is shared by the
group. Third, if you can't find a group, try to sublet an office from
another professional, or share your office. For instance, many psychologists see clients only at night. You might arrange to have the
office from 9 to 5, while your partner works from 6 to 10 P.M. In
this case, it is important to choose your partners carefully. They
should meet your own standards of ethics and professionalism.
Hopefully, they will promote, not detract from, your image.

Equipment

Consultants require minimal equipment: desk, chair, lamp, file cabinet, bookshelf, chairs for visitors, briefcase, appointment book,

stationery, business cards, and clothes. Depending on your typist's abilities, you may want a tape recorder/transcriber or a typewriter for rough drafts. If you hire a secretary, he or she will need a desk, chair, file cabinet, and typewriter. Not counting clothes, you can usually purchase such equipment for $1,000 to $2,000. This is a small investment compared to most businesses.

When purchasing office equipment keep two factors in mind: image and function. For instance, choose a desk with enough work and drawer space to accommodate your needs. At the same time, think of the impression it will leave on your clients, visitors, and personnel. A gray metal desk usually implies a worker, whereas a large wooden desk signifies someone with authority. If the desk is scratched, chipped, and messy, your clients might attribute the same characteristics to your work. Look at your office from the visitor's viewpoint. Do the furniture arrangement, decorations, and cleanliness evoke a professional, competent, trustworthy image? If not, they should. Ask friends and colleagues for their impressions and advice. If need be, call on the services of a professional interior designer to help create the proper image.

Consultants also must pay attention to their personal equipment: business cards, stationery, briefcase, and clothes. The purposes, again, are function and image. Your business card is a reflection of you. For most consultants, the card should be simple and conservative, printed on quality paper stock. It should state your name, company name, type of consulting, address, and phone. If you have a logo or appropriate slogan, you might include it. In some cases, the business card exemplifies your work. For instance, a graphic arts consultant should display his or her talents through the business card. The same holds true for writers and photographers who can incorporate a slogan or a photograph into the design of their business cards.

Your stationery should correspond to the format and image of your business card. Through your letterhead, reinforce your sharp, professional consulting image. Again, keep it simple, conservative, and, if possible, unique. Consider using an off-white color pleasing to the eye. Match the color and paper stock quality to your business cards.

Your briefcase and clothes also promote an image. In addition, they foster personal identification. It is known that people like others who dress similarly to themselves. For these reasons, consultants usually dress in a style that matches their clients. If your clients work in open collars and short sleeves, then a three-piece gray flannel suit is probably not appropriate. A tie and blazer would probably be the upper limit of formality. You want your clients to identify with you and also respect you. Your clothes and behavior should combine to create this effect. For more information on the importance of clothes, I refer you to the many books written on the topic, such as John Molloy's *Live for Success.**

A last set of equipment is determined by the consulting work you perform. More than likely, you will need reference materials such as books, journals, or newspapers. If you are a financial consultant, you will want a calculator and perhaps a computer. Even if you possess these materials, you constantly need to update them. Make a list of all the materials you need, what you have, and where you can secure what you do not have. Rather than subscribe to ten journals, use the library or share the expense and materials with colleagues. Since these materials supplement your consulting practice, choose what you need and include them in your budget.

Secretary

Many new consultants make one of three decisions regarding a secretary. They hire a full-time secretary, or they decide to type themselves, or they have their spouse do the typing. All three are potential mistakes. First, a full-time secretary will not have enough work to keep busy. Second, unless you are an excellent typist, you will waste time typing and produce an amateurish product. Even if you are a good typist, you will make more money by consulting or finding new clients than you will typing. If you charge $30 per hour for consulting and a typist charges $7 per hour, it makes more sense to consult. Third, spouses seldom make good typists, regardless of their ability. Instead, your personal relationship of equals as spouses becomes a business relationship of unequals as boss to worker. Most couples cannot make this adjustment; moreover, the adjustment is usually unnecessary. Secretarial costs are not excessive and any money saved is not enough to be worth jeopardizing a marriage.

The solution to this dilemma is to rent a secretary. Most cities have temporary professional typing services. By availing yourself of these services, you limit the cost considerably. This is particularly true if

* New York: Bantam Books, 1983.

your personal computer's word processing software is compatible with the word processing systems of these services. You can then give the secretary your computer disk with your draft on it. This saves a great deal of time since there is no need to reenter the entire document. Instead, the secretary makes only the corrections and returns a high quality finished product. Moreover, most typing costs are billed to your clients in addition to your fees. (This is discussed more fully in the next chapter).

You should establish a good working relationship with your typing service. Find out how much lead time they need, whether they can transcribe dictation, the turn-around time, and how long it takes to make corrections. Explain your business to them along with the importance of timeliness and professional image. Just as you would interview several potential secretaries, interview potential typists till you find one who meets your needs.

You also need someone to answer your phone. As discussed earlier, contract with a reliable answering service or buy an answering machine. Receiving reliable messages quickly and leaving a favorable impression with your callers are important. Answering services are preferable, even though machines have gained widespread acceptance. Once again, discuss your business needs with your service, indicating the type of callers and questions you expect. Tell them how you would like them to answer callers. One attorney contemplated suing her answering service when she discovered that her service was telling phone callers that she was terribly busy and recommending that the callers seek another attorney. You should constantly monitor your answering service.

Personnel

If you are just starting your practice, you have little need for a staff. As a general rule, do not hire staff unless two conditions prevail. First, you consult and bill at least 80 percent of your time. Second, you can bill at least 70 percent of your staff members' time. The reasoning is that you must preserve at least 20 percent of your time to develop new business and to administer your firm. In addition, a 70 percent staff utilization surpasses the normal break-even point so that you are making a profit on the staff's work.

Instead of hiring new staff when you need specialized skills or additional help, develop a subcontracting network. Identify other consultants whom you can call on when you need assistance. As mentioned earlier, many solo practitioners will take on projects that they cannot handle alone and then subcontract portions of the project to other consultants. This practice works so that both parties give and get consulting work. These same subcontracting networks will enable you to compete with larger firms. In addition, subcontracting expands your capability while limiting your expenses.

Eventually, if you want to exceed your personal income, you must hire a staff, although most firms opt to be understaffed and overworked rather than the opposite. This practice controls expenses, psychologically motivates your current staff, and protects you from laying off employees during downturns in business.

Start-Up Costs and Monthly Expenses

Every business faces one-time start-up costs and regular monthly expenses. You must systematically plan for these expenses. It is impossible here to estimate these costs for you, since they depend on many factors, such as your location, your type of consulting, and your plans. Instead you should use the following list as a guide to the expenses normally incurred by consultants. Fill in the amounts you expect to pay during your first month of operation and an average for each successive month.

Expenses	1st Month	Average Month
Rent (including deposits)		
Office preparation and upkeep		
Utilities (including deposits)		
Phone (including deposit)		
Postage		
Office equipment and furniture		
Stationery and business cards		
Insurance (health, life, liability, theft, fire, etc.)		
Printing and supplies		
Answering service		
Typing/secretarial service		
Accounting and legal services		
Business licenses and permits		

Expenses	1st Month	Average Month
Advertising and promotion		
Dues and subscriptions		
Books and reference materials		
Travel: In town		
Travel: Out of town		
Conventions, professional meetings, trade shows		
Continuing education		
Entertainment		
Contributions		
Gifts		
Salaries		
Unemployment insurance		
Pensions		
Miscellaneous		
Total Expenses	1st Month	Average Month

By estimating these expenses, you have a base upon which to build your fee structure, which is the topic of the next chapter. This chapter has focused on the realities of starting your own consulting practice. By now you should have an understanding of the elements involved in setting up your own firm. With the business plan as a guide, you can move systematically through the steps necessary for maintaining a successful business. With your projected costs in hand, let's now turn to establishing your fee structure.

Additional Sources of Help

Office at Home. R. Scott. New York: Charles Scribner's Sons, 1985.

Staying in Business

5

An optometrist once told me how he determines his fee. He calls it the "Blink Method," noting that it follows the rules of a free market system. At the end of each glass fitting examination, he looks his patient in the eye and tells him "It will cost thirty dollars . . ." While saying this, he watches if the patient blinks. If no blink occurs, he quickly adds ". . . for the frames. There is an additional thirty dollar charge . . ." Again, he looks for the blink. If none is forthcoming, he continues ". . . for each lens. The lens grinding costs fifteen dollars . . ." He continues to add on charges until the patient blinks. At that point, he figures that he has charged what the market will bear.

Charging and Collecting Fees

Your fees are your revenue and your proof that you can make it as a consultant. Unfortunately, the public (and potential consultants) do not understand fees very well. The media reports that consultants charge anywhere from $100 per hour to $2,000 per day. The public mistakenly assumes that those rates are pure profit. With some quick calculations using 2,000 work hours per year times $100 per hour, they arrive at an annual income of $200,000 per year. The public then splits into two groups, each group drawing its own conclusions. The first group concludes that they would like to be consultants. The second group decides that consultants overcharge for their services.

Neither group fully comprehends the relationships of fees to revenues and to the expenses incurred to generate that revenue.

This chapter discusses how fees fit into your consulting practice. (The information presented is the result of numerous discussions with successful consultants.) Specifically, all the business elements included in your fee will be explained. Then, using one of six formulas, you will be able to determine your exact fee. In addition, the various fee arrangements used in the industry will be discussed, and guidelines for collecting your fees—an essential practice for a continuing successful firm—will be provided.

The Fee

A professional's fee represents three factors: the major source of income, an incentive, and a reward. As a source of income, fees are the means by which professionals meet their firm's financial obligations, such as bills, payrolls, and taxes. That same income provides for the professional's personal livelihood. As an incentive, a fee must be sufficient to motivate the consultant to continue in the profession. As a reward, it must be sufficient for the consultant to work and live at a comfortable level. Without these three factors, consultants could not and would not remain in the profession.

At the base of most fee structures is the consultant's billing rate. *Your billing rate is the dollar amount that a client pays for a specified time period.* The time period is usually an hour or a working day. For example, you might state your billing rate as $40 per hour or $320 per day. When expressed as a daily rate, it is called a "per diem." For most consulting firms, the billing rate is the cornerstone of their fee structure and their revenues. As such, it is important to understand all that is included in the billing rate.

Your billing rate must take into consideration the following nine items:

Salary
Research and development
Employee benefits
Overhead expenses
Profit
Competition

Economic conditions
Bad debts
Fairness to clients and your firm

By evaluating each of these items, you can determine your fee. Each item will now be explored more fully.

Salary

Your salary is your worth as a labor commodity on the open market performing the same services you provide as a consultant. In other words, how much would a company pay you to use your skills full-time? If you are now working full-time, your current salary may or may not represent your true worth. Research shows that many people are underemployed and underpaid. Moreover, most salaries increase as a result of a job change from one company to another. In any case, make a note of what your current salary prospects would be if you worked full-time for someone else.

If you have a difficult time determining a salary figure, then consider the following four items: 1) What is the value of your service to the client? Will your clients lose money by not utilizing your services, or will they make considerably more money with your help? In either case, how much money? Will they gain short-term and/or long-term benefits? 2) What client responsibilities will you assume as a consultant? Will your actions and recommendations considerably shape the fate of the client's company? Greater responsibility usually warrants a higher salary. 3) What skills are required for your services? Is there a large or short supply of those skills? The economics of high demand and short supply result in higher salary. 4) What are your previous education and experience costs? Did you spend years in graduate training or apprentice at minimum wage many years? High past costs are generally recouped in your current salary.

As a guide to determining your salary, you might want to contact the Association of Consulting Management Engineers, 230 Park Avenue, New York, N.Y. 10017. They periodically publish a *Report on Compensation for Professional Staff in Management Consulting Firms*. They publish salary ranges by size of firm and level of management consultant. They also provide comparison to studies in prior years. For example, in 1984 the median total compensation level for a senior partner was $99,000 with the highest paid taking in $325,000 per year. Junior partners received a median compensation of $66,000, with the top bracket peaking at $140,000. The median was $52,000 for senior consultants, $37,000 for management consultants, and $26,000 for entry level consultants. Remember that these salaries represent management consultants and may not be applicable to your field.

Your salary plays an important role in determining your billing rate. If need be, interview either consulting firms or companies to obtain your salary range. Once you have this dollar figure, you can use it in the formulas presented later in this chapter.

Employee Benefits

Benefits are the "extras" you receive from an employer, above and beyond your salary. Benefits are normally tax free. For most employees, benefits amount to 25–60 percent of their salary. In other words, they receive tax free an extra 25–65 percent income.

Benefits include items such as:

Insurance: Health, life, liability, legal
Training: On- and off-the-job
Vacation
Sick leave
Pension
Unemployment insurance
Payroll taxes

Many consultants include benefits as part of overhead, which is covered in the next section. Some prefer to separate them. This forces you as a business owner to think about the "extras" you will provide for yourself and any future employees. It also makes you develop policies concerning these benefits—for example, will you compensate for absences due to sickness? Moreover, you can see the relationship between the dollar cost of benefits and your billing rate. You might find that certain benefits are too costly because they elevate your billing rate to an uncompetitive level.

Before progressing to the next section, estimate the dollar cost of your benefits. You will utilize the total benefit costs in the formulas presented later.

Overhead Expenses

Overhead represents the expenses incurred in operating a business. The cost estimates you derived earlier in Chapter 3 are useful here. When analyzing your expenses, you must separate them into two categories. One category involves expenses that are directly related to business operations. This category is overhead. For example, rent, fire insurance, and typing costs for correspondence are overhead. The second category includes expenses incurred while serving your client. For example, long distance calls made on a client's behalf are client expenses, not overhead. Normally, you bill these expenses to the client. Do not include them as part of your monthly operating costs (overhead).

Monitor the following expenses to insure that you are not inadvertently absorbing client expenses.

Typing.   Typing performed for client projects is billed to the client. Some consulting firms bill as much as 50 percent of all typing.

Telephone.   Client-related calls are billed to the client. Nonclient-specific calls are overhead. Remember to invoice the client for time you spend on client-related calls.

Automotive.   Miles accumulated while working on a client project are billed at the most recent Internal Revenue Service rate.

Travel.   Travel includes transportation, hotels, meals, tips, and any other appropriate expenses. Client-related travel is billed directly to the client. All other travel is overhead.

Postage and Delivery.   Whenever material other than monthly statements is sent to clients, you bill the client. Postage and delivery not chargeable to clients is overhead.

Duplicating.   Labor and machine costs of duplicating for clients is billed accordingly.

Securing Projects.   Many costs are incurred when you negotiate and secure new consulting engagements. Labor, typing, travel, and duplicating costs add up when you write proposals and make presentations. Some firms inform potential clients at the outset that they bill these expenses. Other firms recover these expenses after securing the engagement. Fewer and fewer firms are willing to absorb these costs as overhead.

With the above guidelines, review your projected costs from Chapter 3. Separate your true overhead from client-incurred expenses. Add up your total overhead costs. You will use this figure in the formulas presented later in this chapter.

Research and Development Expenses

An important overhead expense is the time and money spent on research and development (R & D). These costs are often forgotten. But good consultants continually refine their current services by improving their skills or streamlining their operations. These improvements and refinements of your consulting may result from continuing education or adding new equipment to your office. Both cost money, which must be included in your billing rate calculations.

In addition to systems R & D, you must devote time and money to developing new services. Every service has a life-cycle. If you do not have a new service to offer when the marketplace no longer needs your current service, your business will suffer. You can avoid this pitfall by setting aside resources for R & D purposes. Continually think of how and when to offer new services that will meet a need in your marketplace. Determine the costs in time, dollars, and other resources that make up this R & D expense. Then, add these expenses into your billing rate calculations.

Profit

Profit is your reward for business risks and ownership. It is above and beyond your salary for labor. Profit generally ranges from 10–50 percent of your salary plus benefits plus overhead. Business owners often make a critical mistake concerning profits. They confuse their salary with their profit. When they receive $30,000 net income from their business each year, they declare a $30,000 profit. In truth, that $30,000 represents both salary and profit. They must subtract what they could have made working for someone else. What remains is their profit and reward for the work, responsibilities, headaches, and risks of being a business owner. You must determine what profit level you require for doing the same.

Competition

When establishing your billing rate, you must be cognizant of the customs of your community and of the industry. Three factors determine your competitive position. First, what are your successful competitors charging? Second, what will your clients pay? Third, what minimum and maximum levels are you willing to accept? The answers to these three questions will give you lower and upper limits for your billing rate. You can then compare these limits to the rates needed to meet your salary, benefits, overhead, and profit. If your rate does not fall within the limits, then you will find it impossible to operate your business without some adjustments.

To obtain the information necessary to answer the above questions, ask bankers, lawyers, accountants, and other consultants. They generally know the customs of your business community and can be very helpful. Also contact your professional and trade associations for information. For instance, the Association of Consulting Management Engineers (ACME) and the Association of Management Consultants (AMC), both listed in the Appendix, provide rate information for management consultants at various experience levels. The author polled several large management consulting firms and found the following:

Title	Range	Average Billing Rate
Partner or equivalent	$600–$2000	$1500
Principal management consultant	$800–$1800	$1300
Senior management consultant	$600–$1300	$1000
Management consultant	$400–$1000	$600
Junior management consultant	$200–$600	$400

These data give you a sample of average national fees for management consultants. The rates for your community or type of consulting may vary considerably. Check with your appropriate trade associations and your local network to determine the normal fee range for you.

You must consider your potential clients' perceptions of your fee. On the one hand, ACME reports that client resistance to consulting fee levels is more widespread now than previously. Managers and owners of client companies are comparing their own visible compensation levels with consulting fee rates. In addition, they seek to reduce high costs in this time of inflation. Unless they clearly foresee benefits that will exceed your fees, they will do without your services. On the other hand, clients familiar with consultants know the acceptable fee range. If your fee is too low, they will assume either that you are a "greenhorn" or that your quality is as low as your price. In either case, they will not engage you unless your reputation is well known and respected.

As you can see, your client's perception of a fair price is important. Again, ask your local network of bankers, accountants, and lawyers. You might conduct a survey of potential clients. Ask what they have paid consultants in the past and what they consider a fair price. Another opportunity to find this information occurs during project negotiations. Whenever you discuss a potential consulting project, you should ask three questions: 1) Have they ever used consultants before? 2) Were they satisfied? 3) What was the nature of the fee arrangement? You will then have rate information for this particular client along with their biases toward consultants.

Make a note of the accepted fee range for your consulting. After you use the formulas to determine your billing rate, you can compare your rate to the accepted fee range. Check where it falls in the range. Is it near the top, middle, or bottom? As a general rule large, well-respected firms are at the top. Small and/or new firms cluster at the bottom. All others fall in the middle range.

Economic Conditions

Your billing rate must take into account not only your clients and competitors, but also the economic conditions that affect you. How are inflation and the recession affecting you? At what rate are your costs rising or falling? How does this compare with the way your clients and competitors are affected? Economic conditions might justify adjustments in your billing rate.

Consider also the financial position of your firm. This includes your solvency philosophy, your growth philosophy, and your profit philosophy. For example, if you are just making ends meet, then an increase in your billing rate may be necessary. On the other hand, if you are content with making a modest profit, you may even lower your rates. When you considered your business plan, you probably contemplated these issues. Now incorporate these issues into your billing rate.

Bad Debts

Bad debts affect every business. A bad debt occurs when you are not paid for services you provided. You can determine your total bad debt rate by subtracting the total fees you collect from the total fees you bill. Bad debts also are expressed through a percentage known as your collection rate. To determine your collection rate, you divide your total fees collected by your total fees billed:

$$\text{Collection rate} = \frac{\text{Total fees collected}}{\text{Total fees billed}}$$

$$\text{Bad debt rate} = 100 - \text{Your collection rate}$$

Professional firms experience bad debt rates from 5 to 40 percent. Very few firms collect all their bills. Most try to maintain a 90–95 percent collection rate, or, in other words, a 5–10 percent bad debt rate. Some large firms become alarmed when their collection rate falls under 85 percent. Few businesses can absorb a 15 percent revenue loss after paying the operating costs to generate that revenue.

To minimize the effects of bad debts, you can take numerous actions. These will be discussed in depth at the end of this chapter. This section will explain how your bad debts affect your billing rate. Once you have minimized and stabilized your bad debt rate to an acceptable level, you must still absorb these losses. If it has minimal impact on your profits, you may wish to do nothing. However, many professionals recoup the expected losses by raising their billing rates. In this manner they spread the bad debt costs across all their paying clients. In effect, they penalize their good clients by making them carry the burden of their nonpaying clients. This is generally not a good practice. More positive approaches are presented later in this chapter.

Fairness to Clients and Your Firm

After considering all the above items (your salary, benefits, overhead, profit, competitive position, economic conditions, and bad debts), you must then make an ethical judgment. What do you think is fair to your clients and to your firm? At what point will your billing rate be excessive, creating an unwarranted burden on your clients? Can you truly justify the value you give with the monetary value you receive? On the other hand, are you selling your services too cheaply? Are you cheating yourself? Many professionals undersell themselves to avoid being rejected by potential clients. They interpret the rejection not in relation to their billing rate but as a reflection of their professional skills. Consequently, they underbid in an effort to maintain their professional pride. This is a self-defeating transaction.

Traditionally, consulting firms have been cost-driven or market-driven when determining their fees. For the past several years, consultants have been adding a new dimension to their fee structure: value-added contribution. They believe that their fee should bear a relationship to the value they provide to their clients. For example, if your services will lead to a $1 million savings, yet the service takes one hour of your time, is it fair to you to receive payment for only that one hour? More and more consultants say no. They incorporate the value they provide into the fee they charge.

Your billing rate is part of an exchange. Research shows that equitable exchanges are the only ones that produce satisfaction for both parties. If you as a consultant feel cheated, then you will attempt to achieve equity by reducing the quality of your work. If your clients feel cheated, then they will either attempt to extract extra services for the same price or refuse to pay. Thus, you serve everyone's best interest by deciding on a fair price and sticking to it. As a result, you can perform your services without the psychological handicap of a guilty conscience.

The billing rate is the cornerstone upon which most consultants build their fee structures. Your billing rate requires you to make important calculations and to exercise good judgment. Some calculations will be precise, such as the dollar amount of your salary, benefits, overhead, and profits. Other calculations will be estimates, such as your competitive position, the economic conditions, and your bad debt rate. You must translate the sum of these calculations into an exact dollar figure: your billing rate. You then make a moral decision as to whether that rate is fair to both yourself and your clients.

How to Calculate Your Billing Rate

The previous section explained the elements included in your billing rate and suggested methods to determine a dollar figure for each element. In this section, you will learn how to plug those dollar figures into formulas used by consultants to calculate their billing rates.

Before the formulas are presented, two more important terms need to be defined: billable hours and utilization rate. Billable hours are the number of working hours you bill to clients. Forty working hours per week multiplied by 52 weeks per year equal 2,080 working hours per year. As a full-time consultant, you will work at least that many hours each year; however, you will not work 2,080 hours on client projects. You will spend some time answering correspondence, administering your practice, keeping up in your field, recovering from sickness, and taking vacations. Seasoned consultants devote 15–20 percent of their time marketing their services to secure new projects. Most of these hours are nonbillable hours. For consultants, the average number of billable hours ranges between 1,300 and 1,700 hours.

Your utilization rate tells you what percent of your total working hours you bill to clients.

$$\text{Utilization rate} = \frac{\text{Billable hours}}{\text{No. of total working hours available}}$$

To determine the utilization rate for consultants, you simply insert the appropriate numbers. For example, based on a 40-hour work week, and allowing for two weeks vacation (or 80 working hours), full-time consultants have 2,000 total work hours available each year. If they bill 1,300 hours each year to clients, then 1,300 divided by 2,000 equals a 65 percent utilization rate. With 1,700 billable hours, the consultant has an 85 percent utilization rate. If you plan to consult part-time at 10 hours per week, and you bill for 5 hours each week, then your utilization rate is 50 percent. Your utilization rate quickly informs you as to how much of your time clients are paying for directly and how much you must absorb as overhead.

By estimating your billable hours, you can use the following formulas, which are examples of how other consultants have calculated their billing rates. Each of them stresses differently the above-mentioned elements of profit, overhead, and so on. Find the formula that matches the emphasis you have placed on these elements.

The Rule of Three. The majority of consulting firms rely on the "Rule of Three" to calculate their billing rates. This rule utilizes your salary requirement as its base. In addition, it assumes that every consultant generates overhead and benefits that equal his or her salary. Moreover, each consultant should produce a profit that equals his or her salary. Multiply each consultant's salary requirement by 3 to arrive at total yearly revenues. One-third of these revenues pays for salaries; another third pays for overhead and benefits costs; and the last third is profit. The total yearly revenues are divided by your yearly billable hours to calculate your hourly billing rate. Thus,

$$\frac{1}{3} = \text{Salary of consultant}$$
$$+$$
$$\frac{1}{3} = \text{Overhead plus benefits}$$
$$+$$
$$\frac{1}{3} = \underline{\text{Profit}}$$
$$= \text{Total yearly revenues}$$

$$\text{Then, your hourly billing rate} = \frac{\text{Total yearly revenues}}{\text{Yearly billable hours}}$$

EXAMPLE:

If Salary	= $20,000
then Overhead =	20,000
Profit	= 20,000
Total	= $60,000 = 3 × $20,000 salary

If your yearly billable hours = 1,500 hours

$$\text{then, } \frac{\text{Total yearly revenues}}{\text{Yearly billable hours}} = \frac{\$60,000}{1,500 \text{ hours}}$$

then, hourly billing rate   = $40/hour
          and
daily billing rate   = $40/day × 8
                            = $320/day

The Rule of Three is a simple and quick method to calculate your billing rate. You only need to know your annual salary requirements and the number of hours you can bill to clients each year. The more hours you can bill, the less you need charge to maintain your profit level. The fewer hours you bill, the more you must charge per hour. However, if your salary requirements and billable hours are within the average range, then your billing rates will compare with the average. The Association of Consulting Management Engineers reports in its *Survey on 1978 Professional Consulting Fee Arrangements* that its members' billing rates have stayed close to this formula over the years.

Modified Rule of Three. The "Modified Rule of Three" follows the same rationale as the Rule of Three, except that you multiply your salary by 2. Some consultants, especially solo practitioners and professors, have a lower percentage of overhead and benefits costs. In addition, some consultants consider exhorbitant the 33 percent profit allocated by the Rule of Three. They are willing to settle for a lower profit. Consequently, their reduced costs and profit margin enable them to offer a savings to their clients through lower billing rates. Thus, if

$$
\begin{aligned}
\tfrac{1}{2} &= \text{Salary of consultant} \\
+ \\
\tfrac{1}{4} &= \text{Overhead plus benefits} \\
+ \\
\tfrac{1}{4} &= \text{Profit} \\
\hline
&= \text{Total yearly revenues}
\end{aligned}
$$

Then, your hourly billing rate $= \dfrac{\text{Total yearly revenues}}{\text{Total billable hours}}$

EXAMPLE:

If Salary	= $20,000	
then Overhead	= 10,000	
Profit	= 10,000	
Total	= $40,000	= 2 × $20,000 salary

If your yearly billable hours = 1,500 hours

then, $\dfrac{\text{Total yearly revenues}}{\text{Total billable hours}} = \dfrac{\$40,000}{1,500 \text{ hours}}$

then, hourly billing rate = $26.67/hour or rounded
and   to $27/hour

daily billing rate = $27/day × 8
= $216/day

You can alter the Modified Rule of Three to fit your particular situation. In this example, the salary was multiplied by 2. You might find that 2.5 is more appropriate for your situation. The important point is that if you can offer lower rates than your competitor without hurting your financial position, then you may have gained a competitive advantage.

Weighted Fringe Benefits Method. The "Weighted Fringe Benefits Method" is another modification of the Rule of Three. It was developed by firms that discovered two facts. First, the overhead generated by each consultant exceeded the cost of his or her salary. Second, the cost of benefits did not remain stable relative to salaries; instead, it rose faster than salaries. As a result, these firms had to add in fringe benefits as a separate factor. Consequently, they derived the following formula:

$$\text{Hourly rate} = \frac{3.25 \times \text{Annual salary}}{\text{Yearly billable hours}} + \text{Fringe benefits}$$

EXAMPLE: First, you must calculate the fringe benefits factor. It is calculated as a percentage of hourly salary. To determine the hourly salary, you divide the annual salary by the total yearly number of hours available. Thus,

$$\text{If Salary} = \$20,000$$
$$\text{If Total yearly hours available} = 2,000 \text{ hours}$$
$$\text{then, } \frac{\$20,000}{2,000 \text{ hours}} = \$10/\text{hr.}$$
$$\text{If Fringe benefits} = 25\% \text{ of Salary}$$
$$\text{then } 25\% \times \$10/\text{hour} = \$2.50/\text{hour}$$

You then place the following values in the formula:

$$\text{If Salary} = \$20,000$$
$$\text{Yearly billable hours} = 1,500$$
$$\text{Fringe benefits} = \$2.50/\text{hr}$$
$$\text{then, } \frac{3.25 \times \$20,000}{1,500 \text{ hours}} + \$2.50 = \text{Hourly billing rate}$$
$$\text{Hourly billing rate} = \$45.83 \text{ or rounded to } \$46/\text{day}$$
and
$$\text{Daily billing rate} = \$366.67 \text{ or rounded to } \$367/\text{day}$$

The Weighted Fringe Benefits Method is most commonly used by large firms. Overhead costs increase with size due to increased management levels and support services. In addition, these firms traditionally offer more fringe benefits in order to attract talented consultants. At the same time, their reputations allow them to charge more than the average firm which uses the Rule of Three to determine its rates.

The Constant Value Method. The "Constant Value Method" is an adaptation of the Rule of Three and the Weighted Fringe Benefits Method. The formula is as follows:

$$\text{Hourly billing rate} = (\text{Salary} + \text{Benefits}) \times .00146$$

It is called the Constant Value Method because the .00146 remains constant even though the salary and benefits amounts change. (I have asked consultants who use this formula how .00146 was chosen as the constant. None of them knew its origin. I discovered its origin from one of my graduate students. After I explained to my students that the origin of .00146 was unknown, the student raised his hand. Having worked fifteen years in the insurance business, he recognized the constant as a number used by insurance companies to determine work disability benefits. When you divide 3 by 2040 (the number of working hours in a year), the result is .00146. Thus, you can see how this formula is an adaptation of the Rule of Three.) If you substitute 3/2040 for .00146, the formula appears as follows:

$$\text{Hourly billing rate} = \frac{3 \ (\text{Salary} + \text{Benefits})}{2,040 \text{ hours}}$$

Rather than total billable hours, this formula uses the yearly total number of available working hours, allowing one week or 40 hours for vacation. It also adds in the yearly benefits as a separate expense.

EXAMPLE:

If Salary	= $20,000
If Yearly Benefits	= 25% of Salary
then 25% × $20,000	= $5,000
Hourly billing rate	= (Salary + Benefits) × .00146
	= ($20,000 + $5,000) × .00146
	= $25,000 × .00146
	= $36.50/hour
Daily billing rate	= $292/day

The main distinctions of the Constant Value Method are its utilization of total available hours rather than total billable hours and its fringe benefits component. The former lowers the billing rate while the latter raises it.

Exact Costs Method. The "Exact Costs Method" does not rely on the estimates and assumptions used by the other formulas. Instead, you determine the total costs of operating your consulting firm. This includes salary, benefits, overhead, and all the other costs you determined in Chapter 3. To these costs, you add your profit requirement. You divide the sum of exact costs plus profit by the total yearly billable hours. Thus,

$$\text{Hourly rate} = \frac{\text{Exact costs} + \text{Profit requirements}}{\text{Yearly billable hours}}$$

EXAMPLE:

If Exact costs	= $40,000
If Profit requirements	= 25% of Exact costs
	= 25% of $40,000
	= $10,000
If Yearly billable hours	= 1,500
The Hourly billing rate	= $\dfrac{\$40,000 + \$10,000}{1,500}$
	= $33.33 or rounded to $34/hour
Daily billing rate	= $266.67 or rounded to $267/day

You should note that the $10,000 profit is not a 25 percent profit margin. Instead, it is 25 percent of exact costs. If the total yearly revenues are $50,000 and the profit is $10,000, then the profit margin is 20 percent.

The Exact Costs Method forces you to determine the precise financial position of your firm. It does away with second-guessing and estimating. You know that your billing rate reflects the true costs of operating your consulting practice. Although it may take more time initially than the other formulas, it allows you to know which costs are rising and at what rates. The other formulas assume that overhead costs rise at the same rate as your salary. Since this is not necessarily true, the Exact Costs Method allows you to adjust accordingly.

Percent of Standard. The "Percent of Standard" formula is used to determine your billing rate in a special situation. Occasionally, you may want to discount your rates. This is known as a "percent of standard." Large firms will discount their rates in order to underbid their competitors and to secure market dominance. For example, the Big Eight accounting firms constantly engage in wage bidding wars with each other. In order to gain dominance in one industry or type of consulting, one firm will regularly underbid by as much as 50 percent. They aim to secure every project over a long time period, say two or three years. At the end of that period, they will be the most experienced firm in that industry or type of consulting. Then, they raise their rates, hoping that clients will pay more for the premier firm. The rates are increased enough to recapture the income lost during the three-year effort to gain market dominance.

Discounting and price wars are dangerous practices. Small firms seldom have the financial resources to support themselves during extended price wars. Even large firms have been "burned" by price wars. Some have found that many clients, especially government agencies, will choose the lowest bidder as long as that bidder has a solid national reputation. As soon as the consulting firm raises its rates, the client switches to a new low bidder. Consequently, the firm never recoups the income lost during its years of underbidding.

The small firm that discounts is seldom taken seriously by clients who use consultants regularly. Experienced clients know what projects should cost. These clients assume that the smaller firm does not realize the project's scope because the firm bid so low. The client attributes the low bid to inexperience or inability. In either case, the client will look for a firm whose rates are within reason. Consequently, if you want to discount your rate, bid at the lower end of the acceptable range.

If you do want to discount your rates, use the procedure followed by most firms. First, calculate your hourly or daily rate by any of the preceding five formulas. Then, determine how much discount you will offer. You must consider two factors: how much discount is needed to secure the client, and how much discount you can afford. You should seldom give discounts that exceed your profit margin.

EXAMPLE: If your Standard daily billing rate = $320/day and you discount 25% of Standard:

$$\text{Then Daily rate} = \$320 \times 25\%$$
$$= \$240/\text{day}$$

$$\text{Hourly rate} \quad = \$240 \div 8 \text{ hours}$$
$$= \$30/\text{hour}$$

Whenever you give a discount (or percent of standard), indicate to your clients that you are doing so. You should show what your standard rates are, the size of the discount, and the reason for the discount. You should also note these in your accounting records. The three most common reasons are 1) to secure new clients: "Since this is our first time serving you, we are pleased to offer you . . .", 2) to help out needy clients: "Since you have been a good client in the past, and given your current financial position, we deem it appropriate to offer you . . .", and 3) to collect delinquent accounts. In the last case, it is better to receive partial payment to cover your costs than none at all.

The above six formulas represent common methods consultants use to calculate their billing rates. Since each formula weighs factors differently, the formula you choose depends on your specific situation. You may find that you must develop your own. In any case, your billing rate allows you to project your total yearly revenues and the number of hours you must bill to achieve those revenues. You now have a set of standards by which to judge the success of your consulting practice. You know the salary, profits, the amount of expenses, the yearly revenue, and the billable hours that you can expect. Each of these is represented in your billing rate.

The six formulas are driven by your operating costs. Most consultants are content to recover their costs and to take home a reasonable salary and profit. Yet there is a growing consensus that a cost-driven approach is less than adequate for services that are knowledge-based, such as consulting. We are beginning to understand that pricing of our services has its roots in the pricing practices of manufactured products. Since cars and toasters are priced based on their costs, we have priced professional services using the same rationale. However, this approach undervalues the contribution of professional knowledge in creating wealth for a firm. As a nation, we now understand that this inappropriate pricing of brainpower has led to international competitive disadvantage.

For example, between 1950 and 1978, Japanese companies acquired 32,000 new technology transfer agreements from U.S. companies. They paid a bargain basement price of $9 billion for brainpowered technology that the U.S. government and companies spent more than $500 billion to develop. This purchased brainpower allowed Japan to avoid the risks inherent in R&D. It also allowed Japan to use the $491 billion in R&D savings for other purposes, such as building new factories and developing international marketing networks. Most importantly, Japan paid only $9 billion for technology that it is now using to create hundreds of billions of dollars of new wealth by taking over American markets. As a nation, we now realize that we underpriced our brainpower.

Once you have calculated your billing rate from a cost-driven perspective, take a look at it from a value-added perspective. Since your client is interested in the value you provide, not in the costs you incur, this value perspective will help you see your fees through your client's eyes. If your value is low, clients will not pay, regardless of your costs. If your value is high, clients are generally willing to pay accordingly.

After calculating your billing rate from both a cost-driven and value-added perspective, put it to a market test by comparing it to the rates charged by your competitors. If it falls within the average range, this is an indication that it is fair to your clients. If it is substantially higher, you may want to review your salary, profit, expenses, and billable hours. Are your salary and profit expectations too high? Can you reduce your expenses? Do you expect to bill too few hours to clients? Your experience and qualifications may warrant your unusually high billing rate. If your billing rate is too low, you must perform the same type of analysis. It is not a sin to offer low rates, but it is useful to know why you are doing so. You may have overlooked something important.

Fee Arrangements

Up to this point, your billing rate has been used in determining your fee because it is the predominant method. However, other fee arrangements exist. Many consultants use different fee arrangements, depending on the nature of the project. For the majority of their consulting work, they charge an hourly or daily rate. For other projects, such as government projects, they might charge a fixed fee.

Before the different fee arrangements are presented, there are three guidelines to be considered pertinent to their use. First, the ethical codes of many professions prohibit certain types of fee arrangements. For example, the Institute of Management Consultants prohibits fees contingent on producing a specific result. The American Institute of Certified Public Accountants allows contingent fees in certain aspects of tax practice, but it prohibits them in general accounting work. Check with your own professional associations to insure that your fee arrangements comply with their codes of ethics.

Second, since fee arrangements are business transactions, they contain an element of risk. In most cases, either you or the client carry the risk. The party that assumes the risk stands to win or lose the most. For instance, if you promise to perform a project for a fixed dollar amount of $5,000, you carry the risk. A budget overrun of $2,000 leaves you absorbing the extra cost. However, performing the project for only $3,000 rewards you with a $2,000 difference. Consequently, you must analyze your fee arrangement with regard to this risk factor.

Third, you may want to use a fee arrangement that is familiar to your client. For example, most lawyers charge by the hour. So, when you consult to lawyers, you should charge by the hour. On the other hand, since construction companies generally charge a fixed fee for their projects, you might quote them a fixed fee. In essence, you should try to speak your client's language if at all possible. It avoids misunderstandings and helps the clients incorporate your fees into their own budgetary processes.

These guidelines are reflected in the ten most commonly used fee arrangements.

Hourly or Time Charges

Hourly or time charges involve multiplying your billing rate by the number of hours you work for the client. As I have mentioned previously, this is the most basic and most common fee arrangement. All you need is your standard billing rate and a method to keep track of how you spend your time.

With time charges, the clients assume the risk, whereas the consultants know they will be paid for time spent. Since the project may require more time than initially perceived, the client could face a substantial bill. This is the risk factor. However, if what the client thought was a big problem is solved in a couple of hours, then the client reaps the reward of a small bill. Since problems are usually more complex than one expects at the outset, many clients try to avoid hourly time charges.

There are three common questions about time charges. First, how do you establish your standard billing rate? This has been discussed in detail already. As a matter of industry practice, billing rates generally are quoted in rounded whole numbers such as $35 per hour or $40 per hour. Very seldom will you see a billing rate of $37.26 per hour.

Second, when you quote a daily rate, how many hours do you include in the day? The general rule is 7½ or 8 hours per day. However, individual firms vary from this practice. Some include 7 hours. If the work is performed out-of-town, some firms put in 10 hours each day. However, these same firms may charge a higher daily rate, multiplying their hourly rate by 10 rather than by 8 for out-of-town work. The decision is up to you. Most clients, though, expect 8 hours' work for a day's pay.

Third, how do you charge for activities such as phone calls and travel? You should keep records of all phone calls with clients or on client projects. The time spent is billed to the client. You should inform your clients at the outset of this procedure. Unfortunately, many clients believe they get free consulting as long as you are not meeting face-to-face. They telephone regularly and for long periods, thinking they will not be charged. You will also bill travel expenses to the client. If you visit more than one client during a trip, distribute the expenses among the clients.

The question of travel time is more complex. As a general rule, time traveled during a work day is generally charged to the client. For example, if you spend 2 hours traveling to and from a client and 6 hours with the client, then you would charge your 8-hour daily rate. However, some consultants do not believe in charging for travel time. These consultants employ a couple of common practices. While traveling, they work on the client's project. In this way, they charge for their work as if they were sitting in their office working on the project rather than in an airplane. Another approach is to charge a higher billing rate for work that requires travel. For example, if their normal rate is $40 per hour, they may charge $50 per hour for work that requires travel. In addition, they have a minimum rate of a half day or a whole day for travel regardless of how much time is spent. If the work requires only 2 hours, they will charge for 4 or 8 hours. The treatment of travel time is an individual firm's decision. Since some consultants want to avoid travel, they charge a higher premium. You need to analyze your own situation to develop guidelines that meet your needs as well as those of your clients.

Fixed Fees

Fixed fees occur when a particular service is performed for a fixed dollar amount. When a lawyer quotes an absolute price to write your will, this is a fixed fee. Many government contracts require fixed-fee contracts. As a consultant, you should utilize a fixed fee only when you have effective cost control of the project. You must be able to estimate your time and costs with a high degree of accuracy. As a general rule, do not use fixed fees for projects with which you have little experience. You should have performed a similar project at least once to charge a fixed fee. Most firms use fixed fees only for projects that have become routine, such as personnel audits or executive recruitment.

In fixed-fee arrangements, the consultant carries the risk of budget over-runs and the reward for budget under-runs. If you quote a certain fee and it requires more time than expected, you absorb the difference. For this reason, clients prefer fixed fees for novel and complex problems. In these situations the risk of a budget over-run is great. Experienced clients prefer to have the consultant carry the risk through fixed fees. The consultant prefers to have the client assume the risk through hourly time charges.

On the other hand, experienced clients prefer time charges for routine projects, whereas consultants desire the opposite. For routine projects, the consultant can take advantage of the learning curve. For example, it should not take as much time and cost to perform a personnel audit the tenth time as it did the first time. If you charged by the hour for the first time, you know exactly how much the project cost. For the tenth time, you charge a fixed fee that equals or is slightly lower than the total hourly charges for the first time. Since you can perform the project in considerably less time due to the learning curve, you reap a sizable reward. However, most experienced clients are aware of the learning curve. As a result, when given the choice of fixed fee or time charges for routine projects, they will choose the latter.

Bracket Fees

A bracket fee combines fixed fees and time charges. In essence, the consultant works on an hourly basis, but his or her fee cannot exceed a specified dollar amount. Bracket fees favor the client. The bracket limit protects the client from budget over-runs. However, since the consultant only charges for time spent on the project, the client is rewarded by any budget under-runs. Cost-conscious government agencies have increased their use of bracket fees in the last few years. Also, experienced clients will opt for bracket fees whenever possible. From the consultant's point of view, bracket fees are a method of instilling trust in clients while quieting their fears of exceedingly large consulting fees.

Contingent Fees

You collect contingent fees once you obtain a successful result for your client. Lawyers commonly use contingent fees in medical malpractice suits. They are paid only if they win. They will usually take a percentage of the awarded settlement. Some executive search firms charge a percentage of an executive's salary after placement. If they do not place the executive, they receive no fees. As a result, the consultant bears the major risk.

As mentioned before, contingent fees are considered unethical by many professional associations. The major reason is that they can pose a conflict of interest for the consultant. The objectives of the consultant and client may differ when payment is dependent on successful results. In the executive search example, the consultant may place an individual inappropriately in order to receive payment. Consequently, many professional associations emphasize that you can charge for time and skills, but not for specific results.

Percentage Fees

When a uniform percentage is applied to the cost of a project, this constitutes a percentage fee. Merger and acquisition consultants may charge a percentage of the entire transaction. Architects do the same with large construction projects. Percentage fees differ from contingent fees in that they are not dependent on a successful result. Instead, the consultant is guaranteed a certain percentage of the total cost. In this way, it is similar to a fixed fee, and the same cautions and guidelines apply.

Value of Assignment Fees

As a consultant, you may perform projects that have intrinsic value beyond the number of days or hours consumed. Value of assignment fees are additional payments for such projects. For example, consultants that turn around a bankrupt business have performed a valuable service not only for the client, but also for the client's employees, creditors, customers, and community. Generally, they charge a substantially higher fee than if they relied solely on time charges. Consultants who prevent union takeovers commonly charge value of assignment fees. These fees can be either fixed amounts or percentages. Since value of assignment fees are attached to risky projects, consultants normally ask for these fees before the project begins.

To underline this point, many consultants use the anecdote about the nuclear plant. A loud knocking pipe created a turmoil at a large nuclear plant. No one could figure out what was making the noise or how to stop it. Finally one of the engineers suggested contacting Charlie, the retired maintenance man. Charlie listened to the knocking pipe. He then followed the pipe's course throughout the plant. After fifteen tense minutes, Charlie located a pipe connection. He asked for a large monkey wrench. Instead of using the wrench to turn the pipe, he hit the pipe connection four times with the wrench. At that point, the knocking stopped. Quite relieved, the management thanked Charlie profusely. In addition, they told him to send a bill for his services. When they received the bill, however, they were quite upset. It merely said, "For services rendered—$1,000." They complained that the fee was exorbitant for fifteen minutes' work. Charlie offered to send an itemized bill if they wanted one. They did. It read:

For 15 minutes' work	$ 25.00
For knowing where to hit	975.00
Total	$1,000.00

Bonus and Penalty Fees

Bonus and penalty fees are based on consultant performance during an engagement. These incentives are usually in addition to one of the other fee arrangements, normally the fixed fee. NASA regularly uses these incentives. Consultants who complete their tasks ahead of schedule receive a bonus for each day they save. At the same time, they penalize firms for each day they over-run their schedules. Many clients facing competitive deadlines will offer bonus and penalty fees. For consultants, this arrangement is similar to a fixed fee. You not only absorb the cost of budget over-runs, but you are also penalized for schedule over-runs. Consequently, the same cautions apply to bonus and penalty fees as to fixed fees.

Retainer Fees

Retainer fees have several meanings among consultants. This may describe an advance payment to "retain" your services for a particular project. In this respect, it is a sign of faith on the client's part to use your services and to insure payment.

In a slightly different sense, retainers are used to guarantee your availability during a time period, even though the client may not use your services. For example, if you have a small practice, you may be working on a large, time-consuming project for Client A. If Client B calls, you may not be available to meet their needs. If Client B wants to avoid this situation, then they may pay retainer fees on a regular basis. Calculate the retainer by the amount of money you require to forego other opportunities, normally a sizable amount, i.e., 10 to 25 percent of your income.

Consultants also use retainers as an arrangement to provide specified services for a fixed fee for a period of time. In this arrangement, you spell out the services and the time period. Services outside the retainer agreement are billed separately. For example, if you consult in the area of executive counseling, you may counsel a certain number of hours each week. Thus, it is important for both you and the client to define your use of retainer fees.

Clients use retainer fees to insure continuity of services. Consultants like retainer fees because they provide a steady income. On the other hand, retainer fees can restrict the consultant's involvement in new and more financially rewarding projects.

Equity Fees

Occasionally, consultants receive payment in the form of business ownership in the client's company. Equity fees are used most often with failing businesses. Clients may not have money to pay you for your services. Instead, they will offer a percentage of ownership in the business if you help turn it around. If it fails, you receive nothing. This places you, the consultant, in a high-risk position since the client has virtually nothing to lose.

Another use of equity fees is an outgrowth of long-term client relationships. For example, retainer fee arrangements over a long time period foster relationships in which the client relies upon and trusts the consultant. At some point, the client may want to obtain partial or total relief of corporate responsibility. He or she may offer you equity if you assume some or all of those responsibilities. In essence, the client is asking you to accept managerial duties in return for ownership.

A third use of equity fees is to create an alternative source of income for your firm. If you consult to start-up or growth companies, you may want to take part of your fees in equity that has a potential to appreciate. Often small, growing companies need consulting assistance but cannot pay for it due to cash flow problems. If they pay you in stock and the company goes public, you can realize a considerable bonanza on the stock you hold. Numerous consulting, public relations, accounting, and law firms in Silicon Valley have become extremely wealthy because they provided services in return for stock in such companies as Apple Computers and Genetech. If you create a well-balanced portfolio of companies in which you hold equity, you can create a steady additional source of income—from dividends or stock appreciation—that does not depend on your consulting fees.

Whenever you accept equity as payment, you should ensure that your equity is protected. It is not unusual for companies to give out increasing amounts of equity until your share is so diluted that it is worth very little. As your stock becomes diluted, you also lose voting power in the running of the company.

In all three cases, equity fees change your role from consultant to part-owner. Your vested interest in the business precludes your ability to act as an objective consultant. Most professionals, including lawyers and accountants, will not perform services for firms in which they have ownership or have positions on the board of directors.

Consequently, you should turn over your consultant role to an independent and objective outsider, if you accept part-ownership of a client's firm.

Deferred Fees

A deferred fee is not really a method of determining your fee. Instead it is a collection method that spreads the consulting fee through installments over an extended time period. Deferred fees are used most often when the client does not have the money to pay you in a lump sum. In other consulting situations, the client may experience dollar savings such as tax recoveries or lower quality-control costs. The client might request deferred fees so that these savings can offset your consulting fee as it comes due. In essence, they are using the cash flow generated by savings to pay your fees.

Deferred fees are not contingent fees. You are entitled payment regardless of outcome. It is simply a method of helping clients who experience a cash bind. By accepting deferred fees, you extend credit to your clients. As a result, you take the risks of default or only partial payments. The client may never have the money or may lose it between now and payment time. To offset these risks, you should consider the following tactics employed by many professionals.

- Charge interest on the total amount. The interest rate usually corresponds to bank rates or credit card rates.
- Charge higher fees.
- Request a sizable retainer fee before you start the project.
- Request collateral if your total fees are substantial.
- Request payment via cashier's check or credit card to insure payment.

Many clients appreciate deferred fees, particularly for large projects. Remember that when you use deferred fees you are extending credit. Like any lender, you must assess the credit-worthiness of your client. Also, determine what rewards you deserve for taking the risk and for allowing someone to use your money. From there, you calculate the best method to insure collection and to receive compensation for your risk.

Time charges and fixed fees are the most common fee arrangements. The fee arrangement you choose is the result of many factors, including your experience with the project, your assessment of the client, the ethical codes of your profession, and your own risk-taking. When in doubt, ask other professionals about their fee arrangements or contact your trade associations.

Limiting Fee Collection Problems

Knowing how to determine your fee is a major step in generating revenues to support your consulting practice. Securing and performing consulting work is the next major step. As the scientists say, however, these are necessary but not wholly sufficient steps for an ongoing successful practice. The third step is the collection of the revenues generated. Without successful fee collection, you cannot meet your own bills. You then run the risk of creditors foreclosing on you. Oddly, new professionals usually ignore fee collections until it is too late; they make three mistakes that can put them out of business. 1) When they first open their practice, they "carry" too many clients. They perform the work and allow clients to defer payment. As a result, they have little incoming cash to meet their business or family obligations. 2) They do not watch their collection rate. As mentioned earlier, the collection rate is crucial to profitability. If they do not monitor their collection rate, they have no way of knowing when it falls to dangerous levels. 3) They do not follow up on unpaid bills. Many people are reluctant to ask for money, yet avoiding the topic creates a desire in both parties to avoid each other. This reinforces nonpayment and dissolution of the relationship. The best way to handle such situations is by gentle reminders. When those fail, you must sit down with the client to work out mutually acceptable arrangements.

Since the success of your business depends on successful fee collections, devote considerable attention to it. Toward this end, most professionals follow three general rules: 1) avoid the problem; 2) limit your exposure; 3) review your billing and collection practices.

Avoid the Problem

You can avoid many fee collection problems through good front-end communications. As early as possible, obtain a mutual understanding with your client concerning the fee. As a general practice, discuss your fees during the first meeting. Also, indicate how and when billing occurs. Then, follow up your conversation with a letter reviewing your mutual understanding. In this way, you avoid confusion and disputes at a later date.

Many consultants find it difficult to discuss fees with prospective clients. Some fear losing the consulting project if their fees seem too high. Obviously, these consultants need either to review their billing rates or to consider another profession. Other consultants think it is unbecoming of a professional to discuss money. Some consultants get so involved in discussing the client's project, they forget to discuss the fees. A final group feels it is predatory to discuss fees when a client is distressed. All four groups commit a potentially costly error.

Remember that many clients have little or no experience with consultants. They do not know how much a particular service will cost, yet they need to know so that they can make budgeting decisions. Not knowing induces anxieties about exorbitant fees. If they have any preconceived fears about high cost, lack of discussion about the fee will heighten the fear. They reason that if the fee was moderate, you would talk about it. Consequently, your silence reinforces their anxieties.

I have found that many consultants use the following approaches to insure understanding of the fee. First, like doctors and lawyers, they post discreet signs in their waiting rooms concerning their fee and billing policies. Second, they provide all clients with a preprinted form that contains the same information. Third, they discuss their fees during the initial interview. Fourth, they send a follow-up letter.

Bringing up the topic of fees can be difficult, since the conversation usually centers around the client's situation. As mentioned earlier, I always ask my clients what prior experiences they have had with consultants. This question serves many useful purposes, which I shall discuss in Chapter 9, "Building Your Practice." For our purposes here, the question serves as an entree to discuss fees. If they have engaged previous consultants, I ask them the nature of the fee arrangement. I then use their reply to indicate how it corresponds to or differs from my fee and billing practices. If they have not used consultants before, I tell them that in my experience most new clients want to know about the fee arrangement. I then explain my fee policies and ask if they have any questions or concerns. In this manner, I insure that fees are discussed and understood.

Limit Your Exposure to Bad Debts

Establishing a common understanding occurs before you begin the consulting project. Too many consultants believe that their collection efforts stop there. Unfortunately, they ignore billing and collections while performing the project. They work many hours and present a large bill at the conclusion of their work. Then, for some reason, the client refuses to pay it. Since the consultants usually cannot undo the work performed, they have no recourse other than the courts. Consultants who do business in this manner forget that fee collection is a continuous process. Consequently, to improve your collection rate, you must limit your exposure during each step of this process.

You can ease your fee collection efforts by following guidelines used in many consulting firms. First, involve your client in handling the assignment. Successful consultants include the client at each step of the engagement rather than ignore the client while performing the project. They delegate tasks wherever possible and hold regular progress meetings. They send documents, progress reports, and letters to maintain constant communication. In other words, these consultants try to keep their efforts in the forefront of their clients' minds. If your clients know that you are working hard on their behalf, they will be less likely to withhold payment.

Second, obtain progress payments by billing frequently. Almost everyone gets paid monthly, biweekly, or weekly in our society, and consultants should be no different. There is no reason for you to wait for payment until the project is completed, unless clearly specified by your fee arrangement. Instead, most consultants send monthly bills for work performed to that date. Sending regular and frequent bills produces many benefits. For starters, several small bills are more likely to be paid than one large one, especially for smaller clients. A business can budget $1,000 per month in consulting fees more easily than it can absorb a $12,000 bill at year's end. Another useful effect is that if payment stops, you can stop your work. Thus, you limit your potential losses by withholding your services. In effect, regular payment of your bill provides positive feedback as to how the client values your services. If the client stops payment, then you know an important change has occurred. You should deal with this change before you resume the project. A final benefit is that regular billing forces you to keep your billing and accounting system in order. When your billing system is sloppy, your collection rate invariably decreases.

A third guideline to improve collections is to bill on time. The value of your service diminishes in the client's mind over time. Regardless of your having saved dollars and customers by designing a new quality-control system, after six months the client will think that your idea played only a minor role in solving the problem, and may even claim your idea as his or her own. Hence, timing is critical, particularly if your work produced favorable results. Make sure that your final bill is presented at the conclusion of the project.

A former graduate student of mine informally surveyed the billing practices of doctors, dentists, and lawyers. She found that professionals who request payment before the client leaves the office have 90–100 percent collection rates. Those who send monthly statements average 65 percent collection rates.

A fourth guideline is to account in detail for all work, time, and expenses related to the client. Note the time, date, and tasks performed, as well as who performed the tasks. In other words, you want to have complete records in case of any disputes. Keeping these records also enables you to budget for similar projects in the future.

A fifth guideline is to send general bills to your client. Usually, you need not provide all the details described in the previous paragraph. Those details are for your records. Instead, most consulting firms send a general bill indicating the phase of the project, the general activities performed, the number of hours, expenses, and the total fee. If the clients request more detailed information, these firms willingly provide it.

The sixth guideline applies to high-risk clients. High-risk clients are those who have a reputation for late or nonpayment or who constantly argue about their bills. For those clients, get disbursements in advance. Many consultants will demand sizable front-end retainers, which they deposit in a trust account. They then subtract their bills from this account. If possible, withhold an essential element that the client needs, such as the final report, until the bill is paid. If you are in doubt about a client's reputation, check with other professionals.

A final guideline is to follow up on your billing. Monitor the payment trends of each client. When this trend begins to change in a negative direction, make note of it. Often it signals financial problems for your client or a client's displeasure with your work. When payments are overdue, send reminders. When the reminders are unheeded, a telephone call is necessary. Inform the client of the situation. In some organizations, your client may not see the bill or realize that payment is overdue. Discuss the late payment with the client to determine the reasons for it. If the client is in a financial bind, set up a meeting whereby you can arrange a mutually acceptable payment plan. If no arrangement is possible, stop the project. Send a registered letter to the client informing him or her of your action.

The above guidelines should make it clear that successful collections require constant effort. The best method to insure payment is by making it clear that your services are valuable to the client and that you are working hard to provide that value. Of course, it is difficult to create that perception if neither aspect is true. The next best way to receive payment is to ask for it. If you don't ask, few people will offer it. You would be surprised at the number of professionals who ask too infrequently due to their haphazard billing system. All of these guidelines, however, must be used intelligently. Rather than rigidly apply them, adapt them to your particular clients and consulting practice.

Review Your Billing and Collection Practices

Successful billing and collection requires a system. The sooner this system is in place, the better your collection rate will be. Unfortunately, too many professionals fail to examine their own system. Once it is established, they are slow to change it. They do not check to see if it is working or if their practice now requires a new system.

To prevent this happening to you, review your billing and collection systems on a regular basis. First, examine your billing rate every six or twelve months. Modifications are generally required, depending on your costs, competitive position, economic conditions, and your worth as a consultant. Second, review your fee arrangements. What type of fees did you charge? How well did they work for you? What lessons did you learn for future fee arrangements? Third, persons not involved in the projects should evaluate your bills and billing procedures. Did you depart from your standard rates or usual fee arrangement? If so, why? Did you give discounts or extend credit to your customers? How often did this occur and what are your justifications? How did they affect your profits? If you force yourself to answer these questions to someone not involved in the consulting project, then you will receive more objective feedback concerning this aspect of your business. Since the individual does not have emotional involvement in the project, he or she can provide the outside input necessary to modify the system. Last, examine your collection procedures. Are you billing regularly and on time? Are you following up on nonpayments? What is your collection rate? These questions will give you important insights to improve your collections.

If you follow the three rules presented in this section—1) avoid the problem, 2) limit your exposure, and 3) review your billing and collection practices—then you will make important strides in improving your collection rates. As in most aspects of life, prevention is easier and less expensive than remedial efforts. The easier you make it for the client to pay, the easier it is to collect. To do this, you must have a system that requires but minimizes continuous effort on your part.

This chapter dealt with what to include in your fees, how to calculate your billing rate, and how to translate that information into a fee arrangement. It is important to note that each fee arrangement requires an analysis of the project, the client, and the risk factor. You also learned how to limit your fee collection problems through prevention and good business practices. The material in this chapter was distilled from interviews with consultants across the country. The guidelines and rules are generalities. You must apply them discerningly to your practice.

Regardless of your situation, to secure a profit you must pay attention to three of the concepts presented in this chapter. First, watch your billing rate to make sure it reflects the financial realities facing your practice. You can increase profitability through your billing rate in two ways: charge more or reduce expenses. Both give your billing rate a higher profit margin. Second, watch your utilization rate to insure that you are billing the number of hours required for profitability. If not, you must sell and perform more consulting work. Third, monitor your collection rate to insure that the revenues produced by your billing rate and utilization rate are being collected. If these rates are kept to maximum levels, then profitability should follow.

Knowing your financial requirements, you now can seek clients—the topic of Chapter 6, "Marketing Your Services."

Additional Sources of Help

Management Consulting: A Guide to the Profession. M. Kubr. Geneva, Switzerland: International Labour Organization, 1976.

Managing Your Accounting and Consulting Practice. M. A. Altman and R. I. Weil. New York: Matthew Bender & Co., 1978.

Contact the major consulting associations and your professional associations for their latest reports on compensation and fee structures.

Marketing Your Services

6

The aim of marketing is to know and understand the customer so well that the product or service fits him/her and sells itself.

Ideally, marketing should result in a customer who is ready to buy. All that should be needed, then, is to make the product or service available.

PETER DRUCKER

Consultants, like most professionals, do not understand the importance of marketing. Consequently, they do not market their services very well. This situation stems from two factors. First, most consultants have neither training in nor exposure to marketing. Engineers, economists, psychologists, computer specialists, and most other professionals disregard marketing. When called upon to market their services, professionals often flounder. Second, professional associations often hinder marketing—until recently they banned advertising as unethical. Many professionals, including consultants, concluded the ban extended to all forms of marketing. Given their acknowledged lack of interest and/or expertise in marketing, these professionals refrained from marketing altogether. Unfortunately, most businesses cannot prosper without marketing. The successful firms, however, saw marketing's value and developed creative approaches. You must do the same.

This chapter will help you formulate a marketing plan. It explains the benefits you will accrue by marketing. You will see how various marketing cycles affect every consultant, and you'll learn the three essential elements of a marketing program: your services, clients, and competitors. Then, you will focus on defining your market niche. Finally, various marketing techniques used by consultants to secure their niches will be discussed.

Additional resources that provide an in-depth look at marketing are at the end of this chapter.

Marketing Benefits

Marketing is the total effort directed at convincing your clients to satisfy their needs and wants through your services. It may occur through luncheon meetings, phone calls to prospective clients, ads in trade publications, or referrals from friends. In any case, marketing is not an isolated activity; it is a total, continuous process. When you integrate marketing into a consulting practice, it yields four distinct benefits:

- Marketing focuses your business and your efforts.
- Marketing makes you do today what is required to secure next year's business.
- Marketing makes you visible to your clients and your community.
- Marketing improves your organization.

Marketing Focuses Your Business and Your Efforts

As discussed in connection with the business plan in Chapter 3, you must identify at the outset your services, clients, and competitors. Marketing takes you one step further. It forces you to examine the interrelationship of those three elements. Moreover, it focuses your attention on your clients, rather than on your services.

Philip Kotler, a highly respected marketing professor at Northwestern University, outlines three marketing orientations: product, selling, and marketing.

The "product" orientation assumes consumers will respond favorably to good products or services that are reasonably priced. Companies with a product orientation believe they require little marketing effort to achieve satisfactory sales and profits. Such companies rely on the consumer seeking the company to bring in enough volume to produce profits.

The "selling" orientation assumes consumers will normally not buy enough of the company's products or services without a substantial selling and promotion effort. The selling orientation does not question the adequacy of the products or services. Rather, a firm develops methods to push them at high volume to produce profits.

The "marketing" orientation demands that the company perform two key tasks. On the one hand, the company must determine the needs, wants, and values of a targeted group of consumers. On the other hand, the company must adapt its organization to deliver the desired satisfactions more effectively and efficiently than its competitors. This orientation begins with the firm's existing and potential customers. After analyzing the customers' needs, it plans a coordinated set of services and programs to meet those needs. The key to profits under the marketing orientation is constant generation of consumer satisfaction.

Marketing, then, familiarizes you with your clients. You must analyze their needs—satisfied and unsatisfied. Then you must develop services that address both types of needs. Marketing also brings you closer to your competitors. Learn how they approach your clients' needs and improve on their techniques. Finally, marketing makes you develop specific methods to reach your clients. The end result is a consulting practice with focus and direction.

Marketing Makes You Do Today What Is Required to Secure Next Year's Business

Consultants frequently neglect the future. Current consulting projects engross them; procuring future engagements receives scant attention. Marketing compensates for this imbalance. Consultants with a marketing orientation realize that certain activities are necessary today to ensure a steady flow of work. These consultants identify future clients and what is necessary to secure projects with those clients. To accomplish this, they use marketing to 1) project future trends, 2) analyze unexploited markets, 3) develop new services, and 4) develop techniques to attract and secure new projects.

Ideally, a consultant has a reasonable backlog of projects. You need enough projects lined up so that as you conclude one, you start another. This requires forward planning based on the historical statistics of your practice. For example, you must know your optimum utilization rate—how many hours you must consult and bill each week. Then analyze what percentage of those utilized hours each week are devoted to each current client. As you plot each week's schedule for an entire year, you will realize that your projects will conclude at different points. To maintain your utilization rate you need to secure new projects now to replace the engagements that will end.

Marketing Makes You Visible

Marketing provides you with visibility among potential clients and potential sources of clients, such as bankers. Marketing helps you—even forces you—to create an image. The style and content of your marketing efforts will communicate who you are and what you do. Create your own image rather than letting it form haphazardly.

Marketing allows you to reach and educate your client. Many clients do not know how to use your services or why your services are important to them. Through planned marketing efforts, you can overcome client ignorance. Without marketing, you reduce your exposure and opportunities to gain new clients.

Marketing Improves Your Organization

Beyond obtaining new clients, marketing also has high internal value to your organization. A good image established through marketing and quality performance often leads to a growth cycle. As you become known and your client base expands, you can charge higher fees. Your increased revenue provides capital to develop new services and to hire additional employees. The combination of a good image and a growing capital base allows you to attract and retain the best staff. Personnel want to work for growth firms with a solid image. Employees realize that these firms provide greater opportunities, more interesting work, and higher status among their peers. In addition, your capital base allows you to pay higher salaries to these top personnel. A quality staff, in turn, increases your growth potential and your ability to charge higher fees. Marketing plays a crucial role in starting and maintaining this cycle.

When you personally market your firm's services successfully, you obtain another internal benefit. You show your staff that marketing and reaching clients are important. Since employees shape their actions to please the boss, they learn by your example. In this manner, you instill a marketing orientation throughout your firm.

From all the benefits mentioned, you can see that marketing not only is necessary but also yields tremendous payoffs. Without marketing, your source of clients and revenue soon dwindles. With marketing, you identify client needs and develop services to satisfy those needs. In addition, marketing provides methods to attract and secure those clients.

Marketing Cycles

Before you gain the benefits of marketing, you must understand four cycles that affect your marketing efforts. Each cycle plays a part in shaping your practice. Utilizing these cycles enables you to market more effectively and efficiently.

Feast or Famine

The "Feast or Famine" cycle is displayed in Table 6. This cycle depicts the common predicament described earlier where consultants ignore marketing. At first, they have no clients. Consequently, they search full-time for a client. After obtaining one, they devote all their time to consulting and no time to marketing. When the project ends, they again have no clients. As a result, they must begin the frantic search for clients. When they land the second client, it is to be hoped they have learned the lesson to break this feast or famine cycle. They try to set aside time for securing future clients. Eventually, they should schedule their workload with 75–90 percent of their time devoted to consulting and 10–25 percent devoted to marketing.

To break the feast or famine cycle you must schedule your projects accordingly. For example, if a project requires 80 hours of consulting, you have a scheduling choice. On the one hand, you can work 40 hours per week for two weeks. This allows no time for marketing. When the project is over, you will not have another project to begin. On the other hand, you can devote 80 percent of each week (32 hours) to the project. Rather than complete the project in two weeks, it will take two-and-a-half weeks. However, you have spent at least

TABLE 6. Feast or Famine Cycle

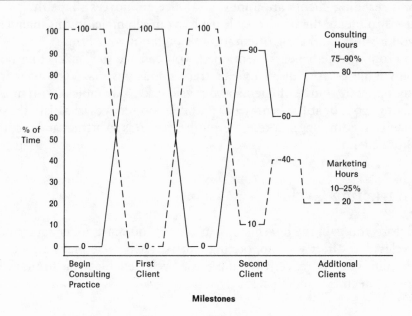

16 hours securing a steady stream of future projects. The difference between two and two-and-a-half weeks' completion time seldom affects the client. However, it makes a substantial difference to the health of your consulting practice.

Industry Buying Patterns

The second major cycle involves industry buying patterns. Most businesses seldom start consulting projects in the summer, since too many personnel go on vacation at that time. Instead, they turn to consultants in the fall and winter when most planning and implementation take place.

The government, which spent $12 billion in 1985 for consulting, has a different cycle. Agency budgets begin October 1 each year. Most agencies conserve their budgets during the fall and winter. During the spring, they can estimate any surplus funds. If they return the surplus, they face a budget cut for the next year. Since this is unacceptable to most agencies, they look for consultants on whom to spend these surplus funds. As a result, late spring to early fall are the good months for government consulting.

To insure that you approach the right clients at the right time, study the buying cycles of the industries in which you consult.

Observing industry cycles also yields information concerning client needs. Every industry proceeds through a life cycle: the company's formation, its growth to maturity, and eventually its slow-down over time. Industries have different needs at each stage of their life cycle. The computer industry provides a good example. Thirty-five years ago, it did not exist. During the early years, it had a high need for technical consultants to develop and improve the product. It also needed personnel consultants to find and train the required staff for a booming industry. As the computer industry reaches maturity, companies need planning consultants to help them find their market niche and to fend off competition. After reaching maturity, the industry will need consultants to infuse fresh ideas for strengthening the industry. By knowing how a particular industry stands in relation to its life cycle, you can develop services to meet that industry's needs.

Life of Your Services

As I explained in Chapter 3, the life cycle of your particular services affects your marketing. Since your services correspond to client needs and since client needs change in relation to their company-industry life cycles, your services must change. Each service you provide has a life cycle. When demand for a particular service declines, you must choose. Either you develop new services to respond to new needs or you can find a new client base whose needs match your developed services. Many consulting firms do both. Consultants with a marketing orientation identify changes in client needs. They develop services in advance to meet these new needs and also seek new markets for their old services. They continually replace old services for which demand has died with new services for which demand is growing. Marketing helps them avoid steady-state thinking about their products. Instead, they realize the service life cycle and react accordingly.

Customer Buying

The final important marketing cycle is the customer buying cycle. Clients move through distinct stages when engaging a consultant.

This cycle resembles buying behavior for any object, such as a car. First, the client becomes aware of his or her needs. This may lead to an interest in meeting those needs. The interest usually stimulates a strong desire to meet the needs. Finally, the client acts to meet the needs. As the client moves through those four stages, the consultant must use marketing techniques appropriate to each stage. For example, during the interest stage, you might phone or meet a potential client. Preparing a major proposal does not suit the situation. However, you'll probably need a proposal to move the client from desire to action. Thus, you must know where the client is in the buying cycle.

The four cycles—Feast or Famine, Industry Buying, Your Services, and Customer Buying—affect both your marketing efforts and the services you offer. Analyze and use these cycles. Without understanding them, you fall victim to haphazard developments and misguided efforts.

Clients, Services, and Competition

Up until now, general aspects of marketing that are important to you have been pointed out. In the succeeding sections, specific marketing information pertinent to your consulting practice will be discussed. This section will focus on your clients, your services, and your competitors.

Know Your Client

To develop a successful consulting practice, ask and then answer the following questions:

- Who are your clients?
- Why do your clients buy?
- What do your clients buy?
- How do your clients buy?

Who Are Your Clients?   In order to market your services and secure a client base, you must know who your clients are. Move from general labels, such as medium-sized firms in the trucking business, to specific individuals in specific companies. Without precise client targets, you cannot really come to know your clients. Acquaint yourself with your clients to specify their unique needs.

- What client *needs* can you satisfy through your services? As mentioned earlier, with a marketing orientation, you begin with the client's needs, not your services or products.
- Which *companies* in which *industries* have these needs? Industries' needs vary. For instance, the trucking industry needs consulting concerning federal trucking deregulation. The computer industry does not. At the same time, only interstate trucking companies need those services. Intrastate companies do not.
- Are there any *socioeconomic factors* pertinent to your clients or their needs? Some consultants work primarily with minority businesses or with Spanish-speaking businesses.
- What is the *geographical location* of these companies? At this point, you must decide if you are willing to travel and to what extent. Your geographical constraints normally limit your client base.
- Do specific *organizational locations* within the company have special needs? For example, finance departments normally need investment consultants, whereas personnel departments seldom do.

After answering the previous questions, you can develop a list of potential client companies. Now, you begin to specify your clients more precisely.

- At what *management level* in the company do these needs exist? For example, chief executive officers (CEOs) are the only clients of some strategic planning consultants.

To define your client, you've narrowed your range of questions from general consulting needs to needs of an industry, a company, an organizational level, and a management level. At this level you can name the client and perhaps his or her position. Aim your marketing efforts at this specific person.

- How does this specific individual *perceive* his or her *needs*? After specifying your clients, you must once again focus on knowing and understanding them. For instance, many clients with personnel problems perceive a need for training when they actually need better personnel selection procedures. If selection consultants did not understand this, then they would not see training requests as a potential source of business.

To understand your clients, you must study the buy-sell psychology: why, what, and how do your clients buy?

Why Do Your Clients Buy?   The reason clients use consultants is the same reason they buy clothes—that is, to *satisfy needs.* Clients' needs are physical, emotional, intellectual, social, spiritual, and economic. Any of these can come into play when a consultant contacts a client. A client may desire a consultant because competitors use consulting services. Other clients enjoy the intellectual stimulation consultants offer. A need for achievement may cause a client to use a consultant to propel his or her company or career. If you understand a client's needs for a consultant, you can market your services to satisfy those needs. Marketing research minimizes your selling efforts. When clients need the services you offer, your consulting sells itself.

What Do Your Clients Buy?   Clients buy *benefits* and *results.* Consultants provide benefits: advantages, satisfaction, and control. For example, a consultant's recommendation may lead a client to a competitive edge. A financial consultant may give the client control over cash flow. Consultants also provide results, even though the consultant may not guarantee it. The client may want to improve productivity by 10 percent or lower accidents by 50 percent. Clients look for specific goal achievements. If the consultant's work leads to these goals, then the client is willing to buy consulting services.

Learn to market your services in terms of client benefits and results, not in terms of your capabilities. Toothpaste companies advertise results—fewer cavities. They do not burden you with toothpaste ingredients or chemical reactions. Yet, consultants too often market their specialty, such as materials requirement planning (MRP). Most clients are unfamiliar with MRP and will not take the time to learn about it. Instead, the consultant should market the benefits clients can gain from MRP, such as increased productivity.

How Do Your Clients Buy?   Knowing both why and what people buy is not enough. You must know how people buy. Previously, I described the buying cycle. People move from need awareness to interest to desire to action. This process is based on the buyer's answers to six questions.

- *What is my need?* The client must differentiate and focus upon his or her need.
- *What will fulfill my need?* At this point the client calculates what will meet the need. It may be new equipment, a new staff member, or a consultant.
- *What sources possess the means to fulfill my need?* Once clients limit their choices to consultants, they examine the resources of each. At this stage, the client has moved from awareness to interest.
- *Can I afford the price of fulfilling my need?* The price and need are related. If a lawyer offered to sue your best friend for no charge, you would not be interested unless you needed it. The fact it is free is meaningless. Price moves the client from the mild interest stage to the strong desire stage.
- *When must I fulfill my need?* Time is critical in the buying cycle. Clients will not move from desire to action unless there is time pressure. At that point where they can no longer ignore the need, they are ready to buy.
- *Why choose one source over another?* Clients choose one source based on their answers to the five previous questions. When the match exists between their need requirements and your capability to meet those requirements, clients will engage your services.

Knowing your client is essential to good marketing and to satisfying your clients. By this time, you should have a clear picture of who your particular clients are. You should understand their needs and how they perceive those needs. By comprehending the benefits and results your clients want, you can educate them as to how your services will provide them. Finally, you can monitor your clients as they move through the buying process. You can match your marketing efforts to their buying pattern. By using this approach, you will reap the greatest return on your marketing investment.

Define Your Services

This topic was more fully discussed at the beginning of Chapter 3. By this time, you should understand fully a rule important to all consultants: *develop your services in relation to client needs.* Consultants who do not follow this rule end up trying to force their services upon clients who have little interest. Obviously, they meet resistance and tend to go hungry.

When defining your services

- be specific
- be clear
- insure that you provide a quality service
- stress how your quality service will meet the client's needs and provide benefits

Identify Your Competitors

Once you have identified your clients and defined your services, you can pinpoint your competition. Now you analyze them in order to compete effectively. Draw upon your potential client list. After each name, record the competitors who provide services to that client. For each competitor specify

- what client needs they attempt to satisfy
- what benefits and results the client receives
- what services they provide to satisfy the needs and achieve the benefits
- whether they are perceived as successful in the client's eyes

As a result of this process, you can assess your competitive position and identify consulting opportunities.

Once you know your competition, their services, and their success rate, you decide if you can effectively compete against them. Again, you must answer a series of questions.

- How do their services compare with yours? How are yours different or better? Do you personally have more appeal as a consultant than your competitors because of your education, skills, experience, or personality?
- What is each competitor's market share of your potential clients? Do you have the same one or two competitors for every client or is it a different competitor for each client?

- What are the strengths and weaknesses of each competitor? How can you minimize their strengths and exploit their weaknesses? Are they too far away to service the client? Do they have limited industry experience?
- What competitive resources do they possess? Are they so big that they can kill you in a price war? Are they a national firm with specialists at their beck and call?

Your competitive analysis will yield the information necessary to market your services effectively. You can then differentiate your services from those of the competition. Also, you will know what responses to expect from the competition. The end result is locating your market niche.

Your Market Niche

By defining your clients, services, and competition, you are carving out your market niche. When doing so, remember three rules. First, each market generally tolerates only one generalist. This is usually the first consultant to provide services to that particular market. If clients are satisfied with that consultant's services, they commonly ask him or her for others. However, most consultants who follow the first one must specialize to differentiate themselves in the clients' eyes. As a result, they end up with a smaller share of the market, as shown below.

The second rule is to avoid direct competition. If you cannot, then you must find ways to circumvent it. Remember that someone who is in the same business as you is not necessarily a competitor. They compete only if they are trying to satisfy the same client needs you are. For those competitors, you must specify what part of their business you want and what part of their business you can get. However, it is always in your best interest to find markets where you are the sole provider.

The third rule is to avoid doing too much. Work overload and frantic growth toll death for many consulting firms. Consequently, select market niches that match your capabilities. Do not branch into new services or new markets until you are ready.

One method of assessing your growth readiness is to look at the learning curve. The learning curve shows that the more you do some-

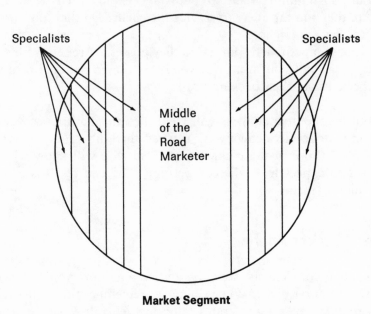

**Each Market Segment Will
Tolerate Only One Generalist**

Specialists

Specialists

Middle
of the
Road
Marketer

Market Segment

thing, the better, faster, and cheaper you do it. If you have taken full advantage of the learning curve for each service, then you are probably ready to expand into new markets. However, it is very difficult to handle more than one learning curve at a time.

You should now describe your market niche in very specific detail. Your market niche should provide you with ample opportunities to consult. It should also allow you to create barriers to competition.

Marketing Techniques

The previous sections focused on the relationship between marketing and your consulting practice. The need for knowing your clients, services, and competitors before you can market or compete effectively was emphasized. In this last section, you will learn in four steps how to reach specific clients with specific marketing messages.

Decide Why You Need Marketing

You can use marketing for several purposes. Most commonly you market to obtain new clients. However, you may want to establish or modify your image. The oil companies spend millions to counter their profit-gouging antienvironmental image. Other companies advertise when the corporate name changes. You may want to educate the public through marketing. For instance, the utility companies currently teach the public how to conserve energy. You may market to recruit new employees. For example, many consulting firms place ads in university placement bulletins. Finally, you may simply provide a public service through marketing. You could sponsor a baseball team or the local symphony for the benefit of your community. Before you can market successfully, you must know why you are doing it.

Decide What You Want to Market

After deciding why you market, you must focus your message on those few items you want to communicate. For example, perhaps you are marketing to obtain new clients. You must ask yourself what messages will attract your targeted clients. Do you simply need to inform them of your availability? Will they engage you if you market new services or new employees? Perhaps they will respond to marketing efforts that express appreciation of the community. In any case, you must limit your message to one that positively motivates the client to accept and act on it.

Decide How to Market

Once you know your client and your message, you must determine the most appropriate paths for bringing them together. All too often consultants randomly select marketing tools. They might hand out brochures, give speeches, and make personal calls. However, these consultants often can't explain why they selected these tools over others. They have not targeted their clients or their message adequately. The client and the message usually point to the appropriate marketing method.

Table 7 indicates the many paths through which you can send your message to your client. As always, you should start with the client. People are most receptive to word-of-mouth recommendations from trusted sources. You should identify which client contacts have the most influence with your client. They may be the client's staff, gov-

TABLE 7. How Best to Reach Your Client with Your Message*

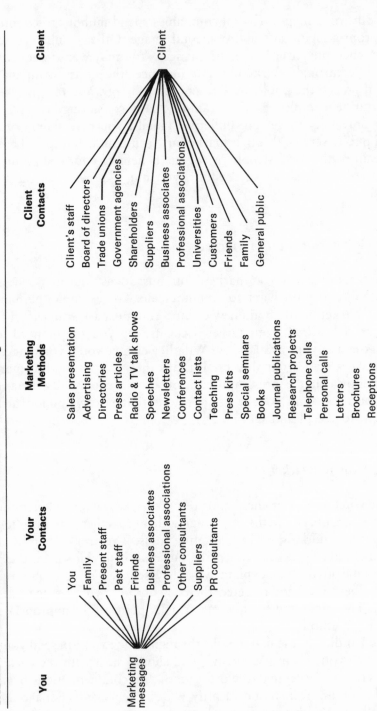

You	Your Contacts	Marketing Methods	Client Contacts	Client
Marketing messages	You	Sales presentation	Client's staff	Client
	Family	Advertising	Board of directors	
	Present staff	Directories	Trade unions	
	Past staff	Press articles	Government agencies	
	Friends	Radio & TV talk shows	Shareholders	
	Business associates	Speeches	Suppliers	
	Professional associations	Newsletters	Business associates	
	Other consultants	Conferences	Professional associations	
	Suppliers	Contact lists	Universities	
	PR consultants	Teaching	Customers	
		Press kits	Friends	
		Special seminars	Family	
		Books	General public	
		Journal publications		
		Research projects		
		Telephone calls		
		Personal calls		
		Letters		
		Brochures		
		Receptions		

* Adapted from a speech by Brian P. Smith, "The Marketing of Management Consulting Services," to the North American Conference of Management Consultants, 1976. Used with permission.

ernment agencies, former professors, or bankers. If you have these influential people carrying your message, then you increase its chances for positive reception.

Knowing clients and their influential contacts, you can then choose the appropriate methods to carry your message. Are they impressed by journal publications? Can you reach them through a speech? How do they respond to telephone calls? Is advertising appropriate for your message? Which methods are best for directly reaching the client and which are needed to convince the client's contacts? By pinpointing the best medium, you avoid a random shotgun approach.

Finally, you must realize that you are not the only person who can or should market your services. Each of your contacts can use appropriate methods to reach the client or the client's contacts. In fact, many of your contacts—satisfied clients, for example—may have influence over the targeted client, especially if they sit on the board of directors. Perhaps past staff members of your firm now work for a targeted client. They will provide a good avenue for marketing to the client.

Your efforts should result in a coordinated marketing program that purposefully chooses people and methods appropriate to each client.

A survey performed for the Institute of Management Consultants evaluated various marketing methods. The results indicate that management consultants hold differing opinions concerning the effectiveness of these methods. The following methods are presented to inform you how one group of consultants views the various methods.

Referrals.   Referrals by past or present clients are the most commonly used means of obtaining new business. The survey suggests that repeat business constitutes 70 percent of all business, while referrals make up 15 percent.

Brochures.   The respondents indicate that brochures are essential since clients expect them. However, they are used most often as a backup device.

Associations and societies.   These received a mixed reaction. On the one hand, if you select them properly, they can generate numerous potential clients. They allow you to meet people and to demonstrate your competence. On the other hand, they can drain your time and attention.

Published articles and books. These can establish both your image and your reputation. More than 7,000 trade publications exist; most of them actively seek material. You should write for journals whose readers can use your services. However, writing is also time-consuming.

Speeches. According to the *Wall Street Journal,* more than 14,000 associations exist. Of these, 71 percent have state chapters. Consequently, a ready market for speeches exists. Speeches give you visibility to potential clients. However, your topic must be timely and your presentation professional. You should obtain the names and addresses of people in attendance, since they are potential clients.

Newsletters. With more than 25,000 active newsletters, the *Wall Street Journal* pronounced it one of the fastest growing industries in the United States. Newsletters are tied to the knowledge explosion. Specific clients want specific information. If you have it, then this becomes an effective means to reach your client.

Mailing lists. These are considered essential by consultants. Many firms arrange them alphabetically, industrially, and geographically. This is a major source for all marketing efforts. However, keeping them up to date is extremely time-consuming.

Advertising. Most consultants still consider this unprofessional. With recent court rulings and increased competition, more firms are using it regularly.

Sales presentations. Formal presentations are frequently used to familiarize clients with the consultant's capabilities.

Formal public relations. Hiring PR professionals is an expensive but effective method to market your services. Large firms utilize PR firms more frequently than smaller firms.

Cold sales calls. Few consultants will contact clients without an invitation. It is also an expensive approach, since it is time-consuming. Instead, firms will arouse interest through letters or brochures. They will then follow up with a phone call.

The results of this survey should not deter your marketing efforts. Since most consultants market poorly, it is not surprising that they find certain methods ineffective. However, if you match your method to your client, then your effectiveness should increase dramatically.

Decide When to Market

If you know who, why, what, and how you plan to market, then you must only decide when. Your timing should consider three factors: 1) when the client is most receptive, 2) when the client is least likely to receive competitors' messages, and 3) when your resources will permit you both to market and to meet the demand created by the marketing. To determine a client's receptiveness, refer to the marketing cycles previously discussed in this chapter. Moreover, assess your own capability to provide the marketed services. Clients unable to meet needs generated by your marketing will seldom return as clients. Thus, timing is critical to the success of your marketing efforts and to your consulting practice.

If you follow these four steps, you can communicate specific marketing messages to particular clients. You should never market without identified clients in mind. If you do not know how to reach these clients, try the following exercise. Assuming that you or someone previously has consulted to them, how did this occur? How were the clients reached? Was it through trade magazines or by referral? Once you determine this, then you can try to improve the method.

Marketing is essential to the success of your consulting practice. Since you must market your services, devise a marketing plan. From the information in this chapter, you can develop an effective marketing plan that creates demand for services. But you must also examine the relationship between marketing, fees, and profits. This will be discussed in Chapter 7.

Additional Sources of Help

Marketing Classics. 5th ed. B. M. Enis and K. K. Cox. Boston: Allyn & Bacon, Inc., 1985.
The Marketing Edge. T. V. Bonoma. Englewood Cliffs, N.J.: Prentice Hall, 1984.

Marketing Management: Analysis, Planning, and Control. 4th ed. P. Kotler. Englewood Cliffs, N.J.: Prentice-Hall, 1980.

The Marketing of Professional Accounting Services. J.J. Mahon. New York: John Wiley & Sons, 1978.

The Marketing of Professional Services. A. Wilson. New York: McGraw-Hill, 1975.

"Marketing Professional Services." E. B. Turner. *Journal of Marketing* (1969): 56–61.

The Regis Touch. R. McKenna. Reading, Mass.: Addison-Wesley, 1985.

The Relationship Between Marketing, Fees, and Profits

7

Profit is a measurable by-product of producing a high quality product or service to enough loyal customers at a price that is fair to them and to you. Profit is not the reason you do business but a condition of doing business.
ANONYMOUS

Your ability to identify a large or growing market niche, to gain a dominant position in that niche, and to price your services properly will in large measure determine your profitability. These three inter-related activities are often viewed in isolation. As a result, profits fail to materialize. This chapter addresses each activity to give you a clear understanding of how they fit together.

Finding a Niche in Changing Markets

Changing Markets

As alluded to in Chapters 3 and 6, the marketplace for consulting services continues to change. As Carl Sloane of ACME pointed out in his presentation to the Institute of Management Consultants, the types of consulting projects requested by clients evolve. In the 1960s, clients sought consultants for business planning, organization structure, marketing, facilities siting, management education, and international business studies. Most of these studies were to help companies respond to the problems and opportunities inherent in a growth economy. Economic expansion and growing markets were the dominant theme of the 1960s. Consultants that succeeded had developed services that corresponded to this theme.

In the 1970s, the world became more uncertain. OPEC altered the world economy. Japan gained the title of Number One. The economy turned sour through unpredicted back-to-back recessions. Inflation ran out of control and unemployment skyrocketed to post-Depression highs. We saw the failure or near failure of some of the nation's biggest corporations. In some cases this was due to fierce foreign competition; in others it resulted from plain poor management. The market for consulting projects in this environment changed considerably. Clients wanted consultants to act as a guiding light out of the economic mess. Strategic planning, economic forecasting, energy conservation, environmental scanning, pollution control, and data processing studies replaced the 1960s' expansion type studies. Many new consulting firms, like the Boston Consulting Group, emerged as dominant players because they developed services in tune with the times. Other firms, like Cresap, Paget and McCormick or McKinsey & Company, lost ground because their services were too tied to the past. Since they failed to adjust rapidly enough, they lost their market niche to new players.

The 1980s have been a time of reassessment and revitalization in the United States. Companies are incorporating uncertainty into their existence and are putting the pieces in place to mount their comeback. Hands-on strategic management studies are replacing abstract strategic planning studies. Implementation assistance is in higher demand than planning assistance. Companies look to consultants for market segmentation studies so that clients can find new market niches to replace lost ones. Productivity improvement and organizational effectiveness studies became popular as a way to improve the client's internal operations. Technology studies, especially of computer, information, and communication systems, were commissioned to use these new technologies as competitive weapons. This shift in emphasis caught many firms flat-footed. The Boston Consulting Group fell into the same trap in the 1980s that had provided the growth opportunity for them in the 1970s—failing to sense the change in the market. Most of the major consulting firms, like Booz-Allen and Hamilton, A.T. Kearney, McKinsey, Arthur D. Little, and SRI International, experienced limited growth in the

1980s because they failed to adjust their services to the changing times. Many smaller and new firms filled the vacuum and flourished. As mentioned before, although the large firms did not grow, the entire consulting industry expanded by about 11% each year. Small start-up firms, solo practitioners, and sharp, aggressive firms like Temple, Barker and Sloane of Boston grew and gained niches at the expense of larger competitors. In a sense, the large consulting firms experienced in the 1980s what large industrial firms experienced in the 1970s: shifting markets and increasing competition.

In the late 1980s and early 1990s, consulting markets will continue to shift. Several major business trends are emerging. The recognition of a global economy has profound impact on business. Besides increases in foreign competition, companies can expect economic fluctuations, such as foreign exchange losses due to the changing value of the U.S. dollar. The consultants who flourish will find many opportunities as their clients try to adjust to this changing global environment.

A second trend is the restructuring of the economy from manufacturing to services, a trend that will provide both opportunities and threats to consultants. On the one hand, consultants can assist clients in this transition by helping them identify new service business to diversify into. For example, computer companies like Control Data have expanded into teaching computer courses in a variety of settings, including prisons. But Control Data has also expanded into offering its own consulting services. This poses a threat to existing consultants.

A third trend is accelerating technological changes. Companies find it difficult to keep up with the latest technologies. They do not know which new technologies will make their existing technologies obsolete. At the same time, they encounter difficulty sorting out or selecting from the wide array of new technologies that could be helpful to them. For this help, they will turn to consultants who can specialize in tracking and assessing new technologies. These trends and others will reconfigure the consulting marketplace in the years ahead. Smart consultants will stay on top of these changes and offer new services accordingly.

New Competition

Traditionally, consultants had few competitors for clients. As noted in Chapter 1, the types of consultants have expanded greatly in the last 20 years to include internal consultants, management advisory services of CPA firms, and government consultants. In the last five years, new competitors have entered the consulting business because of its lucrative growth history. Most notable of these new competitors are firms owned by large Fortune 500 companies. For example, Sears Roebuck owns two consulting firms; one deals primarily with domestic companies and the other is involved in international projects. Control Data's positive experience has inspired similar operations at Xerox.

In addition, traditional service companies, like banks, are now offering consulting assistance to customers, particularly those who have not been repaying their loans on schedule. More and more suppliers and vendors now offer consulting to their clients. A computer company will offer to do the initial feasibility study before trying to sell its products. Accounting firms do executive recruiting for their clients. Insurance companies provide health awareness programs on a consulting basis. In essence, any company that does business with one of your clients should be considered a potential competitor.

The final set of new competitors are information firms. These firms package market, industry, or technological data in the forms of reports or newsletters. Clients buy this information through subscription. Firms like Dataquest in Silicon Valley gather and disseminate voluminous data on segments of the computer business. More and more often, clients ask these firms to interpret the information on a consulting basis. In effect, these information firms are capitalizing on their expertise as a method to diversify into consulting services. They are formidable competitors because their data bases give them a solid foot in the door of clients who desperately need their information.

All of these new competitors are entering the field for one major reason: to get a profitable slice of a growth industry. These new entrants are making the consulting field more competitive as they search for market niches. At the same time, they stimulate the growth of the field as they help create new services and markets. In addition, their new expertise and skills add to the credibility and diversity of the industry.

New Clients

Just as client needs evolve over time, clients that use consultants change over time. In the 1960s, the major users of consultants were those companies that were expanding. These included the industrial firms in steel, automotive, and other heavy manufacturing. In addition, the consumer market companies in everything from appliances to toiletries hired consultants to help them take advantage of our "throwaway" society. Finally, aerospace companies sought help in filling the skies with plane travelers and getting a spacecraft to the moon.

In the 1970s, the heavy users of consultants shifted. Major clients became those facing the greatest impact from the changing economic conditions. Energy, chemical, and natural resource companies paid consultants to help them sort out the new context. Construction companies were at a loss to understand how inflation and unemployment would affect them. These new clients altered the types of assignments given to consultants, as noted earlier.

The major users during the 1980s are firms facing either government deregulation or intense international competition. In the former category, airline, trucking, banking, natural gas, telecommunications, and health companies have used consultants prolifically. Each firm in those industries had to learn how to succeed in a competitive marketplace. They had to move out of a mindset in which the government dictated everything they could do. They hired consultants to help them through this transition. In the latter group, steel and automotive companies, consumer product firms, electronic companies, and textile companies faced intense foreign competition. By offering marketing, technology, and productivity expertise, consultants have assisted in revitalizing many U.S. companies.

In the late 1980s and 1990s, the major users of consultants are shifting again. They are primarily the growth industries of the future with a heavy emphasis on service businesses. Computers, biotechnology, advanced materials, robotics, financial services, health care, and communications companies use consultants to help them take advantage of large, growing markets both domestic and international. These new clients and the new services they need will open up greater consulting opportunities for consultants at all levels.

Changing markets, clients, and competitors are a fact of life in the consulting business. Within this swirling context, you must find a niche if you are to profit and grow. Anticipating changes and responding in the right manner are essential. Establishing a distinctive competence that differentiates you from your competitors is now mandatory. This is the only way you can gain dominance in a market niche. To do so, you need to understand the framework for establishing your reputation within your niche.

Gaining Dominant Position in Your Niche

Finding your niche depends on market perception and market acceptance. Clients must view you as being the most expert person in their area of need. Then they must accept that you are in the best position to help them. In other words, clients look not only for experts but also for experts who can translate their knowledge into solutions for the client. The important point here is that being an expert is not enough—even if your family, friends, and professional colleagues bow to your expertise. You must be an expert and a consultant in your prospective clients' eyes.

To establish these perceptions, you must understand that the consulting industry is characterized by the business mix of three basic segments: hit, custom, and commodity.* A "hit" in consulting is like a hit in any other field. It tops the charts and everyone acknowledges its dominant position. Songs, Broadway plays, books, and fashion designs are industries where a hit is important. In strategic planning consulting, the "growth-share matrix" was a hit when clients clamored to buy it from the Boston Consulting Group. The growth-share matrix helped clients assess the prospects of their product lines by judging them against two factors: the growth prospects of the overall market and the amount of market share held by the product and its competitors.

A consulting hit has several unique characteristics. First, it is generally innovative. More often than not, it creates its own genre with a new way of looking at the world. This stimulates new lines of inquiry, new research, and often new schools of thought. The growth-share matrix, for example, spurred the development of the strategic planning field. Second, the marketplace perceives it as new or different. It attracts a critical mass of the targeted buying public that wants to listen, see, or dance to the hit. They perceive it as adding value to their lives, whether corporate or private. These are the experimenters, the clients who are early adopters of innovative, leading-edge ideas.

Third, in consulting the hit is generally identified with a "star"

---

* This section resulted from the collaborative thinking of Syed Z. Shariz, Michelle Wilcox, Ian Wilson, and the author. The author gratefully acknowledges their contribution.

who personifies the hit. The star develops a persona which lasts longer than the hit. Executives who buy consulting services often do so to rub shoulders with the star. This is why fads in consulting spread. As soon as Company A has had the star speak at a management conference, Company B follows suit in a corporate version of "keeping up with the Joneses."

Fourth, the hit is hyped by the "consciousness industry." In consulting, this is the business press, especially the major periodicals like the *Wall Street Journal, Fortune,* and *Business Week.* Other avenues for hype are the universities, especially those professors who teach executive programs. Consultants themselves act as hype agents when they suggest a new book or latest techniques to their clients.

Finally, the demand for a hit is greater than the supply. As a result, only a few can have access to the hit while it is still hot. Like a sold-out Broadway show, a consulting hit is restricted. This adds to the hype and helps create the persona. At the same time, it spawns imitations, as competitors try to cash in on the hit. Since the star cannot possibly meet all the demand, other consulting firms will see an opportunity to expand into the latest area. They do so by creating customized or commodity versions of the hit.

Custom consulting services occur when either the originator or a bright imitator takes the hit and stylizes it for a certain market segment. For example, many consulting firms took the "growth-share matrix" concept and applied it to a specific market, such as hospitals or banks. In essence, customized services commercialize the hit, making it available to more people. Providers of customized services are generally not inventors or creators. They usually have technical expertise in the field as well as industry experience in the market segment. Value is added to the hit by translating it into specific applications for a particular set of clients. Custom work appeals not to the early adopters but to the "second wave." These clients seldom want to be first. Instead, the second generation of services and products, which have the bugs worked out, appeals to these clients. They are interested more in the service than in the star. In addition, they do not want to pay the premium necessary to get access to the star.

With the advent of custom services, demand begins to equal supply. Rather than a "star" persona, custom services are identified with a firm. Thus, Consulting Firm X has a good reputation for doing Service Y in a particular Market Segment Z. Where a hit is promoted by the consciousness industry, custom services are promoted through concerted marketing by the firm itself. The appeal is that the service is "improved and approved" for the targeted clients. As demand begins to subside due to increased supply, this generally leads to some providers trying to standardize the product into a commodity.

Consulting services become commodities when many consultants provide the service and little distinguishes the delivery or quality of the service. Generally the knowledge is so well known and tested that it can be standardized into a cookbook format. As a result, most trained technicians in the field can apply the knowledge with success. A rule of thumb for testing whether a service has entered commodity status is if it is being offered as a training program at local continuing education centers. By the time these centers begin training non-professionals in the topic, the hit has been around long enough to be fully disseminated into the community.

Commodities are aimed at the mass market. For example, many producers of a hit will develop commodities like video programs, training packages, or books to capitalize on their hits. Commodity products and services are substitutable by nature. One supervisory training film is interchangeable with another that covers the same topics. Commodity products depend on direct marketing for sales. The advertising pitch is that it's almost as good as the real thing, yet it's standardized, available, and cheaper.

Hits, custom, and commodity consulting services can be based on brainpower or experience. A consultant reaches star status either because he or she is known for new ideas, creativity, or analytic ability, or because of how much he or she knows from experience about the industry, discipline, or problems. Consulting firms that offer customized services either sell the brainpower they bring to the client or their years of experience. The same holds true for commodity products firms, although these firms tend to stress experience as their selling point in order to establish their credibility.

Hits, custom, and commodities can take shape as either services or products. A hit might come in the form of a bright idea that solves an important problem for a highly visible client. If the *Wall Street Journal* picks it up, you might be on your way to star status. At the other end of the spectrum, you might write a book that becomes a bestseller. The product is a hit. Similarly, a commodity service could be a standardized three-day workshop on strategic planning or safety improvement. A booklet or training film on either of those topics would constitute a commodity product.

Ideally, a consulting firm would produce a hit and then capitalize on it by offering custom and commodity-serviced products. For example, after *In Search of Excellence* became a bestseller, the two coauthors took different approaches. Bob Waterman, who stayed with McKinsey, began offering customized consulting services that incorporated the book's principles. He also gave standardized speeches and trained colleagues to give standardized two-day workshops. The success of the book and of these new services gave McKinsey a greatly needed boost in image and revenues. Tom Peters, who left McKinsey to start his own firm, took a different approach. He specialized in standardized products, such as training films, speeches, calendars, and workshops. He published a sequel book that used the same formula as the first including similar anecdotes and principles. Then he hired some staff to do customized workshops and consulting for clients. Although Peters and Waterman took different approaches, they each generated profitable consulting practices as a result of their hit. As a postscript, Waterman announced plans to leave McKinsey to pursue the path taken by Peters, reportedly for greater financial return and personal autonomy.

Most consulting firms, however, do not create hits. Instead, they specialize either in customized or commodity services or products. If they emphasize custom services, they either take their experience or someone else's hit and customize it for specific markets. *In Search of Excellence* was followed by a host of other books and pamphlets that capitalized on its success, such as *Managing for Excellence, Creating Excellence, The Excellent Salesperson, Excellence in the Classroom.* All of these were written by consultants customizing a hit for their audience. The same phenomenon happened around portfolio analysis. After one firm made the service a hit and articles describing it appeared in major publications, firms all over the country customized it for clients clamoring for portfolio analysis. Now the technique is so well-known that every graduate business student learns how to do it and many software programs are designed for it. Thus, portfolio analysis is a commodity and you do not need to hire a big-time consulting firm for it.

Some firms specialize in commodity products and services. Most information companies mentioned earlier in the chapter fall into this category. They produce a standardized product, whether it be a report or a newsletter. When clients ask them to interpret the information for their business, they are then offering customized services. Companies that specialize in standardized training programs are also commodity-based. Since the market for services is very large, you can generally reach more clients if you offer commodity-based products and services.

As you try to dominate your market niche, you must understand what mix you will offer. Are you going to continually develop hits that give you preeminence in your niche? Or will you develop the highest quality commodity products that allow you to reach a wider audience? Or will you be the first to translate someone else's hit into customized services for your market niche? Or perhaps from your experience, you can generate some customized consulting services for your niche that will make you a hit in that niche. Each approach has its merits. You must decide which will allow you to gain dominance in your niche.

As you choose your strategy, keep in mind the previous discussions in Chapter 1 and the present chapter about how client needs and expectations are changing. The marketplace has come to expect hits. It is also looking for firms recognized as the most expert in their field. This increases the importance of establishing a differentiating, distinctive competence.

Since the marketplace expects hits, the essence of competition and leadership in the consulting business is "name recognition." Name recognition requires being the first in your market with a hit. Hit producers have a competitive advantage of lead time in gaining the market share of customized work. Clients would rather have as consultants the firm that created the hit rather than another firm that only customized the hit. This requires staff who can produce hits and generate subsequent custom and commodity services to take advantage of the hit.

Hits do not have to be on a national scale. The hit must simply be a hit in your market niche. A genre novel or a jazz record may not make the national bestseller list, but they can still dominate their niches. The same holds true for consulting. You may develop a new analytical framework for the steel industry that draws the attention of the major steel producers. If this is your market niche, it makes little difference to you if computer companies are not interested.

Keep in mind, however, that one hit will not sustain you in the face of proliferating competition and changing client needs. Most competitors are capable of quickly following the bandwagon into "hit" arenas. Consequently, you need to determine how to gain dominance and how to keep it. This generally means producing an ongoing stream of new services and products for your marketplace.

Research and development take on increased importance for the dominant firm. It becomes more incumbent upon you to select and retain staff who are recognized as leaders in their field. Part of their effort must be focused on generating hits that preserve their reputation and maintain the firm's leadership position.

If you choose a custom or commodity strategy, you will also have to change. If you do not quickly incorporate the latest hits into your repertoire of services (or have a good rationale for not doing so), you risk being viewed as out of touch or behind the times. You also risk seeing your market share diminish as clients migrate toward leading-edge ideas and services. So you must keep abreast of the latest changes in your field and react quickly.

As you try to determine your strategy, you can ask yourself whether you are best at innovating, translating, or packaging. The producers of hits are pioneers and innovators. They see things that others don't see. Consultants who customize are translators. They can take someone's bright but often esoteric idea and communicate it to a lay audience. People who know how to package something for mass consumption are best at creating commodities. Each of these skills has its place in consulting. Once you know the niche you are entering, the changing needs of that niche, and your own strengths, you can determine whether you will gain dominance via hits, custom, or commodity services or products. The only thing lacking now is to understand the economics of your strategy.

Pricing Your Services in Your Market Niche*

Hit, custom, and commodity services/products have different sales volume, profit margins, and pricing rationales. As Table 8 demonstrates, a "hit" consulting services is limited in its sales volume by the fact that the star identified with it (whether a person or firm) can provide service to a limited number of people during the course of a 40 to 80 hour week. Yet, over its life cycle, it will produce tremendous profit margins. Since supply of the hit is limited to the star's availability, you can charge a high premium. John Naisbitt, author of *Megatrends,* is in such demand that he charges over $25,000 for a speech. Yet he still gets thousands of offers each year. Profit margins are highest on hits because of the supply–demand phenomenon.

* The information in this section was developed jointly with Dr. Syed Shariq.

TABLE 8. Hit, Custom, and Commodity Service/Product Life Cycles

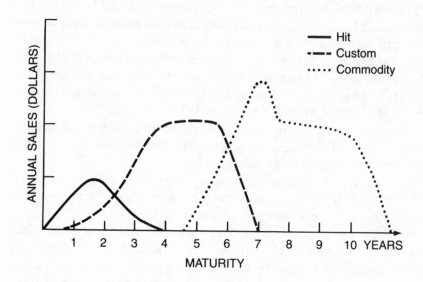

Figure X

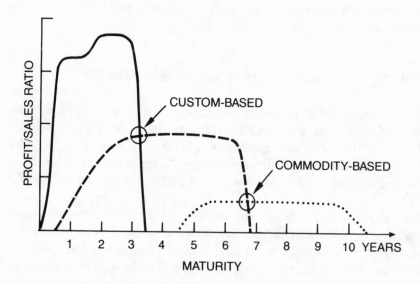

Figure Y

Customized services have a higher sales volume than hits. Since more people can provide customized services, a firm is not limited to the star's availability. Simultaneously, a firm cannot charge a premium for the customized services. So what you make up in sales volume, you trade in profit margins. As custom services increase in availability, they contribute to the eventual demise of the hit. They also lead to others trying to standardize the service as a commodity.

Commodity services and products have the highest sales revenue. This is because you are reaching a mass market with the product. Yet profit margins are low because the price must be in the range of the average buyer. Standardization is the major reason you can make a profit from commodities. Once you have it in cookbook format, it costs relatively little to produce it. Commodity producers are in the position of making a few dollars off of numerous sales; whereas custom and hit producers make higher dollars off of fewer sales. Once commodities become readily available, the market for custom services begins to dwindle.

Just as sales and profit margins differ for hit, custom, and commodity services, so do the rationales for pricing. As stated in Chapter 6, most consulting firms price their services on the basis of cost. Yet this pricing strategy is only appropriate for commodity-based services or products that are in plentiful supply. Costs should play a major factor only when market saturation forces you to keep your prices down. Then your goal is to cover your costs including salary and to take home a modest profit. This is a rational way to price commodity products.

Unfortunately, most consulting firms price their custom and hit services on a modified costs basis. They use their salary or labor costs as the foundation for determining their fees, using some variation of the Rule Three described in Chapter 5. This pricing policy neglects the contribution of services to the client. For customized services, you are adding knowledge to the client. Moreover, you are translating the most up-to-date knowledge into specific application for the client. This knowledge and translation process would be costly for clients to try to acquire on their own.

In return for providing this readily accessible and specific knowledge, you should receive a knowledge premium above and beyond your costs. This knowledge premium is your reward for contributing more than just time to the client. If the client can get from you in a day what would take the client weeks to get otherwise, you should charge for more than one day of your time. Instead, consider pricing on the basis of what it would cost the client to acquire the knowledge on his or her own. At the same time, you cannot price with too high a premium or you will tempt the client to forego the knowledge, to attain it independently, or to seek competitors who will price it on a labor basis. However, if you are truly an expert providing bona fide custom services, your competitors will be few.

Hit services should seldom be priced on a cost or labor basis. With the demand high and the supply limited, market forces are in your favor. More importantly, hits add significant value to clients. You are giving them something brand new that will help them gain competitive advantage. By applying your new knowledge, they stand to gain substantial cost savings, market share, profits, or stock appreciation. It does not make sense for you to charge by the hour. Instead, look to the wealth you are creating for your clients. Based on this estimation, you can charge a value-added premium if they would not attain the wealth without you. For example, a new miracle drug might seem expensive at $1,000. Yet if it helps you avoid a $100,000 operation or lets you live pain-free, the price is insignificant. In fact, some professionals now take part of their fee in equity in order to share in benefits as the stock price appreciates.

In essence, your pricing possibilities lie along a continuum. The lower price range is determined by asking how cheaply the competition can provide the same service you offer. This figure will probably, though not necessarily, be close to your costs of providing the service. In some cases the figure may be above your costs, and in other cases below. Regardless of its relationship to your costs, you will need to match it to stay competitive when trying to offer exactly the same service. The upper price range is based on the value of your service to the client. Ask yourself how you are creating wealth for the client and what the service is worth to the client in dollars. The upper price range focuses on competitive advantage and profit. In rare cases, it is possible to charge prices beyond this upper range, either because the client misjudges the value of your service or because the client is in such a bad situation that any price seems reasonable. However, it is not in your best interest to take advantage of your client's miscalculations, especially if you want to maintain a long-term relationship. Between the lower and upper ranges there is generally a wide middle range that provides the leeway to adjust for competitive, client, and profit considerations of your hit, custom, or commodity services.

If you price your custom and hit services properly, you can increase your revenues and profit margins considerably. This is important because these profits provide the cash necessary for your research and development and for the expansion of your firm. If you decide to enter the hit niche, you will spend considerable funds developing several services, only one of which is likely to become a hit. The success of one hit supplies the cash to continue developing your next generation of services. Out of the next generation, you hope one will become a hit and fuel the succeeding generation. This same cycle applies to custom services. If you fail to price properly, you will not be able to sustain your dominance in your market niche.

Marketing, pricing, and profits go hand-in-hand. Finding your niche in the midst of changing market demands challenges the best professional. You must stay current with your discipline, with the forces affecting your clients (current and potential), and with your clients' evolving needs in light of those forces—no easy task, but essential for long-term success. Then, choose your method to gain dominance in your niche. Will you produce hits and then capitalize on them by offering corresponding custom and commodity services? Or will you take a custom or commodity strategy? Finally, price your services appropriately for the type of services you will offer to your market niche. If you fail to create this bridge between your services and your fees, you will undermine your success and profits. On the other hand, if you tie them together so that you and your clients benefit, you are ready to sell your services. Since selling is an especially difficult aspect of marketing, it will be discussed in detail in Chapter 8, "Selling Your Services."

Additional Sources of Help

Marketing Imagination. T. Levitt. New York: Free Press, 1983.

Selling Your Services

8

The problem with most salespeople is that they don't understand their jobs. They try to take the horse to water and make him drink it. Their job is to make the horse thirsty.
ANONYMOUS

Getting in the Door

Consultants experience difficulty finding clients and selling their services. In fact, consultants find it so difficult they don't even refer to it as selling. They disguise it as "business development." But make no mistake about it. Consultants must sell their services like anyone else. All other factors being equal, the difference between successful and unsuccessful consultants is their ability to sell. In fact, the ability to obtain new clients is an essential requirement to make partnership in most large consulting firms. If you plan to last in the consulting business, become proficient in selling.

This chapter will outline how successful consultants approach selling their services.

Overcoming Fear of Selling

Marketing looks at the big picture of informing the public of your services. Selling is a specific marketing act that results in a consulting assignment. Selling usually takes place in a face-to-face interview.

Consultants, like most professionals, unnecessarily dislike selling. This is partly attributable to our stereotypes of salespeople. Mention the word, and we conjure images of fast-talking used car salesmen or door-to-door cosmetics salesladies. The image oozes with deception and manipulation, pitting buyer against seller. Since we dislike the image, we fear associating ourselves with the activity. In fact, more than a few professionals-turned-consultants have disclosed that they became professionals out of disdain for business and, particularly, for selling. Consultants also avoid selling because they have no training in it. Lacking faith in their abilities makes them uncomfortable, since it directly contradicts their image as "experts."

Most important, consultants avoid selling because they do not understand the selling process. They view it as an isolated activity that occurs at the start of an engagement. Once the project is sold and the consulting begins, they believe the selling is over. They do not realize that consultants should always be selling. In fact, a client is not "sold" until he or she is satisfied. Your best sales tool is providing a high-quality service that results in a satisfied client.

Everyone can overcome his or her fear of selling. To do so, you only need follow three simple steps:

• Realize why selling is in your best interest.
• Understand the emotional response behind your fear.
• Learn the skills that enable you to sell successfully.

As indicated earlier, without selling you will fail in this business. For most people, the fear of failure sufficiently overcomes their fear of selling. However, in a more positive light, selling is a personally rewarding experience. Selling allows you to help someone who is in need. Through your efforts, clients can relax, knowing that competent consultants are solving their problems. This cannot occur unless you sell your services.

To overcome your fear of selling, you must understand the emotions behind it. Fear, an emotion, strongly controls what we do and how we act. However, the fear of selling is what psychologists call a "presenting problem," since it is seldom the real problem. Rather, people talk about it to avoid facing the real problem. If you think about it, what is there to be afraid of when selling? Most consultants do not fear talking to other people about their services. In fact, at parties you can seldom stop professionals from discussing their field.

Yet, in a selling situation, they freeze. Why? The real problem is *fear of rejection* by the client. They fantasize that the client might ridicule them, or worse, tell them, "No, I do not want you as my consultant." Rather than risk rejection, they stay away from selling situations.

Consultants tend to overreact to this rejection. Unrealistically, they want everyone to accept and respect them; in fact, a major reason for becoming a professional is to gain respect. However, to expect this from everyone is unreasonable. Consultants take rejection too personally. They view it as a negative appraisal of their skills, training, personality, and competence. It is seldom any of these. Instead, the client is rejecting the interaction between the two of them. The client simply does not see how working together will satisfy his or her needs. The consultant should not lower his or her self-esteem as a result. Some consultant-client interactions are like hydrogen and oxygen coming together. The result is a new compound—water. However, when sulfuric acid is poured into water, an explosion occurs. They simply do not mix.

To overcome your fears, you must engage in activities that help you succeed. This requires certain skills. In truth, most consultants already possess these skills. It is simply a matter of using them effectively. Success rewards by encouraging those behaviors that led to the success. Hence, the more you succeed selling, the more you will sell.

Understanding Selling

Selling requires a certain orientation. Too often, we view it as a game in which one side wins and one side loses. Selling at its best is a mutually satisfying interaction in which both sides win. On the one hand, the client's needs are met. On the other hand, the consultant generates income, engages in his or her profession, and reaps personal reward for helping the client. Thus, if selling is a game, it should be pleasurable for both participants.

Successful selling demands more than the proper attitude. Numerous activities occur prior to the fact-to-face contact. The selling situation begins with your marketing efforts. If these are executed effectively, then selling simply involves making your services available. Even the best marketing benefits from activities focused toward the specific potential clients—selling. You begin by gaining prospective leads.

Gaining Prospective Leads

A prospective lead is anyone who could use your services. In *Personal Selling,** Ben Enis identifies prospective leads as MAD—Money, Authority, and Desire. Prospective clients have the ability to buy, the right to buy, and the need to buy. The first step, then, is to find MAD prospects.

MAD prospects come from two sources: your marketing efforts and your personal contact system. In the earlier chapter on marketing, you learned how to combine these two sources. Now you will concentrate on developing your personal contact system.

Building a personal contact system seems difficult. Yes, it takes time. But learning about people is easy. The world is a small place. The University of Texas conducted a "Small World" research program. They found that the average distance between any two people in this world is equal to two to three people. On the average, you know someone who knows someone who knows the person in whom you are interested. This applies to the entire world. In your city, chances are that the distance is less.

So you can easily build a personal contact system. First, use your contact system to gather intelligence about prospective clients. To do so, you must concentrate on the client. Learn from your contacts as much as possible about your prospective clients. Salespeople suggest keeping a "Farley File," named after the Roosevelt–New Deal politician Big Jim Farley. He reputedly knew 50,000 Democratic voters by their first names. He kept file cards on each one containing personal information, such as spouse's name, occupation, hobbies, and number of children. Salespeople keep similar information, as well as important business data, such as company size and sales. The more you know about prospective clients, the better you can meet their needs. Information helps break the ice when you meet face-to-face.

Another way to capitalize on your contact system requires putting your contacts to work for you. You want them to carry your message to prospective clients. Joe Girard, in his best-selling book, *How to Sell Anything to Anybody,*† states that the average person knows 250 people well. Thus, each of your contacts can potentially reach 250 people. To do so, however, they must know your message. Unless you know your services and their benefits, your contacts never will. You must inform them in a short, clear, and memorable sentence.

* Santa Monica, Calif.: Goodyear Publishing Co., 1979.
† New York: Warner Books, 1977.

Here is an example of how to put your personal contact system to work for you. In Chapter 6, it was stated that 85 percent of your projects will come from repeat clients or referrals. A marketing consultant demonstrated how one sales call led to 38 clients and 102 projects. The first client requested additional projects. The consultant labeled this "repeat business." This satisfied client referred him to five other clients. These five clients, in turn, referred him to fourteen additional clients. He labeled these nineteen referrals "pass-along business." The final group of eighteen new clients came from staff members who left the original client to work for other companies. These staff members were impressed with the consultant's work for the original client, so they procured his services for their new companies. He labeled this "take-along business." You can see, then, how important one satisfied personal contact can be to promoting your business.

A personal contact network effectively sells your services. To enlarge your network, try the following suggestion. List all the people you know. Then, look at the client list you developed in Chapter 6. Examine both lists to see if any connections emerge. If none occur, then ask yourself questions about the targeted group. In what civic activities do they participate? To what service and social clubs do they belong? Where do they gather for business lunches or for exercise? Pick out the activities at which you are likely to meet them. Then, join.

Most consulting firms, in fact, pay for staff memberships to clubs and associations, realizing that important business relationships form at them. Many firms also promote staff to more prestigious social clubs after the employee has proved effective at the lower clubs.

However, remember the one cardinal rule of all club memberships: make friends, not enemies. No good comes from getting in a fight on the basketball court or ridiculing someone's idea during a Kiwanis meeting. For every person you turn against you, you potentially lose 250 friends. That is bad business.

Planning for Sales

Consultants frequently ask me how much time they should spend selling. The answer depends on your type of consulting and the duration of your average consulting project. From this information, you can plan your own sales schedule.

Table 9 exemplifies a sales planning schedule. The consultant wants to maintain a 30-hour-per-week utilization rate. By scheduling each week, he or she determines when projects will end and when new ones will begin. In this example, the consultant begins Client F's project in Week 6 in order to maintain the utilization rate. Starting with Week 11, his or her utilization rate begins to drop. However, before Week 11 arrives, the schedule alerts him or her to secure new clients to replace Clients A, B, C, and D. Consequently, this consultant must market services well in advance of Week 11.

To create this pipeline, experienced consultants keep track of how much selling effort secures their consulting projects. Using the same example, the consultant would want to secure 30 additional hours of consulting work to replace the 30 he or she utilizes each week. So, during the week, at least 30 hours of consulting must be sold to begin at some future point. An average client provides approximately 45 hours of consulting work. If consultants secure two new clients in a three-week period, they generate 90 replacement hours of work or 30 hours per week.

If it takes two proposals to land one new client, consultants must make four proposals during those two weeks. If it takes three initial meetings to lead to one proposal, they must make twelve initial meetings during those two weeks, approximately one per day. Finally, if it takes five phone calls (or other form of selling, such as letters) to secure an initial meeting, they must make sixty phone calls during those two weeks, or six per day. These marketing activities usually take place in sequence. This week's phone calls lead to next week's initial meetings. Next week's meetings lead to the following week's proposals, and so on. Every week a consultant is making thirty phone calls, having six initial meetings, writing two proposals, and securing one or two clients.

Without a selling orientation, you easily overlook activities necessary for the continuation of your consulting practice. By paying attention to your sales plan, you can prevent the nightmare of running out of consulting projects.

Making the Sale

Selling a service like consulting differs considerably from selling a product like an automobile. Products and services are developed, delivered, and sold in two distinguishable manners. Unlike a car, which

TABLE 9. Planning Schedule for Marketing Purposes

Week #	1	2	3	4	5	6	7	8	9	10	11	12	13	...	...	...	52	Client Total to Date
Client A	15	10*																A = 25
B	5	10	10	10	2													B = 39
C	5	8	15	10	8	2*	2											C = 62
D	3	3	5	10	12	10			2*									D = 50
E	2	6	1	10	5	15	5		2*	10		2*						E = 62
F						10	6	20	5	2	5	1*						F = 48
G							10	5	8	30	10	20	10					G = 83+
I													5					I = 5+
?																		
?																		
Total # Hours Utilized	30	31	31	26	30	32	32	35	30	34	25	23	15					

◯ = Project ends that week
(*) = circled value, i.e. project ends that week

Average client = 46.76 hours

Average week = 28.77 hours

is manufactured in one location and then delivered for sale to the customer in another, a service is often created and delivered simultaneously. As you conduct a consulting project, you concurrently deliver it to the client. No matter how excellent the study, if the delivery is poor, the client will view the study badly. Professor John M. Rathwell of Cornell University contrasted these differences nicely: "Goods are produced, services are performed."*

These differences pose a special challenge to consultants: How do you make relatively invisible services seem real and useful to prospective clients? Professor Ted Levitt of the Harvard Business School tackled this issue in a *Harvard Business Review* article, "Marketing Intangible Products and Product Intangibles."† He suggests that the intangibility of services must be 1) understood and 2) made more tangible. Clients can seldom inspect or try out in advance intangible services like consulting. Since they cannot experience the product in advance, consulting firms try to make clients more comfortable by making their products more tangible.

Tangibility is created through a number of methods. One is image creation. For example, some large firms have glossy brochures of their mahogany-walled offices in major office towers or of the facilities of clients that they have helped. Although the client cannot know for certain that the firm is reputable, these brochures create a tangible image of success. The second method used to create tangibility is metaphors. If you are in the motivation seminar business, you include in your brochures pictures of employees obviously enjoying themselves at your seminar. On the next page, you show those same people hard at work in a team looking eager and earnest to tackle a tough problem. The pictorial metaphor communicates that your seminar works.

A third method is packaging. A proposal delivered in a leather binding leaves a very different impression from one with no cover and just a staple at the top. Your proposal is a tangible representation of the care and quality that your firm provides. If you manage these representations well, your selling job becomes much easier.

As Levitt points out, selling is comparable to courtship. As you pass through the courtship stages, the clients are looking for evidence that you understand and are sensitive to their needs. Taking clients to dinner, sending them a book or article of interest, writing a thank-

* John M. Rathwell, *Marketing in the Service Sector*, Cambridge, Mass.: Winthrop Publishers, 1974, p. 58.
† May–June 1981, pp. 94–102.

you note, calling to say hello—all of these are tangible methods of communicating your interest. However, once you get married, you begin gestation through the consulting project. You begin working closely together. So the prospective client will note every nuance during the courtship, judging your tangible representations as evidence of your probable ability to consummate the project.

How you represent yourself during the sales process is very important. The way you think, dress, hold yourself, and communicate leaves impressions on your client. I remember very clearly a phone call I received during my early years of consulting. A prospective client from a Fortune 500 firm had read an article of mine and asked me to visit a facility in Minneapolis. This client met me at the airport. After we introduced ourselves and he took one look at my 27-year-old face, he asked where my boss was. He could not believe that a young person could have written the article that had left such a positive impression on him. My youthful appearance conflicted with the evidence of my skills that he inferred from the article. Rather than dwell on my age, I focused our conversation on his problem and my article—letting the article, not my face, be the tangible representation of my expertise. After the successful completion of the project, I then talked to him about my age. As expected, it no longer made any difference.

Communication during selling is very important. You can use communication both to get on the same wavelength as your client and to create tangible images. Each of us has our communication style preference. Our preference is generally tied to our sense of hearing, seeing, or feeling. When we write or speak each of us subconsciously organizes our words in a preferred pattern of oral, visual, or felt words. Those who rely most on their auditory sense are apt to respond, "I hear what you're saying." Those who communicate through their visual faculties flash ideas in their mind's eye and often remark, "I see what you mean." People who communicate through touching say "I grasp it now." And those who focus on the physical/emotional might express themselves with, "I feel I understand it now."

As a consultant and salesperson, you can use these communication styles to your benefit. Pay close attention to the words the client uses, the type of questions he asks, the way he describes his problems, and the approach he uses in getting to know you. These all give you clues to his preferred style. Fashion your communication to match your client's preferred style. If your client is a visual person, increase tangibility by creating visual images. Describe what the company will look like after the problem is solved. Do slick visual presentations of your proposal. Give the client pertinent articles to read. However, if your clients are auditory, then none of the above will be very useful. Auditory people do not want to read, they prefer listening. Spend more time talking to them. Or send a tape recording that they can listen to while driving to work. Tactile people require demonstrations that they can participate in. They want to take things apart and reassemble them. Computer demonstrations that they can play with are very effective. Physical/emotional people need to experience something. Invite them to a seminar so that they can experience it themselves or create a demonstration where they have an "aha" experience. Tailoring the tangible evidence in your sales presentation to your audience will go a long way in making the sale.

The words you choose during your presentation can create tangible images. If you match your words to your client's preferred style, you create rapport and increase the chances that your message will be heard. For auditory people, use auditory words, such as, "Your concerns ring true to me," "How does that idea sound to you?" or "Why bark your message when a whisper gets more attention?" Visual people respond better to visual images, such as "Let's try to get a clear picture of the stumbling blocks," or "Your competitor's profits are skyrocketing while yours plummet." Tactile people prefer words that connote touch, such as "Let's get a handle on that slippery problem" or "Let's immerse ourselves in the problem before we wrestle with the solution," or "Let's bulldoze our way through these obstacles." Emotional/physical people attune themselves to feeling words, such as, "My stomach feels queasy over this new production schedule," or "Division X is in sad shape but Division Y is filled with supercharged people." If you pattern your words, you can trigger more positive responses from your clients. Tangible images in the right communication style can help the client understand the services and benefits you provide.

Keep in mind that if you present to more than one person, you will have to adapt your communications. Include images in all four styles so that everyone in the audience feels addressed. If you present only in your dominant style, you risk losing members of the audience who prefer other styles. If you must work through a corporate hierarchy while selling, remember that the next person in the hierarchy may have a totally different style from that of the person you just finished selling. You must communicate in a responsive style, or you will be stopped cold.

After you have made the initial sale, your selling job does not stop. Keeping a client satisfied also requires selling. Intangible services require special attention for holding clients. Very often, the client is unaware of being served well. As Ted Levitt points out, clients of consulting usually don't know what they're getting until they don't get it. Once dissatisfied, they dwell on their dissatisfaction. In acquiring clients, it is important to create tangibility. In keeping customers, it becomes important to regularly remind and demonstrate to them what they are receiving. Periodic phone calls or letters about progress being made cost little. Sending clients articles of interest or socializing with them in a nonbusiness setting affirms the message that you care. Progress reports that inform the client of accomplishments and benefits to date act as tangible reminders of your value. Keeping clients for your consulting services requires constant reselling efforts. You want positive images and evidence to crowd out any possible dissatisfaction. You don't want a minor failure or source of displeasure to stand out due to the absence of positive feelings or reminders. Successful selling demands that you always sell. Whenever someone meets you, they form an image of you as a professional. Whether it occurs at the local chamber of commerce or on a consulting project, you are selling yourself. In the final analysis, clients are buying you to meet their needs.

In this context, selling is a continual and integral part of your consulting practice. If you demonstrate your competence and concern for the client at all times, then selling is no more than an extension of your consulting practice.

Now you are ready to sell your services to a potential client. Turn to Chapter 9, "Building Your Practice."

Additional Sources of Help

How to Sell Anything to Anybody. J. Girard. New York: Warner Books, 1977.
Personal Selling: Foundations, Process, and Management. B. M. Enis. Santa Monica, Calif.: Goodyear Publishing Co., 1979.

Prospecting Your Way to Sales Success. B. Good. New York: Charles Scribner's Sons, 1986.

Secrets of Closing the Sale. Z. Ziglar, Old Tappan, N.J.: Fleming H. Revell, 1984.

Strategic Selling. R. B. Miller and S. E. Heiman. New York: Morrow, 1984.

Building Your Practice*

9

*Surveys of consultant use suggest that roughly 75% of all firms employ
consultants of some kind on something approximating a regular basis.*
GEORGE STEINER AND JOHN MINER

The day arrives when you have a face-to-face appointment with a
prospective client. How did this event occur? More than likely, your
marketing and selling efforts paid off, although this prospective client
may be unknown to you. Perhaps he or she pulled your name from
the telephone book. Regardless of how it came about, having an appointment is an opportunity to secure a consulting project. If you are
like most consultants, you will be nervous, curious, and excited.

In this chapter, you will learn how to turn potential clients into
actual clients through initial interviews, project definitions, proposal
writing and presentation, contracts, and the final sale.

Securing Projects

The initial interview begins the consultant-client relationship. It can
also end it. Most engagements are won or lost at the very beginning.

---

* Professor Arthur Turner of the Harvard Business School contributed greatly to the ideas
presented in this chapter.

In fact, Leonard and Natalie Zunin, in their book *Contact: The First Four Minutes,** suggest that people make "yes or no" decisions within the first four minutes of meeting someone, at parties, sales presentations, and employee interviews. Evidence exists that jurors form their conclusions during the opening statements of the trial. They use selective parts of the trial simply to reinforce their predetermined conclusion. The same holds true for the remaining fifty-six minutes of an hour-long employment interview. There is no reason to believe that this four-minute principle does not apply to initial consultant–client meetings.

The initial meeting has three purposes. During the first few minutes, you should gain client acceptance in order to establish a long-term, positive working relationship. During the remainder of the meeting, the consultant and client should reach a clear and mutually agreed-upon definition of the need or problem. Based on this project definition, you can determine if the client needs your services. If the client can benefit from your services, then take the necessary steps to formalize the engagement. Understanding these three aspects of the initial interview turns your potential clients into actual ones.

The Interview

Since the interview is won or lost in the first few minutes, you must concentrate your initial efforts to secure the interpersonal relationship. Initial interviews provoke anxiety for both you and the client. The surface reason is simple. The four-minute barrier is based on whether or not the two of you like each other. The decision rests on first impressions, not facts. So the initial anxieties stem back to the fear of rejection discussed in Chapter 8.

Additional, more complex dynamics also contribute to the anxiety. From your standpoint, you are walking into an ambiguous situation. You don't know the person or the problems. You may not know if or how you can help. You may wonder how you will fit this project into an already busy schedule. If business is slow, you may need the project's revenues to pay your bills. You may question if your fees are too high. You cannot be sure whether the meeting will lead to a project or waste your time. All these contribute to pre-meeting "butterflies."

* New York: Ballantine Books, 1973.

The client reacts similarly to the consultant, only more intensely. After all, the client is the one who needs your services. If the need is due to a problem, the client may feel desperate. He or she may feel inadequate faced with your reputation and expertise, or interpret the need for consulting help as a sign of weakness and business incompetence. If this is the client's first exposure to consultants, then he or she probably does not know what to expect. Since judging consultant competence is difficult, a large risk is taken when engaging a consultant. On the one hand, the consultant's fee represents a financial risk. On the other hand, the client risks potential damage to the company from the consultant's actions. In other words, the client often gambles on an unknown quantity in an already ambiguous situation. Any of these feelings, alone or in combination, contribute to the client's anxiety.

Anxiety is not the only factor that influences the outcome of the initial meeting. The nature of professional relationships also contributes to the interpersonal dynamics. As mentioned, many people attach a stigma to individuals who seek certain types of help. Although this perception is changing, it's still a factor. Thus, the client may feel comfortable using a consultant. However, if his or her subordinates or business associates view it as a personal weakness, then the client will be affected.

Professional relationships are also fraught with "power" connotations. They place each of you in a dominant or subordinate role. As a result, the client may feel dependent or rebel against feeling subordinate. You may try to prove your superiority. Professional relationships also have a "take it or leave it" quality threatening in any situation.

Your anxieties, the client's anxieties, and the nature of the relationship all play a part in the initial meeting. Often, they produce unproductive, dysfunctional behavior from either the client or the consultant. Such behavior is a "trap" because it snares the relationship into interpersonal dynamics. Either of you can set the trap. It plays into the insecurities of both parties and results in escalating anxieties. Traps seldom permit you to make it past the four-minute barrier.

Recognizing these traps is the first step in developing long-term consulting relationships. Traps can be divided into two types: client and consultant. You can spot a trap by the dialogue. Here are some examples of client traps.

- *Performance trap.* "You are the third consultant I have had in the past ten months." The client puts you on the defensive by implying that previous consultants have not met his or her needs. He or she asserts power by saying "perform or else."
- *Challenge trap.* "How old are you?" The client challenges your qualifications in an indirect manner. If you are old enough, he or she questions the quality of your education. Again, you are put on the defensive so that the client can feel superior.
- *Abdication trap.* "I'm expecting you to get us moving again." The client places high expectation for action and progress on you. He or she abdicates responsibility while challenging you to perform. Consultants with a messiah complex often fall into this trap.
- *Projection trap.* "Could you talk to Joe, my subordinate? He is the weak link in our organization." The client does not acknowledge responsibility for the problem situation. Instead, all blame is projected onto someone else. The client directs your attention toward someone else.
- *Insult trap.* "Sorry, I am late again." The client mildly insults you by continually arriving late, implying that his or her time is more valuable than yours.

Consultants also set traps.

- *Jargon trap.* "I specialize in strategic managerial ecology engineering." The consultant confuses the client in an attempt to impress. The consultant puts down the client by implying that the client is not familiar with the latest developments in the profession.
- *Qualifications trap.* "I am a summa cum laude Ph.D. from Harvard. I am a Rhodes Scholar and Phi Beta Kappa. I have published fifteen books on the topic and have twenty years work experience." The consultant either is insecure relative to the client or wants to establish the client's inferior position. In both cases, the consultant attempts to overimpress the client.
- *God trap.* "Yes, I can solve all your problems." The suggestion that the client become dependent on and, hence, subordinate to the consultant is ego gratification.
- *Pleaser trap.* "I work twelve hours per day and seven days per week for my clients." The consultant views the client as an authority figure. The consultant feels inferior and tries to impress the client.

These examples show how potential consulting projects get side-tracked. Although both consultants and clients develop traps to reduce their anxieties, the end result is that neither makes it past the first four minutes. Consequently, no consulting projects materialize.

If your goal during the first few minutes is to secure the interpersonal relationship, then you must also reduce everyone's anxiety and avoid the traps. Experienced consultants structure interviews to decrease the awkwardness of initial meetings and the potential for traps. At the same time, they increase the information yield and they generate positive feelings.

The first rule when structuring interviews is preparation. Seasoned consultants research the client, the company, the industry, and problems affecting the industry. They familiarize themselves with the client's jargon and way of doing business. To gather this intelligence, they rely on their personal contacts network, annual reports, trade journals, business publications, and their own personal "Farley" files. This preparation enables them both to demonstrate familiarity with the client's business and to focus the interview. Taking time to learn about the client also establishes the consultant's interest and respect.

On meeting someone for the first time, most people find it difficult to "break the ice." Preparation helps at this point. Find out everything you can about this person, such as likes, dislikes, or school affiliation. Then use this information to your advantage. Psychological research shows that the fastest way to make someone like you is to appear similar to him or her. You can do this in numerous ways: your dress, your accent, your hobbies, or your civic affiliations. Expressing interest in your client's interests establishes a link between the two of you. If you know that your client likes golf, then ask how his or her golf game is. If there is a Mexican wall hanging in the office, ask how the client came by it. In other words, capitalize on personal clues to create a friendship.

Once the interview begins, structure your questions to meet the client's psychological and business needs. In other words, the main task on your agenda is to meet the client's agenda. To do so, you apply your professional diagnostic skills to the interview. Ask questions about the client's needs and problems. Quiz the client on his or her previous experience with consultants to discover hidden fears about and biases toward consultants. Find out how the client views the world. Let the client talk while you listen. Clients who need assistance will openly reveal the problem. Give them the opportunity.

Don't be afraid to take notes. They will be an enormous aid should you need to write a proposal.

Pay attention to the client's body language, voice patterns, and behavior. Use them as indicators of the client's feeling toward you, the interview, and his or her needs. For example, if a male client unbuttons his coat and moves his chair to face you directly, then he is displaying openness. If he strokes his chin while leaning back in his chair, he is evaluating you.

A topic important to interpersonal dynamics is money. As discussed in the previous chapter on fees, the client wants to know your fee structure. The guidelines provided before apply here. Additionally, you must discover if the client expects to pay for this first meeting. Usually clients do not pay. Consequently, consultants normally do not give out much free advice or service. However, if the client expects to pay, he or she will expect immediate service. If you withhold under those circumstances, the client will feel cheated. Therefore, explain your policy to the client.

The structured interview goes a long way in establishing consulting projects. First, you make the client feel good. You boost his or her self-esteem by asking important questions and by being a receptive audience. Most people like to be the center of attention. Second, your diagnostic questions about the client's needs properly focus the meeting. With the attention centered on the client, you demonstrate your interest in his or her welfare. The only interest clients have in you is as a vehicle to meet needs; they hold no interest in your problems, family life, or technical trivia. Consequently, limit conversation about yourself to building the trust needed for a long-term relationship. Meet the client's needs and objectives.

The first step in generating consulting projects is tending to the interpersonal aspects of the relationship, thereby increasing the chances of succeeding past the four-minute barrier. Unfortunately, too many consultants ignore this aspect because of their own anxieties. Only by successfully dealing with the client's initial anxieties will you make the client trust you enough to discuss the potential project.

Defining the Project

If you pass the four-minute barrier, gather information about the client's need. This does not imply that the interpersonal dynamics stop. This section will inform you how to use the client's needs as the method of solidifying your interpersonal relationship.

Accurate and accepted project definition is crucial for winning an engagement. Since the client usually has no clear idea of the need, define the project jointly, enabling the client to focus his or her concerns more precisely. Through collaborative efforts, the client begins to know and accept the need. A completed project definition imposes severe limitations on reshaping the engagement. The project definition develops certain expectations in both parties that are difficult to alter. Thus, accurate project definition not only clarifies the need but also determines subsequent behavior.

Needs take three forms for both consultants and clients: perceived, expressed, and actual. Perceived needs are what each party sees. Expressed needs are what each party says. Actual needs are the real needs that may or may not be related to either perceived or expressed needs. For example, a client may perceive a need for more information from subordinates. When talking to the consultant, he or she may express the need for a computer to supply that information. The client may actually need less but more precise information. Both consultant and client must differentiate between these three types of needs.

Since clients want to maintain their self-esteem, they often express needs that are socially acceptable. For example, they may express a need for corporate restructuring, when actually what they want is to fire some department managers. The client's real need might be to change his or her management style. Since the client perceives that planning to fire people is often unacceptable to consultants and that changing management style is personally unacceptable, the client identifies a need that has neutral connotations. The consultant's job is to help the client remove the "blinders." Through diagnostic questions, both consultant and client can shape the project's definition to correspond to the real need.

Related to actual vs. perceived vs. expressed needs is the distinction between symptoms and causes. Clients focus on symptoms such as falling sales. To improve sales they respond with greater promotion, rebates, and motivation training for salespeople. However, if decreased sales are the result of a product no longer appealing to customers, then the clients' efforts will be in vain. The Detroit automobile makers exemplify addressing symptoms rather than causes. As the consultant, you must help clients separate the symptoms from the causes.

Based on the project's definition, you and the client determine four important elements of any consulting engagement: the scope, the approach, the goals, and the terms. First, the scope sets the constraints, such as size of project, who will be involved, what areas you will examine, and the time needed. Second, after discussing several possible approaches, you select a general plan of procedures most appropriate for the project. As the consultant, you provide the primary input when determining the approach. The clients suggest ways to modify the approach to increase its success in their organizations. Occasionally, clients have determined approaches before your meeting. Obstinacy about approach is evidence that the client has rigid motives, which you must uncover. Third, you set goals that describe the type of results anticipated. These goals should reflect the expected expenditures of time, effort, and money. Finally, you will decide the terms of the engagement. These terms include who will do what tasks when, the time required to achieve the goals, and the approximate costs. Any special restrictions, such as patent rights or proprietary information, is also agreed upon.

As a result of defining the project, you discover how you can assist the client. You focus the client's general concern into a specific need. After identifying the need, you determine whether the client can benefit from your services.

During this phase, you also build client acceptance and collaboration into the project. Since the task is mutual, the client reacts positively. This is in stark contrast to those who try the "hard sell" before knowing the client's needs.

Assessing Client Readiness

The last task of the initial interview is to assess the client's readiness to benefit from and to pay for your services. Conduct three distinct assessments during the meeting. First, determine whether or not the person to whom you're speaking can actually engage you as a consultant. (This refers to the MAD client concept described in Chapter 8.) Does this individual have the money, authority, and desire to engage your services? If you targeted your clients properly, you will know before the interview that this person is a MAD client. If not, is there any compelling reason for meeting with him or her? For instance, can this individual arrange a meeting with the appropriate MAD client? In many client organizations, you must meet with several people before consultant expenditures are authorized. In those cases, you follow the chain. Since initial interviews consume both your time and energies, this client assessment is crucial to securing the engagement.

During the second assessment of client readiness, determine how your consulting project fits into the client's organization. In this assessment you judge the potential impact of your work. How does this project fit in with the client's other priorities? Is the need great enough to warrant the client's continued attention and resources? To what extent is the client willing to accept responsibility for the project and its outcomes? Who in the client's organization supports the project and who opposes it? Will the detractors sabotage your project? Will some employees benefit, while others get hurt by the project? What is the power position of the person who engaged you? How does his or her support influence your potential success? In essence, you must determine if your work will make a difference. The client may need your services, but if the organization is not ready to accept them, you will be battling great odds. Exploring the organizational dynamics is important to assessing client readiness.

The final assessment identifies the client for this particular project. In each project, you must specify to whom you will report, whose need you will meet, and who will pay your fees. These issues definitely influence your project, but unfortunately they often remain confused. For example, a client may ask you to review a certain department. If you report back to that client, the department head probably will view your visit as a critical evaluation, and, as a result, will act defensively, hiding evidence of poor performance. However, if you report only to the department head, then he or she is inclined to be more open. Your assurance that information is confidential will make a department head feel more open to questions and assistance. In every consulting project, you and the client must agree on who the client is. If the person paying your fee is not the specified client, then you must establish a mechanism by which they can judge your work. This normally occurs through approval from the client.

Assessing client readiness, then, results in three important evaluations. First, you will know if the client is ready to "buy" your services. Second, you will know if buying your services will satisfy the client's need. Third, you will know if the client's situation will promote or thwart your efforts to satisfy the need. If the results are positive from each evaluation, then you begin formalizing the consulting arrangement.

Structuring an Interview

To capitalize on the initial meeting, you perform a number of tasks simultaneously. Your aim is to design a project that insures success for both the client and you. To accomplish this end, you must establish a solid, trusting relationship with the client to provide the interpersonal base for the project and all subsequent work. Next, you concentrate on the client's need through accurate project definition. Through this process, you demonstrate your ability to understand the client's situation and to offer help. Finally, you determine whether and how the client can use your services. At this point you suggest that the client engage your services as a consultant. Quite often, you will shake hands right then, signaling an agreement. After the meeting, you will send a "letter of understanding" to the client. It confirms your mutual understanding of the engagement's purpose, scope, approach, and terms.

To make the most of your initial interview, you need to plan a structure ahead of time. By preparing questions beforehand, you insure no important areas are overlooked. This is crucial, since clients occasionally withhold information. They do so for several reasons: they may be unaware of the facts or not grasp their significance; they may be reluctant to share the information; the information may not be the kind the client would ordinarily think of telling the consultant; and the consultant may not have requested the information. Consequently, through the structured interview you obtain necessary information or find out why it is withheld.

The structured interview also relieves you of having to think up questions during the meeting, which detracts from your ability to concentrate on the client. Toward this end, utilize the following checklist of questions to ask during the initial interview.* Adapt this checklist to your own situation. For instance, you may develop other questions that are significant to your clients. The important point is that you explore the many areas discussed in this chapter.

- Who is the client?
- What is the problem/opportunity? How is it perceived and expressed?
- How long has this problem existed? (Or how long has the client

---

* This checklist is adapted from "Consulting Process Issues," a paper presented to the American Psychological Association, New York, 1979, by Professor Arthur Turner of the Harvard Business School and the author of this book.

been trying to get some movement toward this goal?) What has been done before? What kind of results has the client had?

- What has happened to motivate the client to use a consultant at this particular point?
- What is the client's prior experience with and attitudes toward consultants? What happened? What perceptions (or misconceptions) do they hold? What fears or anxieties do they hold?
- What was nature of the financial arrangement with the previous consultant? What is the acceptable fee range?
- Does the client expect to pay for the first visit?
- How does the client picture approaching this problem/opportunity?
- If this project is successful, how does the client picture the organization running when the work is completed? How will the organization be different?
- What specific, measurable outcomes (results/products) need to result in order for the engagement to be viewed as successful? Who will use it and how? How will the client know when results are reached?
- What time lines affect this project?
- What are some of the other major preoccupations (and their priority) in the client's organization today? How does this project relate to them? What is the financial health of the client's organization? What resources (personnel, money, etc.) will the client commit to this project?
- Who will be affected by this project or have some influence in its success? How do they feel about the situation? Will there be losers as well as winners?
- How will the client's personnel feel/react to this project and about taking time to participate in it?
- Which parts of the organization are primarily affected by this problem/opportunity?
- Who wants the change to take place and who does not want it to take place? How strongly motivated is each group to hold its position?
- Who will be responsible for carrying out the consultant's recommendations? How do they feel about the project?
- Will the general climate of the organization support or resist change?
- What are the most likely pitfalls and barriers to the success of the project? Have they been adequately assessed and studied?

- Are there certain solutions that will be unacceptable? What other constraints affect this project?
- Does the client have areas of concern about this project and some of the possible results? How will the client be at risk?
- What is the capacity of this particular client to carry out change—in terms of past history and present assessment?
- What is the consultant's interest in this job?

Writing and Presenting Successful Proposals

Most initial interviews result in a client's request for a proposal. In this section, you will learn how to write and present a proposal.

A proposal is usually a document you write for the client that:

1. describes your understanding of the client's need
2. states what you intend to do for the client
3. indicates what anticipated results and potential benefits the client will gain as a consequence of the engagement
4. outlines your approach and qualifications
5. tries to persuade the client to accept your proposal

A proposal is a marketing tool. A successful proposal is appealing as well as informative. Through it, you both hook the client and plan your consulting approach.

Clients request proposals for many reasons. If they are comparing many consultants before final selection, they request proposals from each consultant. Government agencies are required to advertise for consultants through Requests for Proposals (RFPs). They place RFPs in appropriate newspapers, trade journals, and the *Commerce Business Daily*. Based on the proposals received, they select the consultant. Other clients desire proposals to verify the consultant's understanding of the problem. In addition, they have their staff critique the approach before making a decision. The proposal is an important step in securing a project.

Even though a client requests a proposal, you may decide not to submit one. Perhaps you cannot assist this client or you may feel the client is not serious. The project may be beyond your scope of expertise. A competitor may have the inside track. In any case, proposals require time and energy. If you want the project and know you have a solid opportunity, then submit a proposal, but do not waste resources.

Proposal Strategy

To write a winning proposal, develop a strategy for each particular project. Your strategy analyzes in depth what the client wants. Your initial interview notes supply this information. If you are proposing against competition, your strategy should consider what you expect them to offer. You then evaluate what you can offer. Finally, you forge a plan to insure the highest probability of winning.

Having decided to write the proposal, you next create a proposal master schedule. This schedule includes the following milestones:

1. background research completion dates for projects that require additional research
2. "cut-off" dates imposed by the client
3. completion dates for technical, management, and cost inputs
4. scheduled completion date for the proposal's first draft
5. first draft review cut-off date
6. scheduled completion date for the proposal's final draft
7. final draft review cut-off date
8. proposal typing and reproduction dates
9. final sign-off and submission dates

Unless you are skilled in proposal writing, set aside more time than expected. If you set aside adequate time, you can avoid the embarrassment of late submissions. This is particularly vital for government proposals, since those agencies will not consider late proposals.

Some proposals require additional staff either to write them or to perform the project. With a master schedule, you can build the proposal team. In most consulting firms, the people who write the proposals also perform the work. When building the team, you clearly indicate the importance of the proposal effort and the proposed project. You brief the team on the project's purpose, scope, and terms. To avoid schedule conflicts, check how this project fits into everyone's schedule. Then, assign staff responsibilities both for proposal completion and for duties on the project.

As the person overseeing the proposal, you are responsible for the final result. Develop an image of the completed proposal. What topics will you address and what questions will you answer? How many pages do you envision? What format will impress your client? Do you need art work or graphics? Decide on the format and tell your proposal team to prevent gaps in the proposal and misunderstandings.

Most successful consultants arrange an internal evaluation of each proposal before submitting it to the client. They choose colleagues familiar with the technical material and/or the client. It is preferable to select individuals who were not involved in the proposal effort, since you want an objective analysis of and reaction to your proposal. With this feedback, you can modify the proposal to insure its success.

Format and Guidelines for Successful Proposals

Successful proposals follow a certain format. They include elements pertinent to client concerns and expectations. In this section, these elements are described. Not all proposals contain every element. Choose the elements that are appropriate to each of your projects.

1. *Table of Contents.*   Include headings and page numbers.
2. *Introduction.*   Establish rapport with the client. Convince the client that you understand the problem and the underlying factors that influence it. Express conviction that the matter is important and merits professional, outside assistance. Point out that you want to help. Moreover, suggest that you are the most appropriate source of help.
3. *Purpose of the Proposed Engagement.*   Set forth the engagement's purpose and goals. If this section is not accurate, the client will not read further. If possible, state the purpose and goals in the client's own words. This lets the client identify with the proposal. Also, phrase the goals in such a way that you can refer to them. This requires stating the goals as specific and measurable outcomes, such as "develop and implement an inventory control system." Later, you and the client can measure the progress of the project against the goal statements in this section.
4. *Estimate of Benefits.*   Underscore the anticipated benefits the client will receive. Give the client realistic hope, but do not

promise results, even though neither you nor the client would undertake the project without hope of success. In the profession, we call this the "WIIFM Factor"—What's in it for me? Answer this question for the client.

5. *Approach, Scope, and Plan.*   Clarify your plans for meeting the engagement's objective. Define the parameters and limits of the proposed service (for instance, you will be studying only ten of forty warehouses). Explore and critique several approaches to the project. Then, in general terms, explain how you will proceed. Break large assignments into smaller "doable" segments that provide discrete milestones and success experiences for both the client and you. Provide enough information to demonstrate your competence, but not enough so that the client can perform the task without you. Thus, stress the method and techniques, such as the flow of interviews. However, do not reveal the questions you will ask.

6. *Project Schedule and Management Plan.*   To determine the schedule, list the primary tasks required to achieve results. Then specify the timing and flow of tasks according to engagement phases. Finally, detail how you intend to manage the project.

7. *Nature of Final Output.*   Specify any end products, such as reports, new product designs, or graphic material. This avoids later misunderstandings.

8. *Progress Reports the Client Can Expect.*   Progress reports are vehicles for continual communication with the client. Through these reports, you inform the client of problems and of steps taken to resolve them. Indicate the frequency and format of periodic progress reports.

9. *Pricing Summary.*   Explain your fees, type of fee arrangement, billing procedures, and timing of bills. Point out expected expenses the client will bear. The client should understand that the fee estimate is just that—your best estimate of the time and costs involved. Give enough detail about fees so that the client clearly understands the relationship between the cost of your services and the amount of work. Also, include any other terms and conditions that affect the total cost.

10. *Qualifications, Staffing, and Ethics.*   Give a brief resume of your firm and the staff consulting on this project to show you have experience solving problems similar to the client's. Rather than describe your entire background, choose those elements

relevant to this client and this proposal. Finally, include a copy of the ethics code of your professional association: this marks you as a professional and engenders trust.

11. *Use of Outside Consultants, If Any.* If collaborating with or subcontracting to other consultants, specify who they are and what they will do. To avoid later problems, specify whether you or the client is responsible for their technical performance.

12. *Role of Client Personnel.* The client must understand the relationship between your fee estimate and your expectations of his or her effort. Outline how much help you expect from the client's executives and staff. If possible, specify people, duties, and time required.

13. *Support by Top Management.* Most consultants concede that top management support is crucial to success. Make the executives aware of this fact. Moreover, insure that they communicate their support for the project to all concerned. Finally, specify the frequency and purpose of regular meetings with them.

14. *Function of Steering Committee, If Any.* Many consultants require formation of a steering committee. This committee assists, coordinates, reviews, and implements the consultant's work. It gives organizational credence and momentum for the project. It also acts as a decision-making body. In this section, spell out the purpose, composition, and responsibilities of the committee.

15. *Disclaimers.* Clarify your use of any disclaimers regarding the project. At this point, explain that your role is that of an advisor, not a decision maker. Emphasize that achieving benefits is contingent not only on your recommendations but also on the client's decisions and actions. Spell out any other restrictions of your responsibility, such as limitations if a client does not cooperate through personnel support. If your work leads to proprietary information, indicate who has ownership and control.

16. *References.* Consultants are divided as to whether you should provide previous client references. If you do, first obtain written permission from all references listed. You may indicate that references are available on request. Keep in contact with your references to insure that their opinion of you has not changed. Yesterday's supporter can become tomorrow's detractor.

17. *Summary and Closing.*   This section is short. Once again, include your belief that the engagement is "most important." State your availability to answer questions. Indicate that you are prepared to begin the project within a short time period after the client's acceptance.

Using this format, you can develop a winning proposal. Your purpose is to entice the client to engage you as the consultant by including elements that stimulate the client's desire and convince the client that you can satisfy that desire. At the same time, be sure the information is accurate, since this determines the client's expectations concerning activities, approach, benefits, and costs.

Many new consultants have a difficult time estimating the tasks, time, and costs for proposals. This is the topic of the next section.

Methods for Accurately Estimating Project Cost and Time

Most new consultants underbid consulting projects. Even though they can calculate their billing rates correctly, they underestimate the number of hours required for a project. Halfway through their work, they realize they already are over budget. At that point, it is embarrassing to ask the client to revise the budget. With proper planning you can avoid this.

For proposal purposes, every project has four phases: the marketing phase, the data-gathering phase, the analysis phase, and the report-writing and presentation phase. Some projects may include additional phases, such as implementation; but the four-phase project will serve for demonstration purposes.

Know exactly the amount of time spent on marketing to this client. Include preliminary discussions with the client, the initial interview, writing the proposal, and presenting the proposal to the client. Tally these hours as your subtotal for the marketing phase.

For the data-gathering phase, a flow chart will help your estimate (see Table 10). In the first column, list all the questions you must answer in order to complete the project. These questions determine what information you must gather. This, in turn, helps you identify the sources of information.

In the next column, state the purpose for asking the question. Con-

TABLE 10. Sample Data-Gathering Flow Chart to Estimate Time and Cost

Questions Consultant Must Answer	Purpose of Question	Information Required for Answer	Source of Information	Tasks to Gather Information	Hours Required	Personnel Responsible	Completion Date
1. What are essential characteristics of the client's business?	1) To understand client's situation	1A) Market information	1A1) Market studies	1A1a) Read market studies	8	Jones	2/1
			1A2) Marketing director	1A2a) Interview	2	Jones	2/3
		1B) Organization's goals	1B1) Annual reports	1B1a) Read annual reports	5	Smith	2/1
			1B2) President	1B2a) Interview	3	Smith	2/3
				1B2b) Read president's speeches	9	Smith	2/1
		1C) Etc.	1C1)	1C1a)			
2.	2)	2A)	2A1)	2A1a)	#		
				2A1b)	#		
			2A2)	2A2a)	#		
				2A2b)	#		
				2A2c)	#		

sultants often ask more questions than necessary. Irrelevant questions lead to irrelevant data-gathering activities. Since those activities require time, your final cost is higher. By stating the purposes of your questions, you focus your efforts and control your costs.

The next column indicates what information is required to answer your questions. The type of information normally dictates the source. You then list the tasks necessary to gather the information from the source. For each task, you estimate the time required to perform the task. In your estimate include the time needed to get your hands on the information. For example, if you must conduct extensive library research to locate a few facts, base your time estimate on the total research time rather than the time it takes to read the few facts.

By using a flow chart, you break the project into distinct activities. This helps you plan the engagement and prevents your overlooking necessary activities, which leads to underbidding. It helps you assign staff responsibilities and completion dates. This information helps you schedule your activities as in Table 11. In the example, consultant Smith is scheduled to work 13 hours on February 1. A time/task planning schedule enables you to spot these oversights. As a result, you can rearrange the schedule prior to starting the project. The planning schedule also serves as a standard to which you compare your progress.

At the conclusion of these planning exercises, you know the exact number of hours to complete the data-gathering phase. You combine this information with your billing rate and fee arrangement to calculate the fee range for this phase of the project.

Estimating fees for the analysis and report-writing phases is more difficult. Experienced consultants state that each of these phases takes the same amount of time as the data-gathering phase. If it takes 50 hours to gather all the data, you will spend 50 hours analyzing it and 50 hours writing the report. The project total equals 150 hours. These same consultants suggest an additional 10–15 percent above the total for contingency purposes. Thus a reasonable cost estimate would include:

$$
\begin{array}{rl}
30\% = & \text{Data gathering} \\
30\% = & \text{Analysis} \\
30\% = & \text{Report writing} \\
\underline{10\%} = & \underline{\text{Contingency}} \\
100\% = & \text{Total + Hours for promotional phase}
\end{array}
$$

TABLE 11. Sample Time/Task Planning Schedule

Client: _____   Project: _____

| Hours | | | | | Day or Week | Feb 1 | 2 | 3 | 4 | 5 | Feb 8 | 9 | 10 | 11 | 12 | Feb 15 | 16 | ... |
Budgeted	Actual	Task #	Staff	Task Description														
8		1A1a	Jones	Read market studies		8												
2		1A2a	Jones	Interview marketing director				2										
5		1B1a	Smith	Read annual reports		5												
3		1B2a	Smith	Interview president				3										
9		1B2b	Smith	Read president's speeches		9												
?		2A1b	?	?														
?		2A2a	?	?														
?		2A2b	?	?														
?		2A2c	?	?														
Total					Total	23		5										

To this total, add the number of hours from the promotional phase. The report-writing phase may expand or contract, depending on your writing ability. In that phase remember to include time for production beyond the writing, such as editing, partner review, typing, charts, reproduction, and final review.

By using these guidelines, your estimate will accurately reflect the time and cost for each project. This saves you from losing projects by overbidding and from losing your shirt by underbidding.

Proposing Against Competition

When facing competition for a project, remember this rule: *Someone always has the inside track.* Consultants refer to this as being "wired." Very often projects are wired from the start. The client may issue a public RFP to meet government regulations. As a formality, the client publishes the RFP already knowing who will win the engagement. Unfortunately, many consultants expend time and energy developing proposals that are never considered seriously.

Your first question, then, is "Do I have the inside track?" You gain the inside track through a sponsor. All proposals and projects have sponsors within the client organization. This person pushes for you and helps keep you in the running. You must know who has the most influence on your sponsor. Try to keep these key people on your side to broaden your support base.

Competitors also have sponsors. Their sponsors usually differ from yours. You can estimate your chances by comparing the power of your sponsor vs. the power of your competitors' sponsors. Analyze who has power over your competitors' sponsors. Can you sway their opinion on your behalf? When you calculate your power network vs. your competitors' power networks, who has the project wired? If you don't, is there a compelling reason to submit a proposal anyway?

Under certain circumstances, you will not have the inside track, but you should bid anyway. For example, the proposal may provide a chance for person-to-person exposure to the client. If the client is someone you want to meet, then a proposal presents the opportunity. More importantly, the client may have future projects. If impressed with you, he or she may engage you for them, even though the "wired" competitor gets the current project.

When proposing against competition, analyze what you expect the competition to offer. You can discover their approach in several ways. Ask your sponsor. Quiz your business associates and your personal contacts network. Question other consultants who have proposed against these competitors. If your competition has submitted similar proposals to government agencies, read through them. Many clients make all proposals public after selecting one consultant. Utilize these earlier proposals to gather information.

Once you estimate your competitors' approaches, attempt to discredit them in your proposal. Without alluding to your competitors, discuss and criticize their approaches in your proposal. Indicate the shortcomings and pitfalls of each approach. Then, demonstrate how your approach surpasses the other approaches and leads to greater potential benefits. The client will remember your critique when reviewing the other proposals.

Presenting the Proposal

Always ask to present your proposal in person. This serves two purposes. On the one hand, it indicates how serious your clients are. If they will not see you, then they are not very serious. Occasionally, government agencies accept only sealed proposals. More than likely, those projects are wired. On the other hand, a presentation in person increases your chances of clinching the sale.

Since the proposal is a marketing tool, approach its physical appearance and its presentation from the marketing viewpoint. The proposal creates the initial impression of your professional work and your ability to communicate. Make it esthetically pleasing to look at and easy to read. Keep it short, usually one topic per page and one page per topic. Type with double spacing, indentations, capital letters, and margins. Make effective use of space by centering the text. The proposal should look professional and communicate effectively.

To hook the client, structure the presentation from both marketing and psychological viewpoints. From the marketing angle, stimulate the desire, and send a clear message that you can satisfy that desire. From the psychology side, create client identification with the project. You want the client to feel ownership. Car salespeople use this principle: they invite you to test-drive the car; by driving it, you develop a sense of ownership. The same holds true for buying clothes. During the presentation, foster client attachment to the project.

Experienced consultants accomplish these objectives in the following manner. Before the proposal is due, they make an appointment with the potential client to review the progress of the proposal. At such a meeting, they utilize a "rough draft" proposal. With newsprint and magic markers, they review the need, stress the benefits, and suggest alternative approaches to the entire project or aspects of it. They encourage the client to make additions and modifications. As a result, they discover much more about what the client is ready, willing, and able to undertake. In addition, the client becomes a working collaborator. Since the client helped shape the project, he or she will develop a sense of ownership. The consultant then incorporates the results of the meeting into the formal proposal. The final presentation is simply a polished reiteration of the rough draft meeting.

If a rough draft meeting is not possible, experienced consultants try to create the same effect at the formal presentation. To achieve high client identification, the consultant needs to involve the client. Stimulate the client to interact with your proposal. Review your proposal as a "working suggestion" rather than as a "firm finished proposal." Clients are hesitant to mark up or change someone else's typed document; we all learned that rule in grammar school. Instead, we react to finished documents passively: we read and evaluate. You can overcome this barrier by marking up your copy in front of the client. Place large stars or asterisks by your important points. Underline certain sections. You can also use newsprint or flip charts while presenting your proposal. Ask for the client's ideas. Insert them into the proposal. You want the client to invest time and thought in the process.

If you must do a formal stand-up presentation without client interaction, make it professional and polished. Practice your presentation until you feel comfortable. Use audiovisual aids. Keep the presentation brief and pointed, stressing the benefits and results. Do not bore or confuse your client with jargon or technical detail. Set aside time for questions. Finally, thank the client for the opportunity to make the presentation.

Closing the Deal

After presenting the proposal, you will want some indication that the client has selected you as the consultant. Clients seldom offer this indication. As the salesperson, you must take the initiative to finalize the sale. New consultants often fail to take this initiative. They leave the client's office without knowing if they won the contract. Don't make that mistake.

After the proposal presentation, a client should reach a decision. It is only fair to you and the client that you push for closure. If you have led the client through the initial meeting and the proposal presentation competently, he or she should want your services. Some consultants feel they will lose the sale if they push for closure too soon. By this time, however, you cannot lose the sale by asking for it. If the client turns you down, it means no sale existed. No additional waiting time will help your efforts.

To close the sale, simply ask, "When would you like me to start working on the project—tomorrow or next Monday?" Notice that you are not asking *if* the client wants you to work on the project. You ask for a starting date decision between tomorrow and next Monday. Either choice implies that you are the chosen consultant. This type of question helps the client make the initial decision.

Some clients may indicate that they like the proposal, but the cost is too high. By using the project as a carrot, they will encourage you to lower your price. If you estimated properly, you cannot realistically reduce your price without cutting into profits. Instead, offer to reduce the scope of your project to fit the client's budget.

Occasionally clients will postpone their decisions, perhaps to get management approval. Before you leave, find out when they will make the decision. Then make an appointment on that date to discuss their decision. Avoid phone calls, since people have a more difficult time rejecting your services face-to-face. Push for a cut-off date, but do so in a polite and inoffensive manner. A cut-off date keeps you from hanging on and allows you to coordinate this project with your other projects.

Once the client chooses you as the consultant, send him or her a letter of understanding to confirm your arrangement. If the proposal was modified during presentation, enclose a copy of the corrected proposal. You may send a contract, the topic of the next section.

Contracts

Consultants, like everyone else, are turning to written contracts to protect their interests. This is unfortunate. We have created an over-litigated society. Long past are the days of the business agreement when people lived up to their word.

Contracts do have a useful purpose other than self-protection. As has been stressed, the consultant-client relationship is ambiguous. A clear contract provides a guide for both parties. It spells out the responsibilities and actions upon which each party can rely. Thus, even though neither party intends to sue the other, the contract clarifies each party's role and expectations.

Legal Contracts

A legal contract is an agreement enforceable by law. Contracts can be written, spoken, or implied. At one seminar aimed at helping new consultants build their practices, the leader told the audience that he avoided legal contracts. Instead, he wrote a letter that outlined the responsibilities of each party. Then both he and the client signed it. He stated that his method avoided all the hassle of legal contracts and worked as well. Luckily for him, no lawyers were in attendance. Whether he knew it or not, his letter became a contract when both parties signed it. Depending on their previous discussions, they may have a verbal contract, which is just as binding but more difficult to prove.

This section does not provide you with a sample contract. To provide a contract appropriate to every type of consulting, let alone every situation, would be impossible. Instead, ask your attorney to draw up contracts designed for your specific purposes.

To make the best use of your attorney, consider the contract before you ask for one. Why do you want a contract? What are you trying to protect? What do you want to see happen? What do you want included in the contract? Make a list of your thoughts so that you can communicate effectively with your attorney. Ask if you left out anything that is in your best interest or from which you need protection. Your attorney will use this information to draw up an appropriate contract. When creating a contract, you should consider including the following items.

1. *Responsibility of each party.* What does each party agree to do?
2. *Time agreements.* When will each party complete their obligations?
3. *Financial arrangements.* What constitutes payment and when will it take place?

4. *Products or services to be delivered.* Describe the form and method of delivery.
5. *Cooperation of client.* Is this cooperation necessary for good work? If so, then specify your responsibilities and compensation if the client does not cooperate.
6. *Independent contractor status.* Establish that you are not an employee and do not have employee status or obligations.
7. *Advisory capacity.* Indicate that you will not make decisions for the client. Instead, you provide your best opinions only.
8. *Client responsibility for review, implementation, and results.* The final determination of quality and results should lie with the client.
9. *Your potential work with competitors.* If you plan to consult with your client's competitors, specify this in the contract.
10. *Authority of client to contract for your services.* This pertains to corporations only. Some corporate charters restrict corporate employees and owners from entering into contracts. In these cases, clients should state their source of authority.
11. *Attorney's fees clause.* If you must use an attorney to collect your fees, establish who will pay your attorney.
12. *Limitations.* If any special limitations exist, such as limited liability after a certain date, include them. Remember that neither you nor the client can contract away or create a waiver of liability for negligent acts.

These elements will suffice for most consultants. However, ask your attorney if any additional points are pertinent to your situation.

Using a legal contract is a personal decision. The majority of consultants still do not use them. However, if you have been "burned" by clients or if you are taking a substantial risk, then a contract is appropriate. Proper groundwork and continual communication may be an adequate substitute for a contract. Moreover, not having a contract forces you to be explicit and straightforward with your clients. If your intent is to sue your client through the contract, remember that they hold the same option.

Psychological Contracts

Whether you use a legal contract or not, you and your clients always form a psychological contract, a set of expectations that govern the relationship. Generally, these expectations are neither communicated nor agreed upon. Yet the psychological contract usually binds more than any legal contract. If you expect to have an office at the client's building and none is provided, you feel cheated. Once the psychological contract is broken, it is difficult to repair. The injured party usually sets out to sabotage the other's position. Unfortunately, this destroys the relationship. If a legal contract exists, both parties use it for revenge.

To avoid this situation, communicate openly with your client. Remember to address his or her psychological as well as business needs. If you have used the suggestions from this chapter, you will know the client's hidden expectations. Moreover, you will have designed the project with the client to promote client acceptance and satisfaction. If you maintain this approach throughout the project, you will seldom interfere with the psychological contract. The key is to stay alert to the client's needs. This only occurs through constant and effective communication.

Securing client projects separates would-be consultants from successful consultants. Winning a project is the culmination of your marketing efforts. It establishes your ability to listen and respond to a client's needs. During the initial interview, build the client-consultant foundation. Through your interpersonal skills and diagnostic abilities, you will create confidence in your competence and gain valuable information regarding the client's situation. By packaging and presenting this information in the proposal, you convince the client that you are the most appropriate source of help. As a result of all these steps, you will successfully close the deal and secure a client. You will learn how to conduct the engagement in the next chapter.

Additional Sources of Help

Consulting for Change. F. Steele. Amherst, Mass.: University of Massachusetts Press, 1975.

The Consulting Process in Action. G. Lippitt and R. Lippitt. La Jolla, Calif.: University Associate Press, 1978.

Contact: The First Four Minutes. L. Zunin and N. Zunin. New York: Ballantine Books, 1973.

How to Create a Winning Proposal. J. Ammon-Wexler and C. Carmel. Santa Cruz, Calif.: Mercury Publications, 1978.

How to Read a Person Like a Book. G. Nierenberg and H. Calero. New York: Pocket Books, 1973.

Intervention Theory and Method. C. Argyris. Reading, Mass.: Addison-Wesley, 1970.

Management Consulting: A Guide to the Profession. M. Kubr. Geneva, Switzerland: International Labour Organization, 1976.

Organizational Learning. C. Argyris and D. Schon. Reading, Mass.: Addison-Wesley, 1978.

Organizational Psychology. E. Schein. Englewood Cliffs, N.J.: Prentice-Hall, 1965.

Secrets of Closing the Sale. Z. Ziglar. Old Tappan, N.J.: Fleming H. Revell, 1984.

Conducting Projects

10

When problem situations arise, don't do the natural thing and ask "What can I do about it?" Instead ask "What is the true problem in this situation?"

DON KOBERG AND JIM BAGNALL

Frequently the question is asked, "What is it that consultants actually do?" The answer depends on the type of consulting and on the specific project. Engineering consultants differ from real estate consultants by the nature of their training and the problems they face. Yet discussions with various consultants indicate that they all follow a similar pattern. While conducting engagements, they rely on the same general process of data gathering, analysis, and recommendations. In this chapter, you will learn how to design the engagement and collect the necessary data.

Designing the Engagement

If you submitted a proposal, then you have designed the engagement. If not, then you should reread Chapter 9 in order to plan your work. Basically, you want to know who will do what to whom, when, where, and how. By using an engagement flow chart and time/task planning schedule, you can coordinate the entire project.

Your planning up to now concentrated on the technical aspects of the project. The client's problem requires your technical expertise. You have decided on the best approach to reach a successful technical solution. Yet each engagement has a psychological component. For clients to accept and use your technical solutions, they must be satisfied psychologically. You can build success into your projects by incorporating this component.

Three psychological factors are important to the client and the client's organization: progress, resistance, and identification. If clients feel desperate about their problems, then they will need to experience progress quickly. They look for signs that you are effectively solving the problem. Too often, consultants overlook this aspect when designing the project, particularly if the project extends past six months. The consultant can see the light at the end of the tunnel, but the client cannot. When clients do not see progress, their anxiety levels rise with each passing day. When the anxiety becomes unbearable, they dismiss the consultant.

You can avoid this situation by building "success experiences" into the project. Design an initial "breakthrough project" that has a high probability of success. If the project is large, break it into smaller "do-able" segments.

For example, if you are designing a company-wide training program, consider progressing department by department. Accomplishment of each smaller segment is rewarding to both the client and the consultant, since it develops a sense of forward movement. It also underscores your effectiveness and value. Upon completion of each segment, meet with the client to report the benefits accrued during that segment. Also, explain how that segment fits into the overall project. The client will appreciate your efforts.

The second psychological component pertains to client resistance to your work. The client may desperately need your services. At the same time, the client or someone in the client's organization may resist your efforts. They particularly resist when change is initiated by an outside person. Most organizational members have a vested interest in the status quo. They know what to expect. As an outsider, you threaten their stability. Consequently, the organization gathers its forces to neutralize your efforts. Client resistance is the major reason many consultant recommendations are not implemented.

You can handle client resistance in the following manner. During the initial interview, you uncovered substantial information about the client's organization. You know whom the project affects and in what potential ways. Discuss openly with the client the issue of re-sistance. Enlist his or her help in planning a strategy to diffuse the resistance. The tendency is to overpower or to keep out the resis-tance, but this approach usually backfires. It escalates the tension and the resistance. Instead, try to incorporate the resistors into the planning process, since their concerns are often valid. Their input improves the project design and reduces their resistance.

You can also reduce resistance by defining your role. Explain that your purpose is not to change the organization for the sake of change or to threaten employee stability. Rather, the opposite is true. Gen-erally, a company contacts a consultant because its stability is in jeopardy. The consultant's aim is to return stability to the company. This may require certain changes. However, these changes are nec-essary to insure a continuing stable environment. Thus, consultants are agents for stability, although change may occur.

Client resistance relates to the client's need for ownership. As ex-plained in the section on proposal presentation, clients must identify with the project. Without this identification, clients stay at arm's length. At the end of the project, they file your report without us-ing it.

To create client identification, involve the client and the client's staff in the project. Their involvement develops ownership while re-ducing resistance. Include their ideas and allow them to perform many of the tasks during the project. They are more likely to use recommendations they have shaped. In addition, they can create ac-ceptance in other organizational members.

To summarize: it is important to meet the client's psychological needs. Too often, consultants design the engagement from a technical standpoint only. They choose their methodology according to the nature of the problem and the nature of the information needed. If you do not consider the nature of the client and the client's organi-zation, you substantially reduce your chances for success.

Data Gathering: Finding the Problems and the Facts

In most consulting engagements, you first gather all the pertinent information. You began your data gathering during the initial inter-view. At that point, you determined the primary problem. More than likely, you only scratched the surface because the information came from a limited number of sources. Now, during the engagement, you will systematically fill in the missing pieces of information.

Your analysis and recommendations depend on the quality of information you gather. You will constantly be torn between thoroughness and selectivity. In his book *Management Consulting*,* Kubr writes, "The definition of facts and their sources must not be too restrictive. If it is, this might exclude facts from which significant information on causes, effects, or relationships might be drawn, and these are often found in unexpected places." At the same time, Kubr cautions that a virtually unlimited number of facts is available. An excessive accumulation of information becomes unmanageable and cannot be utilized fully in any project. In addition, compulsive fact finding consumes time and money.

During your data gathering, you may uncover problems that went unmentioned by the client. During this phase you verify that the original problem is the real problem. For example, when a client's sales drop, he or she usually points the finger at the sales department. During your investigation, you may discover that lack of quality control is the problem. The solution may require an engineering improvement. Consequently, during data gathering, stay receptive to both facts and problems.

Data gathering collects and synthesizes raw data, the client's interpretation of the data, and the client's opinions, identifying and documenting the issues and problems. From this information, you develop insights into possible improvements and opportunities.

Data gathering also establishes your credibility within the client's organization. You become known through your efforts. Data gathering first exposes you to organizational members besides the client. In addition, the quality of your approach becomes known. The client and his or her staff will compare your approach to how they would approach the problem. Strive to create positive impressions in both instances. Positive evaluations facilitate the conduct and success of the project.

Consultants employ six basic "tools of the trade" when gathering data. They choose the tools most appropriate to the problem and the client.

Literature Search.   During a literature search, you read newspapers, trade journals, books, and any other published information.

---

* Geneva, Switzerland: International Labour Organization, 1976.

In most consulting assignments, you perform two literature searches. In the first, you familiarize yourself with the company and the industry; in the second, you examine the technical literature of your profession for ideas concerning the problem. In essence, you brush up on recent advances in your field. Perhaps a professional colleague published a solution to a similar problem. This can prevent your "re-creating the wheel."

Document Review. Every client possesses documents circulated only within the company. The sources of these documents are both internal and external. Internal examples are organization charts, financial statements, operating plans, procedures books, and monthly management reports. External sources, such as banks, auditors, and the government, issue documents pertinent to the client. For example, CPA firms generally include a "management letter" along with the audit results. This letter describes potential financial problems and recommends solutions. This information is valuable for certain projects. Consequently, request and review documents appropriate to your work.

Interviews. Interviews represent the most common tool used by consultants and will be examined in some detail.

Before the interviews, determine what you want from the interviewees. Always preplan the interview, using a structured question guide. During the interviews, refine the guide if necessary. However, know the information you want so that you fully utilize the interview time. Interviews that get sidetracked due to lack of structure are frustrating for both client and consultant.

Confer with the client when determining your interview schedule. Determine in advance whom you will interview and in what sequence. Consider sampling four types of people:

- internal personnel directly related to the issue
- internal personnel indirectly related to the issue
- internal personnel unrelated to the issue but who may have insights into it
- external people, such as customers, suppliers, trade associations, and bankers, who might have information relevant to the issue directly with this company or with similar issues in other companies

Each of these groups provides a unique perspective on your client and the project.

When conducting the interview, introduce yourself, describe your qualifications, explain the interview's purpose, and reassure confidentiality, if appropriate. The interpersonal dynamics of the initial client interview described in Chapter 9 apply here. Successful interviewing is a difficult skill. You must relax the interviewee, build trust, and obtain the necessary information. Interviewers often commit several common mistakes. For instance, they mismatch questions and the interviewee. A first-line supervisor seldom provides information pertinent to the vice president of finance's job performance. Another common error is accepting opinion as fact. A good interviewer probes opinions for facts to substantiate them. You may also err by allowing the interviewee to plead "confidentiality" to avoid answering a question. To avoid this occurrence, gain confidentiality clearance before the interview. Finally, interviewers face the problem of silence—the respondent may not offer any information. Don't be afraid of the silence. Instead, question the silence. What does it tell you about the question, the person, and the interview? The silence often provides more input than any words can.

For further information on interviews, refer to the resources listed at this chapter's end.

Questionnaires. Consultants frequently administer questionnaires to gather information. They distribute them both internally and externally. For example, a compensations consultant might survey the compensation plans at organizations similar to the client's. In return for providing the survey information, the consultant sends them a summary of the results.

Questionnaires are of two main types: essay and objective. Essay questions are open-ended, requiring the respondent to write in the answers. Essay questions are difficult to summarize since you receive twenty different answers to the same question; yet each answer is often very meaningful. Objective questions require ratings or selecting among provided answers. Consequently, they are easier to tabulate, but constrain the answers. The respondent may have additional input on the question, but no way to transmit it to you. As a result, consultants frequently use both objective and essay questions.

Constructing good questionnaires is a skill. As in the interview, questions can dictate the response. The old barb "When did you stop beating your wife?" best illustrates this point. Regardless of the answer, the implication is that the individual beats his wife. To benefit most from your questionnaires, remove any biased or leading questions.

Direct Observation.   Nothing can replace your own observations. What people report is not always what actually happens. Your observations verify the data gathered from interviews and questionnaires. The Emery Air Freight Company provides a good example. In an effort to reduce costs, they wanted to maximize the number of full shipments sent. The supervisors from each shift reported to the consultant that 95 percent of the shipments were sent full. The consultant sat on the dock to count the number of full shipments. He found that only 40 percent were sent full. Had he relied only on his interviews, he could not have solved the problem.

Your own observations yield important information about the client's organization. For example, how do you feel when you are there? This provides clues as to how the employees feel. Is the building oppressive? Are the people friendly? Is the atmosphere frenetic with activity? Who talks to whom? How are the offices assigned? Who is located next to whom? Where do people gather to gossip? Your perceptions will gather substantial information about the client. As a result, you can better understand both the client and the problem.

Basic Research.   In some projects, you must perform controlled scientific research to arrive at the necessary information. This requires tight experimental design procedures. For example, before companies invest millions of dollars in new products, they want scientific evidence that a market exists. A marketing consultant often conducts this research. In other cases, however, clients have neither the time nor the money for this research. Instead, they will act on the less conclusive evidence gathered from the other five data-gathering techniques.

You can approach data gathering in several ways. Use the various techniques in conjunction with each other. Each provides a unique angle on the problem. In toto, they should produce corroborating evidence.

Inexperienced consultants run into several pitfalls during the data collection period. Most commonly, they fail to

- discuss with the source the purpose of the data collection; consequently, the source provides inaccurate or inappropriate information
- understand the source and its biases; every source has a skewed and limited perspective
- understand how the source gathered its own data; this contributes to the source's bias and may affect the data's validity
- plan ahead in order to obtain what is needed the *first* time; returning to the source due to oversight creates an air of incompetence
- document everything they read, see, or hear immediately; memory is short
- reflect on the data-gathering process: Are they covering each facet of the problem? Are there data gaps? Are they jumping to conclusions that bias their efforts? Is the data well organized?

If you avoid these pitfalls, you can have confidence in your data collection efforts.

Your project's success begins with the quality of your data. They provide the foundation for your recommendations and their acceptance by the client. To secure this function, you must design the engagement to meet your client's psychological as well as technical needs. While collecting the data, do not overlook the psychological dynamics that affect the data. With valid data, you can proceed to the next step: analyzing the data and developing recommendations—the topic of the next chapter.

Additional Sources of Help

Management Consulting: A Guide to the Profession. M. Kubr. Geneva, Switzerland: International Labour Organization, 1976.

Organizational Diagnosis. H. Levinson. Cambridge, Mass.: Harvard University Press, 1972.

Organizational Learning. C. Argyris and D. Schon. Reading, Mass.: Addison-Wesley, 1978.

Personnel Interviewing: Theory and Practice. F. Lopez. New York: McGraw-Hill, 1975.

Process Consultation. E. Schein. Reading, Mass.: Addison-Wesley, 1969.

Research on Human Behavior. P. Runkel and J. McGrath. New York: Holt, Rinehart and Winston, Inc., 1972.

Earning Your Fee: Diagnosis and Recommendations

11

The effectiveness with which the information is used depends on the skill and competence of the user. A technician can take an X-Ray picture; a skilled radiologist is required to interpret it.

HARRY LEVINSON

Most clients hire consultants to make recommendations. Your success depends on the quality and usefulness of your recommendations.

Formulating recommendations involves several steps. You must gather data on the client's problem, as you have already been shown how to do in Chapter 10. Chapter 11 will now guide you in analyzing and synthesizing this collected information so that you can diagnose the client's situation and formulate recommendations. Selling these recommendations to the client will be your final task.

This chapter will help you use some problem-solving techniques to develop high-quality recommendations that your clients will accept.

Analyzing and Synthesizing Data

The information you gathered in Chapter 10 answers specific questions. Quite often, answers from different sources conflict. Each source gives you a different perspective on the client's situation. You will make sense of the data you collected during the process of analysis and synthesis. Analysis sifts through the answers and perspectives for clues. Synthesis integrates the clues to form your picture of the client's situation. Your interpretation of this picture comprises your diagnosis and shapes your recommendations.

Analysis

When you analyze the data, you'll separate them into discrete, topical areas. To differentiate data, consultants favor two methods of analysis: content and statistical. The method you choose depends on how you collected your information. Content analysis, the most common method, is used for information from unstructured interviews, open-ended questionnaires, observations, and written documents. Statistical analysis evaluates data from structured interviews and objective questionnaires. Both content and statistical analysis enable the consultant to identify the client's major problems.

Content Analysis.   You can use content analysis in several ways. For example, suppose you asked the same question of each person—such as, "Why do you think sales have dropped?" Under that question list everyone's answer. Then look down the list of answers; you'll realize how various individuals see the same problem. If you repeat this procedure for every question, you gain insights into the client's organization, which more direct questioning will elucidate further. For example, is there general agreement or disagreement in the organization? Who generally agrees or disagrees with whom? Do some people or groups (such as top management or the sales department) attribute the same causes to all problems? The answers convey not only the problems but the organizational dynamics behind those problems.

Another way to make sense of your data with content analysis is to identify the themes. Review your data and list all topics, such as "Need for Management Training." Set aside a separate sheet of paper for each topic. Then, categorize each piece of data under the proper topic. Next to each data statement, note its source (who said it), the content (what was said), the intent (why it was said), and its emphasis (how the source would rate the statement's importance). As a result of this process, you will discover which topics elicited either the most or the fewest comments. Relationships between the topics will emerge. Most importantly, the discrete topics will give you the full range of your client's concerns. You can synthesize these results into a meaningful understanding of the client's situation.

Statistical Analysis. Statistical analysis differentiates data through the mathematical relationships between each datum. For example, most public opinion pollsters, such as Gallup, utilize statistical analysis when reporting their results. Regardless of your quantitative sophistication, you can use statistical analysis. Data best suited to statistical analysis come from objective questionnaires. Answers on objective questionnaires receive assigned numerical values, such as a rating from one to five. Usually one is low, five is high. Consequently, you can analyze the information and report the results in quantitative rather than in qualitative terms.

After analyzing your data by content or statistical methods, ask yourself the following questions. Did some topics receive great emphasis (such as a 5 on an ascending scale of 1–5)? Are those topics significant, or are they a smokescreen that directs your attention away from more important issues? Similar questions are applicable to the topics that received few comments. Are they truly unimportant or is the organization avoiding certain topics? You may note differences based on level of management or department. Does top management stress certain topics, while middle managers emphasize others? If so, why? As you look at each topic, how do the comments listed under it aid your understanding of that topic and of the organization? How does each topic contribute to the organization's current situation? By asking and answering these questions, you discover the important aspects of the client's situation.

Synthesis

Your analysis yields pieces to a puzzle. During synthesis, you place these pieces into a coherent picture. Synthesizing the data you've analyzed leads to a diagnosis of your client's situation. Synthesis involves three major activities: establishing interdependence, priority ranking, and sequencing. Through synthesis, you'll specify the areas most in need of your and your client's attention.

Most elements of the client's situation are connected. From your data analysis examine each topic's relationship to the other topics and to the whole. To do so, identify connections, trends, and patterns. Some topics may be causes, while others are effects. For example, the need for employee training is directly related to the employee selection process. If the client hires untrained personnel, then training needs will be high. Thus, training and selection are highly interdependent. On the other hand, increased competition in one product area probably has a low interdependence with employee training. To establish this interdependence, draw a matrix (see Table 12) with each topic from your analysis listed along the top and down the side. Then rate from 1 to 5 the interdependence of every pair of topics (1 is low interdependence, 5 is high). From this interdependence matrix, you will discover the complex web of interrelationships among the topics. Also, you can see how actions taken in one area can reverberate into other highly interdependent areas.

The next step in synthesis is priority ranking of each topic. You must determine which topics need the most attention. You can establish priority according to different criteria. Topics important to organizational survival usually receive priority ranking. Topics related to the goals of the consulting project also receive priority. If addressing one topic, such as personnel selection, will resolve another topic, such as personnel training, then that topic gets priority.

A common method of priority ranking also employs a matrix, known as a "forced choice" matrix (see Table 13). Again, list each topic along the top and down the side. Give each topic a number. Compare each topic with every other topic. For each pair, choose which topic is more important. Write the topic's number in the square where the two topics intersect. After completing the matrix, count how many times you rated each topic as most important. Then rank the topics based on the frequency of "most important" ratings. This priority ranking displays the importance of each topic compared to all other topics. As a result, you can determine which topics deserve your immediate attention.

Synthesis also involves sequencing the topics. During this task, you discover the order in which you should address the topics. Some relatively unimportant topics might require completion in order to address higher priority topics. For example, a client might face low productivity due to outdated machinery. The employees might present no problems, being highly motivated and hard-working. Thus, new machinery is selected to increase productivity. Yet, before productivity gains are feasible, the client must focus on two previously

Table 12.   Interdependence Matrix for Problem Areas

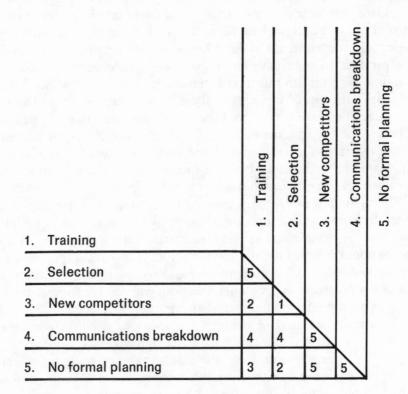

Give each pair a rating based on their interdependence.

1 = very low interdependence

2 = low interdependence

3 = moderate interdependence

4 = high interdependence

5 = very high interdependence

In this example, the training problem has very high interdependence with selection problem and low interdependence with the new competitor problem.

Table 13. Priority Ranking Matrix for Problem Areas

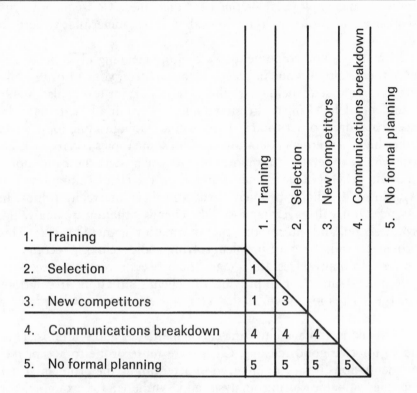

Compare each pair of problem areas as to which is more important and needs immediate attention. Place that problem's number in the intersecting square. Then count how many times you selected each problem as more important.

In this example, training is considered more important than selection. Consequently, 1 was placed in the box which represents problem area 1, training.

The priority ranking results are:

No formal planning:	4 votes = highest ranking
Communications breakdown:	3 votes = 2nd highest ranking
Training:	2 votes = 3rd highest ranking
New competitors:	1 vote = 4th highest ranking
Selection:	0 votes = 5th highest ranking

unimportant areas: 1) how to finance the new machinery and 2) training the employees on the new machines. Consequently, you sequence the topics in their logical order to determine where to start.

In synthesis you combine the data into a meaningful whole. Compare the results of your interdependence matrix, your priority ranking, and your sequencing. Are the most important topics also highly interdependent? Will addressing some topics initially eliminate the need to address other topics? How will attending to one topic affect other highly interdependent topics? Can some topics receive little attention due to relative unimportance? As you answer these questions, you will develop a clear understanding of the client's situation. You will know the major problem areas and their interrelationships. In essence, you will have diagnosed the client's situation by analyzing, synthesizing, and interpreting the information gathered earlier. This provides a solid base for problem solving and developing recommendations. In many cases, this diagnostic process reveals the necessary recommendations for improving the client's situation. If solutions emerge, write them down so that you can refer to them when solving problems.

Many consultants include the client in analysis and synthesis. They do so for two good reasons. Clients are more prone to accept recommendations if they're involved in determining the problem. Their input is valuable during analysis and synthesis; for example, the client's interdependence matrix or priority ranking can provide further insight into the situation, especially if all important client personnel are included. This allows the client to participate actively in diagnosis rather than be a passive recipient. If you involve the client, you must protect the confidentiality of information sources. As a safeguard the consultant alone analyzes the data, categorizing them to prevent identification of sources. The client rejoins the consultant for synthesis.

Problem Solving

The art of problem solving and creative thinking is an integral part of every successful consulting business. Once you understand the client's situation, you must help him or her improve it. During problem solving, you generate recommendations to accomplish this task.

Since experts in this area have treated these topics in depth, the important points to remember will be briefly summarized here. Those desiring greater coverage are referred to the books by Adams, Ackoff, de Bono, Gordon, Koestler, Koberg and Bagnall, McKim, and Osborn listed at this chapter's end.

The first task in problem solving requires you to involve the client. Client involvement at this point is as important as during analysis and synthesis. Since the client ultimately is the one who will accept and use the recommendations, he or she should help develop them. This not only increases the chances of acceptance, but it also emphasizes the client's responsibility for actively solving his or her own problems. In addition, the client provides another creative source of ideas. The extent to which you involve the client depends on your own approach to consulting. Some consultants believe their job means solving problems solo. Others view their role as improving the client's problem-solving skills. Only you can determine how much you need to involve your client for the consulting project to succeed.

Most problems have several possible solutions. The second aspect of effective problem solving involves generating alternatives. As you generate more alternatives, you increase the probability of finding numerous acceptable solutions.

To generate creative ideas, you can follow certain steps. First, set aside the blocks that inhibit creativity, such as your fear of looking foolish or your reliance on tried-but-tired solutions. Suspend premature critical evaluation of ideas. Instead, produce a great quantity of ideas, regardless of quality. During this phase, concern yourself with idea production, not idea evaluation. If necessary, use techniques, such as group brainstorming, to increase your output. If you run low on ideas, try to combine and contrast individual ideas. Often two isolated ideas will spark a new one. If you exhaust your own idea supply, then review how other consultants or companies have approached similar problems. Cross-fertilization is a valuable source of new ideas.

At the end of this process, you should have a goldmine of ideas with which to address the client's problems. Some of the ideas will be irrelevant. Others will be silly. More than likely, though, you will have a large number of ideas relevant to improving the client's situation. Choosing among these alternatives is the next topic of discussion.

Developing Recommendations

During the problem-solving stage, you removed all constraints to free your creativity. Now you will resurrect those constraints to evaluate your solutions. The first step in developing effective recommendations is the realistic assessment of each alternative in light of reason.

Collaborate with your client to evaluate the ideas, since client involvement promotes acceptance of your eventual recommendations. Sometimes clients expect consultants to evaluate the ideas on their own. In this case the consultant submits the best alternatives to the client, indicating a recommended course of action. The consultant then risks rejection. Lack of client involvement in developing recommendations leaves the consultant like an artist unveiling his or her latest creation. The work's reception is either positive or devastating. In either case, the client is surprised. Surprise is a feeling most clients dislike, because it means they're not in control. Methods to handle this situation appear in the next section, "Selling Your Recommendations."

You can evaluate each idea you brainstormed by following a few steps. To start, separate all the ideas into four groups. In the first group, place all the ideas the client *should* use to optimally improve his or her situation. The second group of ideas contains what the client *wants* to use, whether needed or not. These are the biased solutions. In the third group, include all the ideas the client *can* use given the client's resources and constraints. These are realistic solutions. In the last group, list all the ideas that the client *must* use to achieve success. These are the necessary solutions.

Examine each list separately. Does each list present wide-ranging solutions? For example, do all the biased solutions focus on one aspect of the problem? Do too few ideas appear on your realistic solutions list? If so, you might return to problem solving to generate additional ideas. Jot down your impressions of each list as you examine it.

Now compare your lists. Do any ideas appear on all four lists? If so, it is a good indication of their merit and acceptability. As you move from the list of realistic ideas to the necessary to the ideal, does a natural progression emerge? For example, are the necessary solutions present-oriented, while the ideal ones are future-oriented? What criteria separate the lists? For instance, do the necessary solutions require large monetary expenditures, while the biased solutions favor no expenditures? This examination enables you to narrow down your ideas and to order them in relation to your client's needs.

The next step in evaluating solutions for a consulting recommendation is to follow each idea to its logical conclusion. In other words, project what will happen during and after implementation. Who and what will be affected? What are the major benefits? Are there any unexpected side benefits? Can you foresee any unintended, negative consequences? Will the idea achieve what you had hoped, or will it fizzle in midstream? Consult your interdependence matrix from data synthesis. From the matrix you can project how an idea's application to one problem area may have an impact on other related problem areas. By following ideas to their logical conclusion, you can eliminate ideas that sparkle but aren't gems.

Subject the ideas remaining from generating problem solutions to a cost/benefit analysis. You already identified the benefits of the ideas in the previous exercise. Now you must identify the costs. Costs are both obvious and hidden. For example, an obvious cost of management training is the trainer's fee. Hidden costs are the following: salaries paid to personnel while they attend, the production lost while they are not working, and the effects on morale of personnel who do not receive training. Some costs are difficult to determine, such as the social and human costs of closing a plant. However, it is important that you list the benefits and costs for each idea.

At this point, you compare the cost/benefit ratio of each idea. To do so, you must develop a common criterion, such as dollars. Some consultants use a weighting process. Each benefit receives a point value from 0 to 5. Zero indicates no benefit, 5 means extremely beneficial, and 1 through 4 are a continuum between both poles. Costs are assigned a value between 0 and -5, according to the same principles. You then add up the benefits and costs for each idea.

Some consultants combine both dollar values and a weighting process. Regardless of the method you choose, you must develop some way of comparing benefits to costs.

Compare the results of your cost/benefit analysis. Do some ideas yield numerous benefits but incur tremendous costs? Are some ideas too costly with limited benefits?

Compare the analysis with your original four groupings of ideal, necessary, realistic, and biased solutions. Do any patterns emerge? For example, do the realistic solutions yield few benefits with few costs? Are there some necessary solutions with low costs that provide important benefits? Once again, does any natural progression occur?

Do the benefits increase as you move from the realistic to the necessary to the ideal? From this comparison, you can make the judgments necessary for arranging your recommendations by priorities.

Finally, select those ideas to present to the client. If the client has collaborated on the evaluation process, you will narrow down the alternatives together.

Many consultants develop a comparative chart for their recommendations. They begin with the biased and realistic solutions that the client either wants to or can use. They list the benefits and costs of each alternative. They then show how these solutions meet or fall short of the project's objectives. Next, they display the necessary solutions, also listing the benefits and costs of each alternative. If large discrepancies exist between the biased and necessary solutions, the consultant will emphasize the need to move beyond the biased solutions. This same procedure is followed with the ideal solutions. In this manner, the client can see the rationale behind your final recommendations.

At the end of this process, you will select a few substantial recommendations. You then rank your recommendations, indicating which one you would choose if you were in the client's place. If your recommendation includes more than one course of action, sequence the actions. In that way, the client knows where to start and how to proceed.

Selling Your Recommendations

After developing recommendations, your last task is to gain the client's acceptance of them. Obtaining this acceptance is dependent on two factors: the quality of your recommendations and how you conducted the project. Since few consultants experience technical difficulties, you probably produced high-quality recommendations. The remaining factor, then, is your conduct of the project.

If you involved the client at each step, then acceptance is seldom an issue. At a minimum, the client should have read progress reports at each stage. At the maximum, the client helped analyze the data and develop the very recommendations needing acceptance. In either situation, the client is not confronting totally new information. Rather, the client knows that the recommendations are the project's reasonable result. Acceptance in this case is usually a formality.

However, some consultants do not involve the client. As mentioned earlier, they withhold information about the project until the formal presentation of recommendations. This is ill-advised, except in very rare situations. These consultants have a huge selling job ahead of them.

Regardless of client involvement, you generally present your findings and recommendations in person. Your goal is to formalize the client's acceptance of the recommendations. At this point, you should review Chapter 8, "Selling Your Services." The selling process is essentially the same whether selling an initial proposal or final recommendations. You must know your audience and your product. You then shape your presentation to maximize audience acceptance of the product.

Harry Levinson suggests an effective presentation strategy in *Organizational Diagnosis.** Schedule a late afternoon presentation followed by an early morning meeting the next day. The client can read and think about your recommendations during the evening. The next morning, immediately deal with the client's reactions to the recommendations. This prevents negative emotional buildup and increases client acceptance.

As a consultant, avoid presentations unless the probability of acceptance is high. Neither the client nor you should be surprised during the presentation. By this time, you should know your client intimately. Present your findings in light of your client's needs and expectations. This does not mean that you necessarily tell the client what he or she wants to hear. Instead, communicate in a clear, convincing, confident manner. A well-prepared, logical presentation aids this process. Use audiovisual aids prudently and have all the necessary evidence on hand.

Avoid long presentations. Do not overwhelm the client with technical jargon, information, or details. Instead, review the major events in the project. Summarize the important results of your analysis and synthesis. Then describe the evaluation process that led to your recommendations. Present the major alternative recommendations, pointing out their strengths and weaknesses and the costs and benefits. Finally, justify your recommended course of action. If your consulting philosophy precludes making the final recommendation, your task at this point is to help the client choose among the various alternatives. In either case, you must insure that the client understands the risks and ramifications of the selected course of action.

* Cambridge, Mass.: Harvard University Press, 1972.

Your final task during the presentation is to create client owner-ship of the recommendations and commitment to implementation. Many consultants think that their job is over once they present the recommendations. They place all responsibility for implementation on the client's shoulders. These same consultants then complain that their recommendations are never used. However, they could avoid this situation by helping the client plan for implementation.

For those consultants who involved the client, client commitment presents few problems. For those who did not, they must actively seek it during the final presentation. This process is similar to the initial selling process. The client buys nothing until he or she signs on the dotted line. The same applies to client ownership of the rec-ommendations. Until publicly accepted, they remain neutral, theo-retical ideas.

As the consultant, you should push the client to make a decision regarding your recommendations. Some clients will want time to think over your presentation. If so, arrange another time in the near future to reconvene. Help the client understand that acceptance is meaningless without a commitment to implementation. Your last task is to insure that the client assigns duties and responsibilities for implementation. Only this action indicates client ownership and commitment.

Depending on your contract, this may end your involvement, as was previously the rule for most consulting engagements. Today, however, few consulting engagements stop here. At the minimum, you will write a report. More than likely, you will also aid your client's implementation efforts.

Developing recommendations that will benefit the client is a difficult task. It requires the full application of your technical background and your human relations skills. You determine not only what the client needs but also how to insure that the client follows your ad-vice. Successful consultants integrate both these components. This integration culminates during the final presentation. Your next task is to document your work in your report—the topic of Chapter 12.

Additional Sources of Help

The Act of Creation. A. Koestler. New York: Dell Books, 1967.
The Art of Problem Solving. R. Ackoff. New York: John Wiley & Sons, 1978.

Applied Imagination. A. Osborn. New York: Charles Scribner's Sons, 1953.

Conceptual Blockbusting. (3rd ed.) J. L. Adams. Reading, Mass.: Addison-Wesley, 1986.

The Creative Behavior Guidebook and *The Creative Behavior Workbook.* S. Parnes. New York: Charles Scribner's Sons, 1964.

Experiences in Visual Thinking. R. McKim. Monterey, Calif.: Brooks/Cole, 1972.

How to Create New Ideas for Corporate Profit and Personal Success. E. Raudsepp. Englewood Cliffs, N.J.: Prentice-Hall, 1982.

How to Sell New Ideas. E. Raudsepp and J. Yeager. Englewood Cliffs, N.J.: Prentice-Hall, 1981.

New Think. E. de Bono. New York: Basic Books, 1967.

Organizational Diagnosis. H. Levinson. Cambridge, Mass.: Harvard University Press, 1972.

Synectics. W. J. J. Gordon. New York: Harper & Row, 1966.

The Universal Traveler: A Soft-Systems Guidebook to Creativity, Problem Solving, and the Process of Design. D. Koberg and J. Bagnall. Los Altos, Calif.: William Kaufmann, Inc., 1974.

Documenting Your Efforts

12

Everything depends on the degree to which words and word combinations correspond to the world of impression. . . . Has not every one of us struggled for words although the connection between "things" was already clear?

ALBERT EINSTEIN

Most consultants must submit progress and final reports. In some consulting projects the final report concludes the project. Unfortunately, report writing vexes many consultants. "Writer's block" prevents them from completing the project and meeting their obligations.

In this chapter techniques will be suggested for improving both writing style and report organization. The various types and formats of reports will be reviewed. In addition, methods will be outlined to overcome your fear of writing. You'll learn to write reports your clients won't ignore.

Purpose of Reports

Reports are an essential communication link between you and your client. They record what transpired during the project. In rare situations, reports may represent the primary method of informing the client. For most projects, however, reports will complement other forms of communication.

In a report, include information important to the project's success. This information includes the findings and their significance, the recommendations and their justifications, and any decisions. Any substantial departures from the initial proposal or contract warrant documentation. Record both the change and its rationale. Interim decisions that shape or alter the project should be reported. Since memory is short, document these verbal exchanges. In essence, send a report for any new or important event during the project.

Reports also serve other functions. When presented in a clear, logical manner, they facilitate client acceptance of your recommendations. The report can also teach the client the principles behind your methods, findings, and recommendations. The client may then apply those principles to future problems. Reports also act as procedural guides. They describe what must be done to achieve the engagement's objectives. Finally, reports are a continuing reference throughout the entire project; both you and the client know where the project stands.

Continual documentation is in your best interest as the consultant. The client appreciates being informed. Reports provide him or her with a sense of control over you and the project. Moreover, regular communication increases client involvement, acceptance, and gratitude. Reports provide visible evidence that you are working hard on the client's behalf.

Reports also have legal value. Should any disputes arise during or after the consulting project, the reports provide "written proof." By recording all important information, you avoid inconvenient memory lapses.

Reports, then, serve several purposes simultaneously. These purposes directly influence the type of report you choose.

Types of Reports

Consultants classify reports in two ways. On the one hand, there are progress reports and final reports. On the other hand, there are complete narrative reports or short reports. The full report documents the entire project: background, methodology, findings, recommendations, and conclusions. The short report highlights major events, problems, and solutions. These classifications yield four types of reports, such as a short progress report or a long final report. The particular type you use depends on the project, the client, and the report's timing.

Progress or interim reports are generally short documents issued periodically during the project. Upon the completion of each major project phase, issue a project report in which you describe work completed thus far, any interim benefits, the next activities, and all discussions, decisions, and recommendations key to the project's success. Progress reports often include visual or graphic material, memos, and letters. Consultants use progress reports to supplement oral discussions or presentations.

Each particular engagement dictates both the amount of information contained in and the timing of progress reports.

Some projects require long, fully documented progress reports. This commonly occurs in two different situations. Government consulting contracts often stipulate a fully documented progress report at each major milestone. If the contract extends over a two- or five-year period, the government may want a yearly progress report.

The other situation demanding long progress reports involves large capital expenditures. A client's board of directors or top management might demand full progress reports after each phase. Based on their evaluation, they then authorize expenditures for the project's next phase. In both these situations, you must schedule both the time and the expense for report preparation and presentation.

Most clients demand a final report. For some consulting projects, it represents the only permanent and tangible output. Traditionally, final reports were long, comprehensive, and boring. Consequently, clients seldom read or referred to them. Today clients and consultants favor shorter reports or a short summary report to accompany the longer report.

When determining the type of report to use or the information to include, keep the client in mind. Since the client is the reader and user of the reports, determine what he or she needs to benefit most from your efforts. Does the client value or disdain written reports? Does he or she encourage written reports within his or her own organization? Are they long or short? Is the client detail-oriented or conceptual? Is he or she too busy to read long reports? Does he or she prefer graphs and charts or written documents? From the answers to these questions, you determine the type of reports that will inform and inspire the necessary client actions.

Format and Organization

The report's structure aids the client in understanding the material. Choose a format appropriate to the report's purpose and the client's preferences. Clients generally favor reports that present the information in a logical sequence.

A report's major sections typically include the following:

1. *Table of Contents.* This essential element allows the reader to visualize the report's content and organization.
2. *Executive Summary.* Many busy clients will not read the entire report. A summary of your findings, recommendations, and benefits insures that this key information is transmitted.
3. *Project Background.* A short history of the project helps the reader place the project in perspective.
4. *Objectives and Scope.* This section highlights the project's purpose and its limits. Your findings and recommendations are directly related to this section.
5. *Data-Gathering Methodology.* Since your methods influence the results, describe your data-gathering methods in nontechnical language.
6. *Analysis and Synthesis.* The client often wants to know your methods and the results of analysis and synthesis. Remember to protect confidentiality in this section. Excessive detail, statistics, or charts belong in appendixes.
7. *Findings and Conclusions.* This section documents your major findings and conclusions based on your analysis.
8. *Recommendations.* Your recommended course of action should correspond to both the project's objectives and your findings.
9. *Projected or Realized Benefits.* In this section, you highlight the benefits achieved by the study and those achievable through your recommendations.
10. *Implementation Guide.* This guide considers specific methods of implementing the recommendations. It addresses the sequence, timing, and constraints involved at each step.
11. *Appendixes.* These include necessary charts, exhibits, tables, or analyses. Keep appendixes to a minimum.

The exact structure of your report depends on the project's requirements and client's needs. A report that parallels your conduct of the project and your initial proposal has two benefits: it is logical, and it reinforces the process in your client's mind.

Overcoming the Fear of Writing

Most professionals in our society fear formal writing. A blank sheet of paper freezes their writing hand. In essence, they suffer from "writer's block," the inability to express themselves in writing. As the deadline approaches, the block becomes a wall, completely disabling the author. At the last moment and in a fit of desperation, the author stays up all night to produce the necessary report. The outcome may be acceptable but it is generally not satisfying. The author resolves not to let it happen again, but it usually does.

Writer's block results from two factors: a poor approach to writing and a lack of writing skill. You can overcome both these obstacles. Since writing is a skill, you can learn it. You might never resemble the renowned science writer Isaac Asimov, who produces ninety words per minute, but the following suggestions will help you develop sufficient skill to fulfill your writing obligations.

Reduce "writer's block" by increasing your ability. Greater skill builds confidence. Locate an experienced writer who can develop your skills. Take formal classes or arrange informally to work with a skilled writer. Your teacher should demonstrate good writing and critique your efforts. Do you know a technical writer, a journalist, an editor, a poet, or a published author? Any of these people can help improve your writing.

If you cannot find or afford a teacher or tutor, then learn indirectly. Find books, reports, magazines, or letters that impressed you. Study the writing to discover what impressed you. Is it concise, clear sentences or the use of descriptive words? Perhaps the writing flows logically. Derive principles of "good" writing from these examples. Now contrast your selection with writing that bores or confuses you. What do you notice about the bad writing? Are the sentences too wordy? Do the writers rely too heavily on passive sentence structure? Are the writers repetitive? From this contrast, develop a list of dos and don'ts to guide you in your own writing.

Writing teachers encourage their students to copy in longhand entire passages of good and bad writing. Although this task sounds childish and tedious, it makes you experience physically the difference between good and bad writing. While you copy, notice the author's writing style. What types of words do effective and ineffective writers use? Where do they place their words? How do they form their sentences? Do they vary their style? How do they develop their logic and make their points? Again, list the dos and don'ts you discover.

Practice.   Writing, like any skill, requires practice. Devote time each day to writing and critiquing. Write letters to the editor or to your elected representatives. Write speeches you'd like to give. Write that magazine or journal article stirring in your head. Critique and rewrite old reports or proposals. Write new brochures. In other words, write, write, write. Critique your writing. Examine it at a later time. Compare it to your examples of good writing by other authors. How do you rate? Note where you succeeded and failed. Rewrite your piece. Concentrate on your weak areas. If possible, have someone critique your rewrite.

Place your ego aside.   Book and journal editors tell me that their most difficult authors are professionals, especially consultants. These groups, they say, have tremendous egos and can't accept criticism. This is understandable. Since consultants are experts, they are seldom criticized. When they are, it threatens their self-esteem. However, to improve your writing, accept constructive criticism. This makes it easier on both you and your critic.

Focus your efforts on report writing.   Since writing makes many consultants uncomfortable, they avoid the task. They procrastinate until the due date is tomorrow, or, worse yet, yesterday. The nature of consulting work contributes to this unfortunate situation. Report writing occurs as the project is winding down. More than likely, you will be starting a new project. The corresponding excitement and novelty easily consume your attention, detracting from the report writing. Remember that report writing takes as long as data gathering or analysis—it always takes longer than you planned.

Schedule "high energy" time blocks for report writing.   Consultants often squeeze writing in between other activities or at the day's end. Instead, give yourself 3 or 4 hours to formulate your thoughts and write. Choose times when you're at your peak and your mind is clear of distractions. Writing is a deceiving activity. It requires little physical movement, but it demands intense mental concentration.

Allow more than one day and one draft for report writing.   Don't expect yourself to write the report in one sitting. Using an outline, divide the report into small, "do-able" sections. Complete a rough draft of one section per sitting. Plan separate time periods to rewrite and finalize each rough draft section. This makes the task manageable. It releases the time pressure that leads to writer's block.

Create a favorable writing environment.   Choose a place free from interruption and distraction. For example, if you are a people watcher, a populated library is not for you. The physical surroundings should signal work, not rest or recreation. At the same time, make the place positive, not oppressive. If you like lamplight, put a lamp on your desk rather than using the overhead flourescent light. Turn the thermostat down a few degrees, since a cool room increases your alertness. A clean desk top provides work space and eliminates distractions. Fill your thermos with your favorite nonalcoholic beverage. You won't get hung up in the coffee room if you don't go to it. Equip yourself with all the books, notes, pencils, rulers, paper, and other supplies you will need. Put a "Do Not Disturb" sign on your door and ask your secretary to hold all calls.

Get an editor.   Always have someone else read your writing. Sharing the burden reduces writer's block. As the author, you often get too close to the material. An objective outsider can spot your mistakes, misspellings, and faulty logic. A professional editor can improve your writing style as well. Often you cannot use an editor due to client request or the top-secret nature of the report. In those situations, set your final rough draft aside for at least a week, preferably two. Then return to it. Your editorial judgment usually improves with the time lapse.

Reward yourself.   If writing is drudgery, work to make it pleasant. Psychologists know that rewards increase the response. Develop your own reward system to reinforce your writing. Each time you complete your writing goal, do something enjoyable for yourself. For example, if you wrote successfully from 9 A.M. to 1 P.M., reward yourself with a delicious lunch or take the afternoon off for a golf game. Use small rewards during the entire process and plan a big one upon final completion. When you pair undesirable activities with desirable rewards, another benefit can occur. The undesirable activity, in this case writing, often becomes desirable.

Writing constitutes part of a consultant's job. Rather than avoid it, use the above suggestions to overcome your fear. Only by writing can you improve your skill.

Improving Your Writing Style

Your writing style, by definition, is peculiar to you. The problem is that it may often seem peculiar to your reader. Incorporating generally used techniques into your style enhances your writing's readability and reader acceptance.

Experienced writers and consultants suggest the following rules.

Know your audience. Consider everyone who will read the report. What are their needs, backgrounds, and preferences? How will they use the report? What can you assume they know and don't know? What style will increase reader acceptance?

Write your report in a positive tone. Emphasize needed improvements and projected results; don't denigrate the client.

Write short reports, if possible. Shorter reports not only appeal to busy clients but they also reduce the amount you must write. Longer reports provide greater opportunity for poor writing displays.

Break your report into sections. Use headings and subheadings to focus the reader's attention.

Limit each topic to one page, if possible. This forces you to write concisely, summarizing the major points of each topic, and prevents the reader from confusing topics.

Avoid long, complex sentences and paragraphs. They confuse or bore the reader. Lawyers refer to this as the KISS principle— "Keep It Simple, Stupid."

Avoid jargon, slang, and unnecessary technical terms. Write in plain language, using words familiar to the reader.

Use direct descriptive words rather than euphemisms.   For example, use the word "fired" instead of "he found himself out of a job."

Use the active voice, not the passive.   Action verbs portray the image you want. Shoveling is more precise than digging.

Vary your sentence structure to avoid monotony.

Use graphs, pictures, charts, and tables when appropriate.   A well-constructed graph often tells more than an entire written page. Keep complicated material in the appendix, while summarizing its content in the report.

Use numbers selectively.   Use absolute values, percentages, or ratios, depending on their content in the report and their understandability. Recheck your numbers for accuracy.

Emphasize major points through indentations, underlinings, asterisks, bullets, or capital letters.   Visually, the major points should jump out at the reader.

Your goal is a concise, punchy report that both informs and convinces the reader. Since the report affects your consulting reputation, devote the time and effort necessary to polish your style. Work with your editor to improve your writing ability. It will pay off throughout your consulting career.

Producing Reports

Production ruins many well-written reports. You'll be to blame if you waited till the last minute to write the report. Typing errors, ink smears, and similar embarrassments mar the report. Worse yet, delayed production holds up the report, resulting in a missed deadline. In either case, the report loses effectiveness.

Production scheduling is important. Know how long it takes to type, proofread, and correct reports of varying lengths. Add reproduction and binding time. Schedule these into your project. Respect the needs and instructions of your production people. Common courtesies and a smile contribute to quality production.

Since the report reflects your image, make it professional. Use high-quality paper, typewriter, cover stock, binding procedure, and printing. The reader's initial reaction plays an important role in report acceptance.

The report should please the reader visually. Use margins, indentations, and double spacing to ease reading and to create a calm impression. Avoid crowding or cramming the page.

You are responsible for the report's final appearance. Before it leaves your office, read it carefully. Look for spelling errors, misplaced pages, and miscellaneous markings. Have your editor do the same. Only after this final approval should the client see the final report.

Using Reports

Unread reports frustrate consultants. They interpret neglected reports as signs of a client's disinterest or stupidity. In either case, it discourages future report writing.

You can prevent this situation in various ways. If the client helps write the report, then you know he or she will read it. Many consultants distribute the report during a formal presentation. The client will then follow the presentation with the report. The consultant should refer to the report to highlight major points. Finally, reports with implementation guides are most often used. Clients will refer to the report for guidance in carrying out your recommendations.

More consultants are turning to view-graph presentation to increase the usefulness of their reports. Rather than turn out a thick document of prose that goes unread, smart consultants distill their key findings into outline form. Then they develop a slide presentation with one point and two or three subpoints per slide. Effective presentations use a mix of text slides and picture slides, keeping in mind that one good graph or chart conveys information better than a slideful of words. During their presentation, they use the slides as they follow the outline. The detail and the transitions of a report are given orally during the presentation. Clients only receive a printed copy of the slides that contain the major points. Clients can then make notes of any interesting details on these copies. In this manner, the clients receive only a thin collection, from 10 to 50 pages, of the most important findings and analyses of the study. In addition, they have not only read and heard the important results of the study, but they have made notes relevant to them. To most clients, this format beats long, dry reports. It is more digestible, useful, and action-oriented. In addition, the brief format makes it easier for clients to communicate the study's findings to others throughout the organization.

Report writing is an essential activity for most consultants. Writing, like any skill, requires learning and practice. Since your effectiveness is partly measured by your reports, well-written reports are important to your success. In addition, they improve your reputation.

A final report, however, does not necessarily end your client involvement. Often, the client will ask you to help implement the recommendations contained in the report. This is the topic of Chapter 13.

Additional Sources of Help

The Elements of Style. 2nd ed. W. Strunk and E. B. White. New York: Macmillan Publishing Co., 1972.

Getting Things Done. E. C. Bliss. New York: Charles Scribner's Sons, 1982.

Guide to Managerial Communication. M. Munter. Englewood Cliffs, N.J.: Prentice-Hall, 1982.

Guide to Professional Practice: Interim and Survey Report Practice. New York: Association of Consulting Management Engineers, 1966.

Prentice-Hall Handbook for Writers. 6th ed. G. Leggett, C. D. Mead, and W. Charvat. Englewood Cliffs, N.J.: Prentice-Hall, 1974.

The Presentation of Technical Information. 2nd ed. R. O. Kapp. London: Constable & Company Ltd., 1973.

Writing for Results in Business, Government, Science, and the Professions. D. W. Ewing. New York: John Wiley & Sons, 1979.

From Ideas to Action: Installing Your Recommendations

13

More important and more difficult is to make effective the course of action decided upon. . . . Nothing is as useless as the right solution that is quietly sabotaged by the people who will have to make it effective.
PETER DRUCKER

The entire consulting project culminates with installing your recommendations. In effect, the project's goal is not met unless the client acts on your recommendations. In the past, consultants seldom assisted their clients in implementing recommendations. Instead, they withdrew from the project after issuing their report, leaving the client on his or her own during implementation. Without the support and professional guidance necessary for successful implementation, the client often files the final report, once read but unusable, in a desk drawer.

Increasing numbers of consultants, however, now include implementation in their services. This chapter describes the steps involved in successful implementation. Initially, you and the client determine your respective responsibilities. Then, you design methods that utilize organizational resistance to build support for the recommended new system. This involves pilot projects, client personnel training, and the effective utilization of organizational dynamics. Once the recommendations are in place, you monitor the system for possible problems and modifications. Finally, you stabilize the new system so that it can sustain itself.

Who Is Responsible for Implementation?

The client is ultimately, but not solely, responsible for installing the recommendations. As the consultant, you must preserve the client's decision-making authority. However, if the client does not implement the recommendations, then you have failed in some way. Perhaps you misunderstood the client's needs or expectations. In some cases, the client has a "hidden agenda" for the project, publicly professing one purpose, yet secretly planning to use the results for other purposes. Did you fail to identify the hidden agenda? If no hidden agenda exists, did you fail to prepare the client for your recommendations? Did the client need more involvement, information, or persuasion? Did you expect the client to do too much too fast, given his or her resources? If you neglect these behavioral issues during the project, you will seldom be able to implement your recommendations.

If the client decides to implement, clarify your role prior to any action. You and the client should evaluate the client's capacity to install the recommendation. If the client has prior implementation experiences and a highly trained staff, then you can play a minimal role with limited participation. When implementation is extremely complex, then your involvement generally increases. In any case, you and the client should elucidate each of your responsibilities before implementation commences.

The client, however, retains absolute authority over all decisions. The organization and its future belong to the client, both legally and practically. Occasionally, a naive, beleaguered, or conniving client may desire to transfer this authority to you. Not only should you decline, you should tell the client why. Management, policy decisions, client staff control, and day-to-day operations are the client's responsibilities. You advise, encourage, explain, guide, and/or train. In addition, you help the client assume increasing responsibility for implementation. Your aim is to withdraw from the project once the client is capable of successful installation without you.

Strategies for Successful Implementation

Your recommendations are at the mercy of the people installing them. Preoccupied with technical details, consultants often develop blind spots regarding the human reaction to their recommendations. The client's personnel either support or undermine implementation. Effective installation of recommendations, then, requires attention to behavioral and organizational dynamics.

In this section, strategies will be described that utilize these dynamics to aid implementation. Initially, you must win organizational support by effectively handling resistance to your ideas. Next, you must establish organizational conditions that support your recommendations. Once the conditions are set, you must train client personnel in the skills necessary for implementation. With trained personnel, you can test your recommendations in a pilot project. The pilot project helps win further organizational support and indicates necessary modifications. By laying this organizational groundwork, you thereby insure the success of your final action—full-scale implementation.

Handling Organizational Resistance

For too long, consultants have voiced the maxim, "People resist change." They imply that people prefer the status quo and that resistance is bad. Both premises are faulty. As a rule, people both seek and resist change. Which behavior they choose depends on their current state. If present conditions dissatisfy them, they generally seek change. Satisfied personnel, on the other hand, repel change. However, when you expect people to resist change, you increase the likelihood that they will. You create a self-fulfilling prophecy. If you treat them as stubborn people who won't buy your ideas, they will resist you.

Resistance is generally a positive phenomenon; an important survival mechanism, it protects against outside threats. When consultants see their work undermined, they blame the client's staff. From the staff's viewpoint, consultants are like bacteria entering a body. The staff must block the potentially dangerous invaders before they harm the system.

You can handle resistance through two actions: understanding the staff's viewpoint and involving the staff. Although you may want to overpower the resistance, don't. Listen and learn from it instead. Before implementation begins, assess potential individual and organizational reactions to your recommendations. Ask these questions: Who will support or resist the recommendations? Why? Who benefits or suffers from the change? Who benefits from the status quo? How are individual and organizational needs affected? How will the changes disrupt important social and emotional relationships? Does one person or group perceive a loss of status? Will you interrupt long-standing and satisfying work relationships? To understand resistance, then, perceive the potential changes from the employees' perspective.

Meaningful client personnel involvement also lowers resistance. Throughout this book, client involvement has been stressed. If you forego this involvement prior to implementation, you risk implementation failure. Staff involvement aids acceptance. When the staff contribute practical ideas, they feel valued. In addition, they develop ownership of the recommendations. With staff involvement you can gather immediate evidence of what threatens or satisfies them. Staff involvement also serves as an emotional inoculation. Pre-implementation planning meetings prepare the staff for future changes. By giving an early taste, you prevent later shock at implementation activities.

To handle resistance effectively, don't try to overpower it. Rather, consider how your recommendations might produce resistance. Then involve the client's staff to make the recommendations workable.

Checking Organizational Infrastructure*

Before implementing your recommendations, check them against the organization's six key infrastructures. These infrastructures— technology, organization, staff, management practices/systems, knowledge/learning, and legal/financial—can either help or hinder your ability to implement successfully. The technology infrastructure includes existing technology, such as data processing or assembly lines, and emerging innovations in technology, such as communica-

---

* The material in this section is adapted from *The Gold-Collar Worker* by Robert E. Kelley (Reading, Mass.: Addison-Wesley, 1985).

tions or robotics. The organization infrastructure includes the formal structure, review processes, integration mechanisms for interdependent work units, corporate culture, and the climate for innovation. The staffing infrastructure encompasses the number, level, skill mix, tenure, and attitudes of the entire work force.

The management practices/systems infrastructure envelopes the rules, procedures, superior–subordinate interactions, job design, human-resource programs, incentives and compensation, and computer, financial, control, and other such systems. The knowledge and learning infrastructure includes the mechanisms for creating, acquiring, accessing, synthesizing, utilizing, institutionalizing, and advancing the knowledge bank critical for the organization's current and future performance. The legal and financial infrastructure takes into account the legal and financial position, strength, opportunities, and constraints of the firm along with their effects on future business success.

These infrastructures are to organizations what electricity, plumbing, heating, and structural supports are to a building: the systems by which the organization conducts its business smoothly.

When all six infrastructures work effectively, no one notices their presence. When they malfunction, however, they can bring the entire system to a halt, much as a blackout of electricity does to a city. Often, consultant recommendations focus on improving one infrastructure. Yet they ignore how counterproductive aspects of the other infrastructures undermine their efforts.

For example, in one chemical company, the research-and-development and marketing departments were charged independently with developing new products. After a full year with no progress, top management decided to institute a team-building program that focused on joint problem-solving meetings. Although both departments found the team-building sessions useful, no new products were forthcoming. A thorough analysis of the major infrastructures revealed that the formal organizational structure, bureaucratic procedures, dominant corporate culture, and incentive systems all undermined the intended results of the team-building program. The infrastructures actually discouraged interdepartmental teamwork.

An outside consultant helped the company to finally address these obstacles. She suggested that it form an entrepreneurial unit to develop new products. The R&D and marketing personnel in the unit reported to one new department head instead of two separate department heads. The traditional rules and procedures were set aside, and the incentive system rewarded teamwork and new-product development instead of the traditional performance measures. Within a year the new department had developed five new products, two of which became major commercial successes.

Before beginning your implementation, examine the six key infrastructures. Analyze how they either support or throw counterproductive roadblocks in front of your recommendations. Then, identify how those infrastructures must be modified if your project is to be successful. Do not ignore the easy gains yielded by the simple removal of counterproductive barriers. Too often people believe that traditional practices or barriers are sacred and untouchable. More often than not, a seemingly immovable obstacle can be eliminated merely by bringing it to the attention of those who do have control and suggesting the appropriate changes. Your objective is to modify the infrastructures in order to reinforce the success of your project's recommendations. If the staff does not have the skills to carry out your recommendations, you must help the client alter the staffing infrastructure. Otherwise, your recommendations will be useless. If the legal structure of the firm constrains certain actions, consult the company's in-house counsel or an outside attorney to determine what other alternatives exist.

Professor Ralph Kilmann uses the above approach in his organizational consulting work.* At a more detailed level, he describes the five areas that consultants and managers must pay attention to if they are to bring about substantial change in the organization. Kilmann argues that recommendations cannot be installed piecemeal. Quick fixes never work and often make the situation worse. Instead, the organizational infrastructures must be fully integrated. Kilmann describes five tracks that enable successful change to occur. The five tracks—culture, management skills, team-building, strategy–structure, and reward systems—are important subunits of the organization and management practices/systems infrastructures. They act as powerful leverage points for achieving sustained change in an organization.

The culture track identifies the shared but unwritten rules for each member's behavior. In many cases, cultural norms create or reinforce mistrust among organizational members and discourage any new ideas or programs. If you try to implement your recommendations in the face of a dysfunctional culture, you will not get very far. In-

---

* Ralph Kilmann, *Beyond the Quick Fix*. San Francisco: Jossey-Bass, 1984.

stead, you must help the client understand how the culture undermines the needed changes. Then, identify what new norms and cultural beliefs will foster a more positive environment.

The management skills track fosters the interpersonal, conceptual, analytic, and administrative skills necessary to manage complexity. Unfortunately, too many managers latch onto the first quick-fix solution and then try to ram it into implementation. They do not probe or understand the root causes of the problem. Or they may lack the interpersonal skills necessary to work with others. Sometimes they need a new conceptual framework for viewing their world. As a consultant, part of your job is to help develop your client's management skills. Help him or her identify implicit assumptions and replace illogical ones. Help supplement his or her current skills bank with the new skills necessary to implement successfully your recommendations.

The team-building track is essential for many recommendations. Since many problems facing business are complex, they require the participation of many people to solve them. This often involves cooperative efforts across work group boundaries. If these groups do not have a history of working together, then team building is a must. To insure that all available expertise and information will come forth to manage the complex problems, pay attention to the team-building track. A collaborative, participative effort among all parties seldom happens on its own in traditional companies.

The strategy-structure track provides the organizational vehicles to support your recommendations. By aligning your work with the client's overall mission and goals, you promote an internal coherence for the client. Clients see that you are actively helping them achieve their goals. However, you may need to alter some of the organization's systems and structures that interfere with goal attainment. Always identify how the existing systems either support or impede your recommendations. For example, bureaucratic red tape can hinder a client's being innovative in the face of competition. If you can help the client streamline structures and systems to achieve the desired goals, then your value increases substantially.

The organization's reward system must support your recommendations. If people receive no intrinsic or extrinsic rewards, they have no reason to cooperate with the changes. If their performance reviews and compensations are tied to the old, they will continue to do the old. This does not mean that they prefer the old or are dissatisfied with your recommendations. It is simply not in their best interest to change until the reward system justifies the change. A well-functioning, performance-based reward system that is aligned with your recommendations is a necessary prerequisite for successful implementation.

The reward system includes both extrinsic and intrinsic rewards. Extrinsic rewards are those generated by the organization. They can be tangible or intangible.* Pay, bonuses, office size and furnishings, promotions, glamorous business trips, and physical work conditions are tangible extrinsic rewards. Status, praise, and participation in decision-making are intangible extrinsic rewards. The extrinsic reward system is what is visible to all the employees. The tangible and intangible displays must be consistent with each other and supportive of the company's overall direction.

Intrinsic rewards, those generated by the individual or by the work itself, can be tangible or intangible. Mastering a new job is tangible. The sense of satisfaction that comes from instituting a major change in organization is an intangible intrinsic reward. If these intrinsic rewards can be channeled in the direction of the project recommendations, you have a powerful source of support. For example, many workers will put in overtime in order to help institute a new program that they think is necessary or will be beneficial to them.

When examining the reward system, also analyze how people get punished. For what activities do they lose pay or get demoted? Look for less explicit but equally punishing actions, such as getting reprimanded, being labeled as less than competent, or being exploited. These intrinsic and extrinsic punishments powerfully influence the client's behavior. If the punishment system forbids people from supporting your recommendations, your implementation efforts will face an uphill struggle.

By assessing the six major organizational infrastructures and the subsystems described by Kilmann, you will know whether they will support or obstruct your implementation efforts. By identifying organizational barriers to change, you can avoid many pitfalls. You will also know what system-wide changes are needed if your efforts are to succeed. Often these changes involve people. Moving from organizational to individual change is the next step in implementation.

---

* Adapted from *The Gold-Collar Worker*, by Robert E. Kelley. Reading, Mass.: Addison-Wesley, 1985.

Ten Conditions to Promote Individual Change

Changing is seldom easy, even for the highly motivated. Lack of motivation or resistance compounds the problem. Psychologists have discovered that certain conditions ease the transition from old to new. These conditions create the social, motivational, and cognitive climates necessary to unlearn old behaviors and learn new ones. Effectively using these conditions with the client's personnel will aid your implementation efforts.

1. *Establish a positive working relationship.* Client personnel are more likely to accept change from someone they trust. By this phase of the project, you should have developed a solid working relationship. If not, then select someone who does have such a relationship to introduce the change.

2. *Establish open and two-way communications.* Nothing can replace clear, front-end communication. Regularly inform the client's personnel of future plans before the grapevine does. Then respond to their feedback. Pay attention to both their obvious and hidden concerns.

3. *Provide necessary knowledge.* Considerable research suggests that people should learn the new information before they try to apply it. Fully explain what will occur, how, and why. As a result, client personnel can form mental maps to use during implementation.

4. *Provide a social role model.* Social role models wield enormous influence over others. Select role models who meet two conditions: 1) they are similar to the target person(s)—that is, the individual(s) whose behavior you want to change—and 2) they are held in high esteem by the target person(s). A social role model produces several positive effects: he or she clearly displays the desired change from which others can learn, legitimates the change, and encourages others to change.

5. *Obtain public commitment to change through a direct and open process of negotiation.* Tie public commitment to actual goal-setting. Target goals through open negotiation. Client personnel must view the goals as possible, desirable, and realistic. As a rule,

avoid both easy and impossible goals. Instead, establish moderately difficult goals that result in feelings of achievement. To generate a positive self-fulfilling prophecy, express confidence in their achievement capability. If possible, write down the goals for both parties to sign. This further emphasizes the public commitment. Express goals in measurable, not vague, terms. State exactly what will occur, when, and how often.

6. *Restructure the environment to support the change.* Too often, people approach individual change from the wrong direction. They exhort and persuade to no avail. A changed environment produces the desired change more quickly. By restructuring physical or social settings, you force people to behave differently. For example, one executive team decided they needed greater awareness of the production operation. To insure that they spent more time there, they moved their offices onto the production floor. This move supported their desired change. Another group could never start its staff meetings on time. Tired of exhortation, the president installed two new policies. He locked the meeting room door at the prescribed time to keep out latecomers. Next, he tied part of the yearly bonus to the number of staff meetings attended. The problem stopped immediately.

7. *Provide practice.* When change involves learning difficult, new behaviors, people require practice. Psychologists suggest the following guide. First, demonstrate the new skill. Second, guide the client's personnel in practicing the skill. Third, allow them to practice on their own. Keep practice sessions relatively short with regular rest periods. Space the sessions over a period of time. Neither one-shot nor long, continuous practice is effective. Fourth, allow the client's personnel to demonstrate the new skill. Finally, give feedback to improve their performance.

8. *Once change takes place, give feedback on performance.* Feedback serves two functions. It displays how people stand in relation to their goals, and it modifies and corrects performance. Keep feedback objective by basing it on data, not adjectives. Instead of saying "You're doing a good job," say "Your goal was $10,000 in sales. You sold $15,000." In addition, provide feedback on a regular and frequent basis. Immediate feedback after performance works best.

9. *Shape behavior through reinforcement.*   Change accompanied by rewards endures. The client's personnel should value the rewards, whether monetary, praise, or privileges. In addition, tie the rewards to actual performance. Immediate reinforcement strengthens this connection. Once the new behavior is firmly established, intermittent rewards can usually sustain it.

10. *Promote internalization of change.*   Individuals who incorporate the change into their value system maintain it longer. If you use the preceding nine conditions effectively, internalization generally results. Help people identify with the change effort and its ensuing benefits. Once internalized, they can maintain the change with dwindling assistance from you.

Integrate the above ten conditions into your implementation efforts. They make changes easier by attending to the human and organizational aspects of change. As a result, the change should occur successfully while generating fewer problems.

Training Client Personnel

Effective implementation generally requires training of client personnel. Usually, you will need to train two separate groups. In the first group are the staff members who will install the system. In the second group are staff members who will supply the data and utilize the output. For instance, suppose you recommend a computerized inventory control system. You train the staff who will operate the computer. In addition, you train the purchasing department on how to supply the data. Then you demonstrate how to use the results for inventory planning and control.

You do not necessarily lead all the training. You might train supervisors who in turn train their subordinates. Occasionally, you will arrange for special outside trainers or outside training courses. The previously mentioned conditions for change apply to training situations. Effective training incorporates sound learning principles.

Ultimately, you aim to build client competence in operating and maintaining the new system without you. A secondary benefit is a more highly trained staff. Ideally, your training efforts will foster further interest in employee development.

Pilot Projects

Whenever possible, avoid untested, full-scale implementation efforts. Instead, try the recommended changes on a small scale. For instance, suppose you recommend a new productivity measurement program. Rather than install it untested throughout the entire organization, select one department for a pilot project.

Pilot projects yield several benefits. Even though clients may commit themselves to a new program, they usually harbor some doubts. Some consultants refer to this as "post-decision regret." It results from taking a risk. A pilot project reduces the client's fear of disrupting the entire organization. The client can see the change and its positive effects on a small scale. This early success experience reinforces his or her earlier decision; it also encourages the client to install the change throughout the organization.

A pilot project provides opportunity to "debug" the new system, since problems will undoubtedly occur. In a pilot project, you can quickly spot and cope with any problems that arise. Should last-minute resistance occur, you can handle it on a small scale. Once large-scale efforts begin, the sheer size compounds each minor problem. Cumulatively, these minor problems overwhelm the project and destroy its impact. Pilot projects prevent this. They also teach you what to expect once your large-scale efforts begin.

Pilot projects prepare the entire system for the pending changes. Other departments can observe from a distance and see the positive results. Pilot projects quiet fears. During the briefing sessions, the client's personnel may not have believed your assurances that, for example, the productivity program would result in higher pay. A pilot project will show them. Personnel involved in the pilot project will often advocate it to other employees.

During the pilot project you can evaluate important aspects of the new system. Test the standards and procedures for operating the new system. Check whether the client capably administers the new system. How effective were your earlier training efforts? Will the system maintain itself in the long run? Did you meet your work schedule? From this information, you can make necessary modifications. Then, incorporate your learning into a revised implementation control manual and schedule.

As a result of your consulting project and implementation efforts, your client should have learned some things that are useful. Professors Chris Argyris and Don Schon define organizational learning as the process of detecting and correcting error.* They describe two types of learning. Single loop learning enables the organization to carry on its present policies or achieve its objectives. Single loop learning is similar to a thermostat that turns the heat on or off when it senses that the room is too hot or cold. It takes corrective action to readjust to the desired temperature range. Consultants are often called in as an organization's single loop response to a problem. Something is out of order and the consultant is supposed to fix it. Once the situation is taken care of, the consultant is thanked, paid, and sent away until the next problem surfaces.

The second type of organizational learning is double loop learning. If the thermostat could question itself (or the homeowners) about whether it should be set at 68° or whether a thermostat is the best method to regulate temperature, it would exhibit double loop learning. When you question the underlying goals, policies, and norms of an organization, you make it possible to detect higher-order errors. When consultants are called in to improve the marketing of a product and they design a successful marketing plan, they are providing a single loop learning response. If they question whether the product should be manufactured at all, they are exhibiting a double loop learning response.

In most organizations, it is taboo to question organizational goals, policies, and norms—especially if top management is excited about them. This leads to "error hiding" since no one is allowed to question the emperor's dress habits, let alone reveal that the emperor has no clothes. As a result, error hiding, camouflage, and games are a part of life in most organizations. If the CEO is committed to a path, you risk your job if you tell her she is on the wrong track. A large bank in Texas encountered this problem in spades. A headstrong CEO wanted to lend heavily in the energy sector and in Latin America. The chief economist and loan officer advised against it. Both were demoted. Their replacements understood that their job was to support the CEO's decision, which they did. Today, the bank is in deep financial trouble as countries and energy companies default on their loans. The CEO has since been replaced by an embarrassed board of directors.

Although consultants are often called in for single loop reasons, they offer a disservice if they do not play a double loop learning role. Coming from the outside, consultants can ask the unaskable ques-

---

* Chris Argyris and Donald A. Schon, *Organizational Learning*. Reading, Mass.: Addison-Wesley, 1978.

tions. They can help counteract organizational blind-sidedness and rigidity. Instead of going along with organizational games (and thus becoming part of the problem), consultants should foster double loop learning. Help your clients produce, listen to, and deal with multiple sources of valid information. Assist them in making informed choices on the basis of competent, valid knowledge, rather than value-laden organizational norms. Don't be so obliged to them that you will do anything they ask just to keep getting projects. Even if you are providing single loop solutions, do the work within a double loop context.

Part of organizational learning involves error detection and correction. Most organizations first try to hide error. Once error is uncovered, they try to fix it quickly. As a consultant, you can help them take a different attitude toward error. Consultant Don Michael suggests that rather than hide or avoid errors, consultants and clients should become error-embracing.* They should see error not only as a problem but as a learning experience. Errors not only indicate that something wrong needs correcting (i.e., single loop learning) but also that something may be wrong with the system. Several errors may seem unrelated; yet if they are embraced and dissected a pattern may emerge that can lead to significant improvements in the system. Moreover, error-embracing reverses error from being something negative to be avoided to being something positive. Thus, consultants must examine their pilot projects to discover both the successes and the errors. Help the clients use both in a double loop fashion during the entire implementation process.

Monitoring the New System

Having laid the necessary groundwork, now assist the client in large-scale implementation. Aim for a smooth transition from old to new. In the early stages prepare yourself to handle immediate crises. Your pilot project should have corrected all major problems. Individual people or departments, however, often require certain modifications. Quick response to these minor problems prevents later difficulties.

Do not undertake large-scale implementation without two accompanying tools: control systems and contingency plans. You should

* *On Learning to Plan—And Planning to Learn.* San Francisco: Jossey-Bass, p. 197.

have tested both tools during the pilot project. Based on that experience, modify them for the large-scale effort.

A control system is a procedure by which you measure the effects of implementation. You prescribe the desired goals or plans, such as a certain production rate or taking actions in a certain sequence. Then you monitor actual performance and compare it to desired performance. The control system lets you know when you've strayed from the prescribed plan or goal. Frequently measure performance against the desired plan. Then provide these results to personnel with authority to make corrective changes. Monitor the corrected action to insure that it works.

Most control systems fail for one of six reasons: 1) inaccurate measurements, 2) unimportant or overwhelming measurements, 3) infrequent measurements, 4) untimely reporting of results, 5) failure to take corrective action, and 6) failure to follow up the corrections.

An effective control system requires minimum effort for maximum results. Too often, consultants design complicated control systems, which are undermined by the client's staff. Work with the client's staff to develop controls that are useful and usable to them. If the client's staff does not help develop the control system, then train them in its use.

Contingency plans prevent panic at the first crisis. Despite your best effort, occasionally the recommendations will not work. Rather than blame the client (or vice versa), shift to your contingency plans. This reassures the client's staff that all is not lost. A well-planned transfer based on solid performance data is a sign of strength. Contingency plans provide reasonable flexibility in controlling events.

During implementation, you and the client will evaluate progress. Check whether goals are met, benefits materialize, and schedules are maintained. Document these assessments in progress reports. Jointly agree on modifications and future evaluation dates. As implementation progresses, periodic evaluations usually suffice.

Stabilizing the Change

New changes often have a short life. Like kindling, they blaze brightly and die. Once the client and consultant see initial benefits, they overlook the need to stabilize the change; the client then regresses to old patterns or significantly alters the new system. To avoid this situation, help the client build supports for the new system.

Utilize managerial, structural, and motivational supports for the new system. The client should assign authority and responsibility for every phase of the system. The individuals so assigned must know their exact duties and rewards for maintaining the new system. Too often, everyone is assigned general responsibility; each person believes the next person will perform the job. Instead, legitimate the new change by assigning specific control.

Structural supports contribute to long life. Make it impossible to revert to the old system. For example, if you develop new reporting forms, collect and destroy all the old ones. If the grapevine is overactive, develop a formal communication system that is more effective and efficient. Then work at dismantling or clogging the grapevine. In essence, create barriers to alternative systems.

The client's staff also needs motivation for continuing the change. Regular feedback and new goal-setting increase motivation. Design multilevel reward systems that include compensation, status, praise, self-satisfaction, and privileges. The rewards of success foster repetition. If performance falls below expectations, remove rewards while offering constructive methods for improvement. Periodically, hold refresher training sessions to solidify the new skills. Continually reinforce their maintenance of the new system.

By combining these supports, you stabilize the change. Without these supports, you risk its early demise.

Implementation tests the quality of your recommendations. Moreover, successful installation demands a keen insight into human and organizational dynamics. This quality separates the professional consultant from the theoretician. Integrating psychological principles with your recommendations promotes both their acceptance and their use. This benefits both the client and the consultant.

Successful implementation is more than its own reward. It encourages the client to use your services in the future. Client satisfaction is the best advertising, but you will never know the extent of your success unless you evaluate your efforts—the topic of Chapter 14.

Additional Sources of Help

Behavior in Organizations. L. W. Porter, E. E. Lawler, and J. R. Hackman. New York: McGraw-Hill, 1975.

Beyond the Quick Fix. R. H. Kilmann. San Francisco: Jossey-Bass, 1984.

Changemasters. R. M. Kanter. New York: Simon & Schuster, 1983.

Consulting for Organizational Change. F. Steele. Amherst, Mass.: University of Massachusetts Press, 1975.

Corporate Cultures. A. Kennedy and T. Deal. Reading, Mass.: Addison-Wesley, 1982.

The Gold-Collar Worker. R. E. Kelley. Reading, Mass.: Addison-Wesley, 1985.

Organizational Behavior and Performance. 2nd ed. A. D. Szilagyi and M. J. Wallace. Santa Monica, Calif.: Goodyear Publishing Co., 1980.

Organizational Psychology. 3rd ed. D. A. Kolb, I. M. Rubin, and J. M. McIntyre. Englewood Cliffs, N.J.: Prentice-Hall, 1979.

The Planning of Change. 3rd ed. W. G. Bennis, K. D. Benne, R. Chin, and K. E. Corey. New York: Holt, Rinehart and Winston, 1976.

The Skilled Helper. G. Egan. Monterey, Calif.: Brooks/Cole Publishing Co., 1975.

Evaluating Your Performance

14

Evaluation is a time for accounting; for comparing actions with consequences; for detecting flaws and making improvements; for planting the seeds of future challenge.

DON KOBERG AND JIM BAGNALL

When you evaluate your consulting performance, both you and your clients benefit. Evaluation, performed properly, acts as a quality-control mechanism, a learning device, a legal protection, and a marketing tool. In this chapter, you will learn the specifics of evaluating your consulting performance. In addition, you will find ways to publish your efforts in appropriate professional forums. By chapter's end you will view evaluation as a professional opportunity, instead of a burdensome responsibility.

The Professional's Test

Consultants who forego evaluation usually do not understand its far-reaching benefits. Evaluation insures that you achieved the project's objectives. If you have, the evaluation results build the client's confidence in and satisfaction with your work. If you have not, you can take necessary corrective action. Without evaluation, you lack this quality assurance, and neither you nor the client knows the full extent of your success or failure.

Evaluation promotes learning for both you and the client. If you achieve positive results, the client learns that consultants are a valuable resource. Having gained benefits in the project, the client will be more likely to utilize consultants in the future. The client also discovers how to evaluate projects and can apply these principles to other projects.

Evaluation teaches you several lessons. By adding each project to your experience base, you take advantage of the learning curve. Comparing this project to previous projects improves your efficiency and effectiveness. You learn how to conduct each step of the assignment better. You determine the time, cost, and resources required for this type of project. Your technical strengths and weaknesses will surface, perhaps indicating need for continuing education. In sum, each project improves your services.

Evaluation provides legal protection. Malpractice suits against consultants are increasing. In our age of litigation, people look for scapegoats. A client experiencing business difficulties may blame the consultant. Since memories are short, you must document your evaluation results. In case of later legal action, evaluation demonstrates both your professionalism and your effectiveness during the disputed project.

Finally, evaluation is an excellent marketing tool. Documented project success encourages the client to use your services again. Remember that repeat clients form the basis of most consulting practices. In addition, they refer potential clients. Evaluation supplies data necessary for the referral. With substantial facts and figures, your client can convince more potential clients to use your services. As a result, your reputation spreads more quickly. While protecting client confidences, you can use evaluation results during sales calls. Actual previous results sway prospective clients more than unsubstantiated promises. Finally, if you publish your results, you reach a large user audience. Without evaluation, you lose all these marketing benefits.

Evaluation, then, benefits both you and the client. It clarifies everyone's perception of the project's success. This, in turn, prevents later misunderstandings. If you fear an unfavorable evaluation, its importance increases. Failure to conduct an evaluation will not ameliorate the client's dissatisfaction. More than likely, it will add to it. Learn what went wrong and try to correct it. If you don't, you endanger your consulting practice.

What to Evaluate

Project outcome, client satisfaction, consultant satisfaction, and consultant effectiveness are the criteria for evaluation. Regarding the client, you initially assess whether your work achieved the project's objectives. Did you fully accomplish what you promised in the initial proposal? If you and the client modified the initial proposal, did you meet the modified objectives? In addition to completing work objectives, did your efforts lead to the desired results? Did the client benefit from your services? If not, why? Had you performed your duties differently, would the outcomes have changed? Did the results occur even though you did not complete the work as promised? Did the consulting expense exceed the possible benefits? Why? These questions assess your primary responsibilities: satisfying your work commitments and providing client benefits.

You should also evaluate client satisfaction, although this assessment is tricky. For the most part, you seek unqualified client satisfaction. Occasionally, you and your clients will disagree. They may indicate that you must change your report. At this point, judge the client's long-term, best interests. If client dissatisfaction will do more harm than an unchanged report, compromise. If changing your report will do more harm, refuse. Compromise is acceptable only in light of the client's best interest, not your own. When you do compromise, document it for the client. Specify your reasons and the possible ramifications of the compromise. Although complete client satisfaction is desirable, you cannot always attain it.

In addition to client satisfaction, assess your own satisfaction. Were you pleased with the project's conduct and success? Did you enjoy consulting on the project? How do you feel about your relationship to the client? Were you able to establish professional trust and rapport? Would you consult to this client again? A professional takes his or her own feelings into account. You are a valid data source for evaluating the project. Unfortunately, too many consultants rely only on this source.

Another self-evaluation examines your consulting effectiveness. How could you improve your initial selling efforts? Did problems arise due to an inadequate proposal? Did you conduct the engagement in a professional manner? Did you change the project's scope during the engagement? Why? Did you apply sound techniques appropriate to this project? Did you meet your schedule? Did cost or time over-runs occur? Was the project fully documented in a timely fashion? Were meetings held regularly? Were these meetings effective? Were all your recommendations accepted by the client? If not, why? Was implementation successful? Could you have interacted better with the client? What did you learn that you can apply to future projects? These questions critically assess your consulting skill. From these results, modify your functioning for increased effectiveness.

These four evaluations—project outcome, client satisfaction, consultant satisfaction, and consultant effectiveness—are the basic, minimal criteria for every project. They provide sufficient information for quality control, legal protection, and marketing.

Some consultants conduct additional assessments for specific purposes. For example, you may want to know how widely your work improved the organization. Is the organization more effective and efficient? Other firms assess client costs. Could they achieve the same results with fewer client expenditures? Still other firms evaluate client learning. Does the client know how to handle similar problems in the future? Each of these evaluations is valuable. However, maintain a balance between pertinent and simply desirable information.

How to Evaluate

Many consultants do not evaluate their consulting projects because they do not know how. Proper evaluation considers sources, methods, and timing. Use sources that provide the necessary data. For example, if your aim is to reduce absenteeism, check employee records. For determining client's satisfaction, ask the client and question individuals familiar with the client's reaction to the project. To determine your own effectiveness, examine yourself. You might also want the client's assessment of your performance. In essence, tap the direct sources, if possible. If not, use indirect sources. The evaluation's validity and usefulness increase with the number of appropriate sources.

Timing affects your evaluation results. If possible, begin evaluation before the project commences. At that point gather preproject data. For example, before you install a new productivity program, obtain current productivity rates. If you plan to design a new marketing strategy, gather current market share statistics. This preproject data gives you a baseline. After completing the project, gather similar data. Your evaluation compares the pre- and postproject figures to measure your impact.

Not all consulting lends itself to such comparisons. If you help a client choose between locating a new plant in Texas or in Colorado, pre- versus postevaluation is difficult. The same dilemma arises over machinery selection. However, too few consultants consider collecting preproject data when it is feasible; therefore, they have no comparative base against which to evaluate their effectiveness.

Gathering postproject data poses problems. Most consultants suggest evaluation immediately following project completion to avoid client or consultant memory distortion. In addition, if evaluation results uncover problems, you can take prompt, corrective action.

In some projects, beneficial results do not appear for months or even years. If you help a client restructure from a functional to a divisional organization, the benefits seldom appear immediately. Instead, the change usually disrupts the organization and temporarily reduces organizational performance. If you evaluate only at that point, you would judge the project unsuccessful. However, if you evaluate over an extended time period, organizational performance will probably show improvement.

When feasible, evaluate your efforts after they've stood the test of time. Compare your immediate postproject results with this long-range evaluation. Did the client sustain the immediate benefits? Did other benefits occur at a later point? Was the project sabotaged? How does the client feel after six months or a year? This long-range evaluation better assesses your lasting impact. Combined with the short-term evaluation, it realistically appraises your effectiveness.

Many useful evaluation methods exist. Approach evaluation as you would a consulting assignment. Ask yourself what you want to know, such as project effectiveness. This leads to both the source of information and the possible methods of obtaining it. For methods refer to Chapter 10, "Conducting Projects." Review the section on data-gathering tools, such as observation, interviews, surveys, and basic research.

In general, design your evaluation process when writing the initial proposal. For each proposed objective, determine how you will assess its achievement. Specify what, when, and how you will evaluate. Including evaluation in the proposal yields several benefits. Making it part of the project insures that it will occur. When evaluation is not included, questions later arise as to its necessity and cost. As a result, either you or the client may resist it. Evaluation also forces you to state practical and achievable objectives. Since you must develop evaluation methods for each objective, you avoid superficial, unrealistic, or nonmeasurable goals. You will know what you plan to do and when you have done it. Finally, evaluation is a good sales tool. It marks you as a professional. When clients appraise your proposals, they notice your interest in achieving and proving results. This gives you a competitive edge over those who do not evaluate.

Documenting Evaluation Results

When evaluation results are tabulated, document them fully for the proper audiences. For instance, report project outcome and client satisfaction to the client. If appropriate, inform him or her of your own satisfaction. Clients appreciate feedback. Many new clients are still learning how to be "good" clients. Since the role is new to them, your feedback helps them improve their future utilization of consultants.

When you document results, present the entire picture. Neither overstate benefits nor hide problems. Present evidence of your achievements and failures. Where possible, explain why the results occurred. Applaud everyone involved, not just yourself. Where results are unsatisfactory, avoid blaming the client or the client's staff. Instead, explore what happened and how to change the situation. Use the evaluation as both a reward and a self-correcting device.

Consultants too often neglect documenting their efforts for other audiences. With solid evaluation data, many consulting projects are suitable for professional publications. You should publish whenever possible. Suggest to your clients that you write the article together, or obtain permission to publish alone. If necessary, disguise the client information to insure confidentiality.

Professional publications normally benefit everyone. You and the client will receive professional recognition, and this will build both your reputations through positive exposure. Potential clients learn of your services, your approach, and your effectiveness.

The entire profession also gains. Your publication adds to the common knowledge base. Other consultants can learn your methods, which will prevent them from reinventing your wheel. In addition, a respectable publication improves the profession's public image. Unless we inform the public of the benefits of consulting, they rely on questionable, third-party accounts.

Publishing opportunities abound. Magazines, trade journals, newsletters, newspapers, and books offer numerous possibilities. For example, the *Directory of Publishing Opportunities* lists 2,600 academic and special-interest journals. *The Writer's Handbook: What to Write, How to Write, and Where to Sell* includes 2,500 markets. Determine what audience you want to address. Who would benefit from your knowledge? How would you benefit? In some cases, you may want to inform several audiences, stressing different aspects of the project to each. Select the publications read by your audiences. Write the editors for publication guidelines and their interest in your topic. Then, drawing upon your evaluation results, write an article suitable for the particular publications.

Evaluation generally completes the learning cycle. A professional reflects on his or her experiences to foster future improvement. Successful consultants are their own most uncompromising critics. They realize that honest evaluation promotes their consulting practice. Utilizing hard objective data, these consultants insure success. In addition, this success secures client satisfaction and future projects.

Evaluation also completes the project cycle. Occasionally, it leads to periodic follow-up visits. More often it signals the end of the consulting relationship—the topic of Chapter 15, "Terminating the Project."

Additional Sources of Help

Directory of Publishing Opportunities. Chicago: Marquis Academic Media, 1975.

Evaluation Research. C. H. Weiss. Englewood Cliffs, N.J.: Prentice-Hall, 1972.

Evaluative Research. E. A. Suchman. New York: Russell Sage Foundation, 1967.

How to Control the Quality of a Management Consulting Engagement. New York: Association of Consulting Management Engineers, 1972.

How to Get Happily Published. J. Appelbaum and N. Evans. New York: Harper & Row, 1978.

Literary Market Place: The Directory of American Book Publishing with Names and Numbers. New York: R. R. Bowker, published annually.

Some Guide Lines for Evaluative Research. E. Herzog. Washington, D.C.:
    U.S. Department of Health, Education, and Welfare, 1959.
The Writer's Handbook: What to Write, How to Write, and Where to Sell.
    Boston: The Writer, published annually.
Writer's Market. Cincinnati: Writer's Digest, published annually.

Terminating the Project

15

The key notion is that every consultation relationship must have some plan for a healthy, mutually satisfying termination of the working relationship.

GORDON LIPPITT AND RONALD LIPPITT

All consulting engagements eventually end, but the transition often thwarts consultants and their clients. Either the project stops abruptly without proper follow-up, or it lingers unfinished. This chapter addresses those readers who experience difficulty in terminating projects.

This final task involves both psychological and administrative elements. Endings are laden with emotion. The client's dependency and your postengagement depression influence how and when you terminate the relationship, and may also interfere with tasks needing attention, such as sending the final bill. This chapter teaches you how to control both the psychological and administrative aspects of terminating a project so you can conclude your project in an efficient, timely, and satisfying manner.

Termination, like a good symphony, must be structured and orchestrated. Except in a few isolated cases, the consulting project should never just end. If you do not prepare the client and yourself for termination, the end will come as an abrupt shock that can leave your client quite dissatisfied.

Your final presentation, whether the project includes implementation or not, should never be your last meeting. Schedule a minimum of one to two additional meetings. These successive meetings are to insure that the client understands your recommendations. They give you time to convey the nuances and to help the client plan to make them permanent changes. Also, you have time to meet with the client to discuss next steps and the conclusion of the project.

A useful tool for termination preparation is a transition plan or action guide. This documents for the client just who is responsible for what action steps and when the steps are to be performed. Every recommendation you make needs translation into an action step if it is to be implemented successfully. Good transition plans differentiate both the sequence and importance of each action step. In this way, the client knows what must happen when. Also, the client can see how the work involved in carrying out the action steps will affect the other ongoing activities of the firm. With a transition plan in hand, you and the client avoid undermining the recommendations. If the recommended action steps put too much stress or overwork on those responsible, they will not be carried out satisfactorily. Since organizations have limited surge capacity for incorporating additional work activities, the transition plan enables you to see whose workloads must be shifted to take on responsibility for certain action items. Also, it helps you determine what sequencing pattern for the action steps will work best for your client.

The transition plan also points out when you will be stopping your efforts. This sends an important signal to the client as to when your involvement ends and when the client must assume total responsibility for the project's continuation and success. If the timing does not work for the client, he has the opportunity to negotiate a different termination strategy.

The final benefit of the transition plan is that it makes the client think realistically about how fast things can change and how long it might be before benefits start to accrue. Once the client sees the schedule of action items and the expected dates for improvements to become visible, she or he can gear up for them. By establishing time frames, the client avoids the unrealistic expectation that everything will be better immediately. Also, the time frames reinforce the notion that the project and its benefits continue even after you leave.

Follow-Up Prior to Termination

As a professional you must guarantee that a client has access to your services. The client should feel free to contact you at any time. Moreover, following a project, you should periodically check its continuing effectiveness. Ideally, this follow-up should be combined with your evaluation efforts. If you don't evaluate the project, however, plan a series of client contacts to monitor the project. In addition, encourage the client to call you if problems arise.

Follow-up is important for many reasons. Primarily, it acts as an early warning system. You can observe both the operation and the results of the system you recommended. Sometimes a client inappropriately alters the implementation plan. With frequent follow-up, you can detect such changes before disaster occurs. Follow-up also instills client security because the client won't feel abandoned when difficulties occur. Finally, follow-up encourages frank discussion of the project and the client-consultant relationship.

The question of who pays for the follow-up often arises. Usually, a consultant includes follow-up in the scope of the original project. In that case, the client pays for it. However, if you over-ran a fixed-fee budget, normally you absorb the cost. In certain situations, you can renegotiate the contract. For example, delays instigated by the client may increase the project's cost. By the time you reach the follow-up stage, you might have exhausted your budget. Since the client action led to this problem, you have a right to renegotiate the contract.

Occasionally, follow-up identifies needed corrective action. If deficiencies in your work necessitate such action, then you perform the work at your expense. For example, if you overlooked important data during analysis, or if you used statistical analysis and later found computational error, you would redo the work free of charge.

Sometimes factors beyond your control will cause problems. The client may not follow your advice. One of your client's competitors may take unexpected actions that affect your recommendations. Important client personnel may quit. Since these are beyond your control, you are not responsible.

Sometimes, you and the client will disagree on what led to the problem. The client may expect you to absorb the cost, regardless of the source. When in doubt, ask yourself if other professionals would judge your work to be of high quality. If still in doubt, seek impartial review from your peers, being careful to maintain client confidentiality. If they are satisfied with your work's quality, then you have met your responsibility. However, client dissatisfaction may dictate performing the additional work regardless. Only you can judge if the cost of client dissatisfaction is greater than your costs for performing the work.

Follow-up, then, fills the important gap between implementation and termination. Professional consultants realize their responsibility for regular checkups. Follow-up allows modification of the current project and prevention of future problems, so the client continually benefits from your services.

The Psychology of Termination

Saying goodbye evokes many fears, anxieties, and some sadness, be it a child leaving home, a good friend moving cross-country, or a consultant and client ending a project. As a result, people in our society postpone or avoid goodbyes. In consulting, this phenomenon surfaces in many forms. Some clients have created make-work projects to keep the consultant in the organization. Some consultants have left final reports unwritten for as long as one year after project completion. They claim that other projects diverted them. In truth, they don't want the project to end. If they don't finish the report, then, by definition, the project is not over. One consultant never sends a final bill for the same reason. All these examples underscore the emotional difficulties of terminating the consultant-client relationship.

Two major psychological issues emerge during termination: client dependency and consultant depression. If you established a solid, trusting consulting relationship, neither you nor the client wants to end it. For the client this may be the first such relationship in the work setting. Clients may miss having you as a regular and confidential sounding board. They might not want to lose the intellectual stimulation you provide. In addition, the relationship supplies interpersonal and social rewards such as friendship and status. Consequently, the client comes to rely on you to meet many needs.

These same factors can affect the consultant. The project furnishes professional challenge. The client's dependency makes you feel needed and important. The fees constitute an income source. There are many such reasons for prolonging the relationship.

To insure a smooth and satisfying ending, you can follow a number of steps. Initially, you must realize that human needs permeate consulting relationships. In this way you can prepare both the client and yourself to handle them. For example, you should discourage client dependency throughout the entire engagement. Foster client acquisition of skills that will allow the client to stand on his or her own feet. Avoid becoming economically dependent on any client. Such dependence interferes with your judgment and creates a conflict of interest. Mutually decide on a termination plan with your client. When you feel that no further work is necessary, do not unilaterally decide to stop. Instead, explain your perspective to the client, who may see the situation differently. The reverse also occurs: the client may no longer desire your input when you think it is still necessary. In either case, you should candidly discuss your viewpoints. Talk about your feelings and how hard it is to say goodbye. Enough trust should exist by this time to encourage mutual decision making. As a result, you can arrive at an acceptable and rational conclusion.

Don't stop cold turkey. Arrange some future date for your last meeting, then begin a weaning process. Space successive meetings further apart until your final meeting. During that time assure the client that the project possesses the necessary support systems for continued success. For example, you may provide additional client training. Reduced involvement prior to termination allows you to assess your mutual decision. At a later point you may find your decision to terminate is premature. You and the client can then negotiate further involvement appropriate to the situation. Had you already terminated, you would not have this opportunity.

Upon terminating, emphasize to the client that only the project is over, not the relationship. Emphasize that your services are always available and that you have a continuing interest in his or her welfare. Moreover, lack of contact does not end a relationship. If you have a good relationship, you can re-establish it quickly, even though months have passed.

If possible, plan a termination celebration. Have a business lunch to toast the project's success. Plan to publish an article together or to present your experiences at a professional meeting. In other words, designate some personally satisfying method to acknowledge that the project is over.

During termination you should prepare for your own psychological depression, which often follows the completion of a consulting engagement. Consultants experience "postpartum" depression after successfully finishing a major project. Their enthusiasm wanes, and their work concentration ebbs—normal reactions to both major accomplishments and saying goodbye. Successful consultants learn to handle this depression. Some reward themselves with a vacation after the project. Others find it impossible to relax. Idleness deepens their depression, so they consume themselves in new projects. The workload helps them overcome depression. A few consultants simply prefer to acknowledge their mood while maintaining their normal schedule. In any case, you must realize that the low feelings are normal. Plan to expect and cope with them.

Attending to both the client's and your own psychological needs, conclude the project on a positive note. Avoiding these issues does not make them go away. If anything, they surface in obstructive ways, such as delaying the final report, which angers the client. Instead, prepare a mutually satisfying way to meet your needs and end the project. With your needs gratified, you can focus on the necessary paperwork and administrative details. Thus you can meet your professional obligations in a timely manner.

Final Administrative Tasks

To conclude the project to everyone's satisfaction, do not overlook your business obligations. Make sure the client has received all the reports, charts, and information you promised. When a client does not receive an expected document, dissatisfaction follows. A shortchanged client seldom returns to the same consultant. Prevent this situation by asking the client if you have provided all expected products.

Document your termination by sending the final bill with a termination letter. Officially inform the client that you completed the project. The client must know when your current services have ended. Briefly summarize the benefits that accrued as a result of the project. Express your appreciation at serving the client. If you enjoyed the association, tell the client. Thank the client and his or her staff for all courtesies extended to you. Since you want to insure client satisfaction, encourage him or her to contact you if problems arise. Finally, extend an offer to maintain your working relationship during future projects.

Don't forget to send your final bill simultaneously with termination. The client is more likely to pay when the project is still fresh. Monitor your collection. If necessary, review the section in Chapter 5, "Limiting Fee Collection Problems." Remember that the client may withhold payment because of dissatisfaction or to keep the relationship open-ended. In any case, gentle reminders help. You may need to meet with the client to discuss the situation.

Finally, plant the seed for future projects. Maintain a low-level client contact, even though the project is over. Some consultants regularly send brochures or new services announcements. Others distribute newsletters. One mails professional articles of interest, suggesting application to the client's situation. Some have annual client parties. After a substantial time period, an occasional phone call is acceptable. Express your sincere concern for the client and your responsibility to maintain contact. This provides a face-saving method for clients who have difficulty asking for your help. In essence, create opportunities for clients to utilize your services in the future.

Now that you know how to begin, conduct, and complete an entire consulting engagement, you are prepared to serve your clients. Now you must shift your emphasis from consulting to administering your consulting practice—the topic of Chapter 16.

Additional Sources of Help

The Dynamics of Planned Change. R. Lippitt, J. Watson, and B. Westley. New York: Harcourt, Brace & World, 1958.
Organizational Diagnosis. H. Levinson. Cambridge, Mass.: Harvard University Press, 1972.

Continuing Your Success: Administering Your Practice

16

If clients are expected to take the consultant's advice seriously, they must be able to recognize that the consulting unit itself provides an example of sound organization, competent management, and efficient administration.
M. KUBR

In this chapter the focus is shifted from conducting a consulting engagement to administering a consulting practice. The individual assignment is placed within the context of an entire firm. The administrator's skills differ from the consultant's skills. Rather than reviewing the entire management field, three administrative roles pertinent to consultants are described: the paperwork processor, the project manager, and the owner. By the end of this chapter, you will know the administrative requirements of a consulting practice.

Consultant As "Paperwork Processor"

Throughout this book the emphasis has been on documenting your consulting projects. Control over a consulting engagement requires complete documentation throughout the engagement. Paperwork abounds. Producing, cataloguing, and filing this paperwork can overwhelm you. Some consultants' offices have files scattered over the desk, chairs, and floor. Consultants often lose their way in a morass of paper.

To prevent this situation you must devise a method to store and retrieve information on consulting projects. Knowing what information to collect and how to file it depends on your producing a format for the work papers. Then you can create a way to retrieve work papers efficiently. Storage and retrieval tame paperwork.

Storage

A format many consultants use to produce and file necessary documents is shown in the following checklist.

Index.   List all documents and page numbers in the file.

Summary.   Summarize in one page the client, industry, problem, method, and recommendations.

Bench-mark documents.   These documents correspond to the major events during the engagement.

> Engagement notice (this documents what initiated the project, such as a published Request for Proposal or a phone call from the client)
> Proposal letter and the proposal
> Letter of either confirmation or understanding
> Contract (if used)
> Engagement plan
> Letters indicating any changes in the original agreement
> Final report and minutes of final presentation
> Implementation plan, if not included in final report
> Progress reports and minutes of progress meetings
> Correspondence and memos-to-file documenting meetings, phone calls, letters, and staff meetings both with the client and within your own firm
> Letter of termination

Engagement control.   These documents specify your plans, budget, schedule, staff, expense, and billing control over the project. Include any flow charts.

Engagement plan and checklist showing what you plan to do and how you plan to do it

Engagement budget estimate for each phase and for each staff member

Engagement staff and scheduling, describing who will complete what tasks when (include flow charts)

Engagement time and expense reports for both the client and your staff (compare these to your budget estimates)

Billing notices and paid receipts

Background data.   Include all the data you gathered for this project.

Research data, such as interview notes, surveys, observation records

Client documents, such as annual reports, records, policies

Company background material, such as popular press articles or industry data

Literature review documents concerning either your client's company or the problem

Notes if you consulted with others about your client's company or the problem, such as suppliers or specialists within your firm

Analysis and research findings.

Copies of all analyses and their results

Conclusions based on your analyses

Development of recommendations and alternatives.

Alternatives developed to address your conclusions

Comparison of alternatives

Recommendations you will incorporate into the client report

Progress reports and meetings.

Outline of all progress reports

Drafts and final copies

Presentation materials

Minutes of meetings (for each meeting document names and titles of all present, place, time, points covered, client reactions, modification, conclusions reached, and actions to be taken)

Final report and meeting.

Outline of report
Drafts and final copies
Presentation materials
Minutes of meeting (include same information listed for progress
  reports and meetings)

Implementation plan.

Outline of plan
Progress reviews
Changes and modification after installation

Follow-up. Document results of all follow-up activities.

Engagement evaluation.

Evaluation forms used for client and consultant evaluation
Evaluation results
Actions taken as a result of the evaluation

Lessons learned. Document all relevant lessons regarding this
firm, industry, problem, engagement administration, or consulting
process.

Other information important to this client or engagement.

The preceding format will help you collect and collate each project's pertinent information. Modify and adapt the format checklist
to your own situation. Simply remember that your consulting obli-
gation is unfulfilled until you properly document the experience.

Retrieval

To aid information retrieval, many consultants maintain four files.
The first contains all client folders in alphabetical order. These folders hold the complete work papers described in the preceding checklist. Then, separate files are established by industry, problem, and
method. Place a copy of the one-page client engagement summary in
each appropriate file. For example, within the industry file you may

have electronics, automotive, and other industries. If your client is an electronics firm, you insert the engagement summary in that folder. Follow the same process for your problem and method files. Then, when you face a future project, you have access to your past experiences by industry, problem, and method. This saves you from reinventing the wheel. You cross-fertilize from project to project.

Being an effective "paperwork processor" improves your consulting practice. You maintain an ongoing record of client involvement and improvement that you can quickly review before each new project for the client. It also protects your practice by preserving all important documents. In case of later litigation, you need not rely on your memory.

Consultant As "Project Manager"

Continued consulting success requires administration of both single and simultaneous projects. You must mind your "Ps"—product, personnel, process, and paperwork. By diligent project management, you complete your work in a timely manner; you satisfy your clients.

Project managers initially focus on the project's requirements. You specify the end product and what's necessary to produce it. You plan the work so the project concludes in the manner you and the client agreed on. A final product that is professional and acceptable within the time, money, and resource allocations is your responsibility; in fact, overseeing the product is your *first* responsibility.

Project managers also supervise personnel. Directly, you manage your own staff assigned to the project. Indirectly, you manage client staff connected to the project. Selection, motivation, coordination, education, and performance evaluation fall within your purview. The personnel make or break a project's success. Servicing their needs and directing their efforts is your second responsibility as project manager.

Project managers monitor the process or work flow. Through proper scheduling and control, you move tasks toward completion in an efficient, effective, and timely manner. Moreover, you require that all work contributes positively to the client's needs. Managing the work flow, then, is your third responsibility.

Project managers process paperwork. When you send paperwork to the client, arrange it systematically. Communicate regularly. Paperwork for the firm should be complete, accurate, and filed for easy retrieval. Paperwork is your final responsibility.

The four Ps—product, personnel, process, and paperwork—apply to your entire consulting practice as well as to a single project. Controlling multiple, simultaneous projects, however, increases the complexity of your practice. You must compare and coordinate schedules, staffing, and performance. Utilizing your resources efficiently to meet your obligations is a major undertaking. If your staff is large, you will spend more time administering and less time consulting. Your responsibilities shift from performing the work yourself to insuring that all the work is performed.

Consultant As "Owner"

As an owner of a consulting firm, you are responsible for your firm's survival and direction. This differs from your role as either consultant or project manager. As consultant, you work on projects. As project manager, you supervise projects and the staff assigned to them. Your duties may also include finding new clients. If you own the firm, you provide the firm's financial, marketing, personnel, and management base. You delegate duties and give directions. Most importantly, you take the risks and reap the rewards.

It would help to reread Chapter 3, "Starting Your Own Practice." As owner, your first task is setting a goal. You decide the firm's intent and its future purposes. You know your customers' needs and develop services to meet them. Instead of focusing solely on day-to-day problems, you look into the future. You create a vision that guides your firm.

Next, you formulate a strategy for reaching your goals. A comprehensive game plan allows you to implement your strategy and includes organizational structures such as charts, communication systems, compensation plans, and personnel paths. Moreover, you develop an integrated set of policies to complement your structures.

Your next task is leading your enterprise. You are the model for your employees of how they should perform. When they see you following the game plan, they will too. Your vision and determination inspire them. You maintain their focus on effectively delivering your firm's services to satisfied clients.

Finally, you insure your firm's survival. Internally, you provide the necessary resources of people, money, and equipment. Externally, you secure markets and financing. You protect the firm from hostile parties such as competitors. You represent the firm to the public: press, unions, community groups, or professional associations. In other words, you create, personify, and defend your organization. You are responsible for every action within and by your firm. If you take the task lightly, you will fail. If you concentrate on effective ownership, you reap the monetary and personal rewards of being your own boss.

Your consulting firm contains many administrative roles. Your firm's success depends on each role being filled. Someone must administer each individual project as well as simultaneous projects. In addition, someone must manage the entire consulting practice. The most challenging and complex role is ownership. As an owner, you are responsible for every action within and by your firm.

Additional Sources of Help

Competitive Advantage. M. Porter. New York: Free Press, 1985.

Handbook of Strategic Management. K. Albert (ed.). New York: McGraw-Hill, 1983.

How to Control the Quality of a Management Consulting Engagement. New York: Association of Consulting Management Engineers, 1972.

"How to Set Up a Project Organization." C. J. Middleton. *Harvard Business Review* (March–April 1967): 73–82.

Management Consulting: A Guide to the Profession. M. Kubr. Geneva, Switzerland: International Labour Organization, 1976.

Management: Tasks, Responsibilities, Practices. P. F. Drucker. New York: Harper & Row, 1973.

Managing Your Accounting and Consulting Practice. M. A. Altman and R. I. Weil. New York: Matthew Bender & Co., 1978.

Managing the Paperwork Pipeline. M. Kuttner. New York: John Wiley & Sons, 1978.

Personnel Management. 6th ed. H. J. Chruden and A. W. Sherman. Cincinnati, Ohio: Southwestern Publishing Co., 1980.

Professional Service Management. W. Joseph. New York: McGraw-Hill, 1982.

Strategy Formulation and Implementation. A. A. Thompson and A. J. Strickland. Dallas: Business Publications, Inc., 1980.

The Issues of Consulting

17

In consulting, the idea of permanent, life-long education is not new. An individual who becomes a consultant should realize that s/he is joining a profession which has to change continuously, because its object . . . also changes rapidly.

M. KUBR

At this point, you know how to conduct consulting engagements and set up a consulting practice. This chapter completes your background with a discussion of current issues. Readers who lack consulting experience, printed references, or consultants as resources will benefit most from this chapter. Choose random topics of particular interest. However, for your individual protection, please read the ethics and malpractice sections.

Ethics of Consulting

A sense of ethics distinguishes professional consultants from non-professionals. Ethical codes protect both you and your clients. As a consultant, you usually stand in a special relation of trust, confidence, and responsibility to your clients. This is known as a fiduciary capacity. Adhering to ethical codes assures your client that you will not exploit this fiduciary relationship. Ethical codes also protect you from unwarranted client accusations.

Review the ethical codes of the major consulting associations identified in the Appendix. Based on collective consulting experiences, these codes address the major ethical dilemmas faced by consultants. They advise on confidentiality, conflict of interest, objectivity, professional involvement, and other practices. Also, re-read Chapter 2, where general ethical standards are discussed.

Since no universal consulting association exists, no universal ethical code applies to all consultants. Instead, individual professional associations should guide your consulting behavior. If you consult in law, follow the American Bar Association's code. Real estate consultants adhere to the National Board of Real Estate Brokers code. Psychologists submit to the American Psychological Association's ethics statements. Engineers comply with the Society of Professional Engineers code. By combining your profession's code with a consulting association code, you build a solid ethical foundation and thus protect yourself and your clients.

Active discussion about ethical standards promotes better standards and increased utilization. To enhance your thinking on the subject, read the following:

"Ethical Dilemmas and Guidelines for Consultants." In *The Consulting Process in Action*. G. Lippitt and R. Lippitt. La Jolla, Calif.: University Associates, 1978.

"Ethical Issues in Social Intervention." D. Warwick and H. Kelman. In *The Planning of Change*. 3rd ed. W. G. Bennis, K. D. Benne, R. Chin, and K. E. Corey, eds. New York: Holt, Rinehart and Winston, 1976.

"Professional Codes." In *Management Consulting: A Guide to the Profession*. M. Kubr. Geneva, Switzerland: International Labour Organization, 1976.

"Professional Ethics and Competence in Management Consulting." D. C. Moseley. *California Management Review*, Spring 1970, p. 44.

"Some Ethical Problems in Group and Organizational Consultation." K. Benne. In *The Planning of Change*. 2nd ed. New York: Holt, Rinehart and Winston, 1971.

Malpractice and Liability in Consulting

As mentioned in Chapter 9 under "Contracts" and in Chapter 14, malpractice suits are rising. This trend received attention in an article by William Brockhaus, "Prospects for Malpractice Suits in the Business Consulting Profession," in the *Journal of Business* (January

1977). Dissatisfied clients commonly resort to legal suits. However, not enough case law has developed to specify particular consultant liabilities.

It is to be hoped that you will never face a malpractice suit. Yet, in our litigation-oriented society, the odds are against you. Brockhaus found and revealed in his article that few consulting firms take action to protect their interests. This is disturbing. It is better to be unnecessarily prepared than caught unaware. If you are a sole proprietor, you stand to lose your personal and business assets over a malpractice suit.

Protection comes in many forms. Most important is to establish positive and open client relationships. Display and distribute your ethical codes. Encourage your clients to contact you immediately should problems arise. Then you can work out mutually satisfying solutions.

Provide highest quality service and stand behind it. Take the extra steps needed to insure client acceptance. Remember to evaluate and document all your work; orderly and complete documentation leaves a good professional impression with judges and juries. If possible, have colleagues periodically evaluate your work to assess your practices and standards. Constant self-regulation by professional peers attests to your concern for high quality.

Contact your attorney for further advice on legal protection. If necessary, use contracts to specify your and your client's obligations.

Finally, carry malpractice insurance. Most professional associations offer it to their members at reasonable rates. Although it increases your expenses, it protects your assets and income.

Certification and Licensing

Certification and licensing is a controversial issue among consultants. One group views it as a means to regulate practitioner quality, reduce the number of hucksters, protect the public, and improve consulting's public image. The other group perceives it as an encumbrance designed by the "in-group" to protect its market share. This second group questions who can develop standards applicable to all consultants. Moreover, who will sit in judgment?

Currently, no government laws regulate consulting. Some consulting associations award certificates to consultants who meet certain minimum standards. These certificates carry no legal meaning, nor do they indicate that consultants without them are inferior in training or competence. In fact, few consultants hold such certificates. Since the public is unaware of these certificates, they act primarily as status symbols within the profession.

Problems of dual licensing also arise. If you possess an engineering or CPA license, must you obtain another license to consult in that field? In most cases, the additional license is redundant. For those fields where no primary license exists, such as marketing, what meaning would a consulting license have? What could a licensed marketer do that an unlicensed one could not?

Licensing or certification seems premature at this time. Since consulting applies to all fields, one general licensing procedure approaches the impossible. Until someone accurately defines consulting for each field, no one can establish licensing requirements.

The cost/benefit of licensing is also questionable. There is little evidence to show that licensing in any field insures service quality. However, licensing restricts the number of consultants who can practice and increases certain consultants' fees. In addition, public taxes and licensing fees rise to support the regulatory agency, so the government and a few licensed professionals benefit economically at the public's expense.

Licensing is necessary only when the individual client does not have enough resources to adequately protect himself or herself. In those cases, the state assumes the protective responsibility. Most states traditionally hold that the size and increased resources of organizations allow them to defend themselves adequately. Hence, a business can judge the competence of its professionals. Ideally, the free market system supports the effective consultants and forces the hucksters out of business. When the business community rightly accepts regulatory responsibility, licensing consultants is less necessary.

Continuing Education

Successful consultants continue their education. The knowledge explosion and increased specialization quickly outdate a consultant's usefulness. To stay on the leading edge of their profession, consultants attend university courses, seminars, lectures, and professional meetings. Current books, journals, magazines, and newspapers consume their reading time. Periodically, they meet with other consultants to discuss new trends, techniques, and experiences. In other words, effective consultants conscientiously upgrade their knowledge and skills.

Consultants need continuing education in two areas: technical expertise and consulting. Updating your technical specialty is usually easy. Most universities and professional associations offer regular programs.

Improving your consulting skills was previously difficult; however, several opportunities currently exist. Many universities now offer graduate courses in consulting. You can find these courses in business, engineering, education, psychology, architecture, social work, and medical schools or departments. Professional associations increasingly devote training time to consulting. (I have presented papers and led consulting workshops at the annual American Psychological Association convention.) The established management consulting associations such as Association of Consulting Management Engineers (ACME), Association of Management Consultants (AMC), Institute of Management Consultants (IMC), and Association of Internal Management Consultants (AIMC) hold training sessions across the country. Finally, you can apprentice or collaborate with other consultants. Working with others, you learn new methods and skills.

You should be cautious about some continuing education opportunities, such as newsletters, seminars by "a consultant's consultant," and recent associations that claim to be professional. Some current newsletters tend toward gossip and trendiness. Despite professional-sounding titles, they lack quality information and professional standards. Be wary of self-proclaimed "consultant's consultants." Through effective PR, these individuals have created a public image as experts in consulting. However, they're better at marketing than consulting. Through excellent marketing, they entice you to their seminars on consulting. Once at the seminar, you learn little about consulting. Instead they reveal advertising tricks. Then, they try selling you high-priced booklets, materials, and newsletters about the field.

In light of consulting's growth, new businesses and associations have formed to service consultants. They offer certificates, supplies, seminars, and other material. Some are get-rich-quick scams, while others provide a valuable service. Exercise caution. For example, no need currently exists for new professional associations. Too many already exist. However, service businesses are different. If they sell books by reputable authors from reputable publishers, this is a solid service, since most bookstores do not stock material on consulting. However, if their books are high-priced vanity press material, don't be fooled.

Since high-quality continuing education opportunities are available, critically appraise unconventional ones. As a consumer, question these resources, just as clients question you. In general, stay with legitimate sources such as universities and well-established professional associations to meet your continuing education needs.

Clients' Expectations

Each client has an image and reputation to protect. As the consultant, you reflect that image. Your behavior and effectiveness extend beyond the project results. They affect organizational politics and career mobility. Consequently, your demeanor can outweigh and hinder your effectiveness.

Clients criticize consultants who overlook these considerations. For instance, some consultants cling to one style of dress. Some prefer business suits; others wear corduroy pants with plaid shirts. Their dress becomes part of their image. Unfortunately, they do not adapt their dress to the consulting situation. In many cases, their clothes are inappropriate, such as jeans at a board meeting or a three-piece suit on the factory floor. This can embarrass the client. Late reports, gossiping with secretaries, arguing with client employees, tardiness, condescension, typographical errors, and poor performance all damage the client's image. Promote your client's welfare by behaving professionally. A professional always places the client's best interest above his or her own.

Solo Practitioner vs. Consulting Teams

Consulting alone or with others is a personal choice. Solo consultants enjoy complete autonomy from clients, schedules, policies, and profits. Team consultants work on larger, more complex projects. They benefit from the synergy of different members' backgrounds and approaches. They also share responsibility for the outcome. However, the price of increased stimulation and challenge is less autonomy and control.

Some consultants work both independently and with teams. The majority of their practice remains their own. Occasionally they undertake a project with other consultants, maximizing their benefits with minimal costs.

Scrutinize potential collaborators carefully. Working with them reflects on your image. Their ethics, reputation, expertise, and work standards should equal yours. Since team efforts require positive dynamics, assess your working relationship. In essence, build success into the project by carefully choosing coworkers.

Working with others forces you to reflect on your own practices. Team members normally challenge each other's assumptions, techniques, and solutions. This process results in new learning and improved effectiveness. You should plan either to work or to confer with other consultants periodically.

Internal vs. External Consultant

In 1979, I published an article, "Should You Have an Internal Consultant?" in the *Harvard Business Review.* This section is based on that article. It resulted from a national research study of internal consultants across the country, sponsored by the Association of Internal Management Consultants. Internal consultants, unlike externals who work with numerous unrelated organizations, work with only one company's divisions, subsidiaries, and new acquisitions. Appearing during the 1970s, internal consultants are gaining the credibility that management attributes to outside experts.

In many large organizations today, internal consultants perform many of the functions external consultants once performed. Internals aren't replacing externals. Companies sometimes turn to their internal consultants because they deliver high-quality service, rapid response, and accountability, all at lower cost to the company. However, the organization's political atmosphere can limit the internal's application. For example, when outside objectivity is required by government regulatory agencies, then internal consultants are insufficient.

A decision to use an internal or external consultant is best made in light of the advantages and disadvantages each brings to the particular situation. Neither is satisfactory for all consulting problems. In many cases, the skills of both internal and external consultants are similar. Each group possesses different attributes, however, such as timeliness or objectivity. Consequently, clients will use internal and external consultants in a complementary manner.

As internal consultants become more common, your role as the external consultant will necessarily change. To begin with, the internal consultant will replace the external one as the management generalist. As a result, the external consultant will become more and more expert in specialized areas. Clients will limit external consultant utilization to the following five situations:

- The organization cannot afford or does not need a full-time internal consultant.
- The organization requires extra help for a short period of time (such as for data collection) or on projects for which the internal person does not have time.
- The internal consultant or other company members do not possess either the specific expertise or broad experience needed for a particular situation.
- The political atmosphere surrounding the problem requires the appearance of objectivity or political neutrality.
- The executive desires an outside opinion on a major decision in addition to the internal consultant's recommendations.

The relationship between internal and external consultants will also change. They will work more in teams where each party contributes his or her own expertise and perspective. As internal consultants become the organizational filter through which external ones pass, both must become increasingly collegial and collaborative.

After the article appeared in the *Harvard Business Review,* an interesting reaction occurred. It received tremendous positive responses from solo external consultants and internal consultants. Only a few negative responses came—each from representatives of the large external consulting establishment. Unfortunately, they seemed to misinterpret the purpose of the article, which did not intend to threaten or denigrate external consultants in favor of internals. Instead, it reported on a phenomenon of interest to all consultants.

Most external consultants need not fear internal consultants. Only a few thousand businesses can afford them. In addition, they offer increased consulting opportunities. Since they are more attuned to problems and needs, they will generate more work. Finally, for consultants who do not want their own firm, internal consulting offers job opportunities.

Time Management*

Time management is critical for consultants. Consultants have two major resources: brainpower and time. Consultants must work hard to maximize these two resources. The first step in leveraging the time resource is learning how to prioritize activities, an important step for both managers and workers. Of the dozens of time-management philosophies and practices, most begin by categorizing one's work according to priority. Usually, employees are asked to divide the tasks at hand into one of four categories: 1) activities that are important and urgent, 2) activities that are important but not urgent, 3) activities that are not important but are urgent, and 4) activities that are neither important nor urgent. These four categories can help consultants prioritize tasks and activities along meaningful lines. Activities that are both important and urgent require immediate attention. Next come those activities that are important but not so urgent. Next you can attack those activities that are not very important but urgent, if there is either time or good reason to do so. This category generally includes activities that others want you to do. Finally, the not important–not urgent activities should be worked on if time allows or as a creative diversion.

Unfortunately, most people put everything into the important and urgent box, which means they have not done a very good job of planning. Or they may spend too much time on activities that are in the unimportant but urgent box. As a manager of a consulting firm, you must not be the cause of that poor planning. If you frequently give employees odd jobs, small, unimportant assignments, or last-minute, I-need-this-yesterday requests, they will always be in a reactive mode and never be able to move into the proactive mode of working on important but not urgent problems.

People spend 95 percent of their time in the urgent and important box. By then they are so exhausted that they may try to escape by working on things that are neither urgent nor important. Thus they may come in on a Saturday morning but, rather than working on the

* This section is adapted from *The Gold-Collar Worker* by Robert E. Kelley.

report that might be due, end up straightening their desks or reading magazines. This is simply because they are so worn out from pushing themselves on the important and urgent things all week long that they do not have the energy or the attention span to do anything but unimportant and nonurgent tasks. The ideal is to develop a mix that is comfortable for you as a manager or a worker. For many people, 30 percent of their time should be spent on important urgent activities, 60 percent on important but not urgent activities, and 10 percent on urgent but not important activities.

Avoiding Consultant Burnout

Consulting, like most professional jobs, can produce stress. Pace, complexity, and responsibility add up. Unless you cope with the stress, you can end up incapacitated.

Successful consultants utilize four methods to prevent burnout. First, they manage their time effectively. Too many commitments and poor scheduling often afflict professionals, weakening mental and physical defenses and leading to fatigue and illness. Good time management overcomes these situations. Plan for only 40 to 50 hours of work per week. In the face of your workload do not expand your hours. Rather, figure out more efficient ways to utilize your 40 to 50 hours. Remember that nothing fatigues like the persistence of an unfinished task. For help in this area, see the suggestions for further reading at the end of the chapter.

Managing client relationships also reduces stress. Clients often become very demanding, running you ragged. However, you don't have to hop on a plane every time your client wants to see you. Often you can handle the client's problem over the phone. Explain to each new client your scheduling practices, then communicate your schedule to them in advance. For instance, if one client's project will occupy two weeks next month, inform your other clients now. If they need you, you still have a month to work it in. If not, then at least they are informed of your upcoming unavailability. By managing your client relationships, you can schedule and adhere to your schedule.

Professional support systems also defend against burnout. You need colleagues with whom you can talk shop. These people provide the stimulation that prevents professional staleness. They also commiserate with you over the profession's trials and tribulations. If you need another opinion, you can call them. If you are in a jam or need assistance, they respond. By building this professional support system, you protect yourself against burnout.

A related insurance against stress is a healthy emotional support system. On the one hand, you must find ways to relax. Reading, physical exercise, naps, a drink, and friends all help let off steam and tension. On the other hand, you need intimate relationships that tolerate your emotional release, massage your ego, and build up your confidence. Also, this support system reduces your need to seek emotional comfort from the client.

Finally, reward yourself regularly. Feel satisfied at attaining your work goals. Acknowledging your success is important. External rewards are also necessary. Visible evidence such as vacations, time with friends, new clothes, a gourmet meal, and a movie physically reinforces your mental health. In addition, rewards make life more enjoyable.

How to Avoid Giving Away Free Advice

New consultants give away free consulting in their attempts to win a project or please the client. This occurs during the proposal or the sales presentation. By being too specific at this stage, however, you show the client how to do the work. Rather than provide a comprehensive technical proposal, demonstrate your understanding of the problem and your ability to handle it. Utilize flow charts, time lines, and procedure statements instead of giving away your methods. For example, indicate that you will conduct interviews in a certain sequence. You need not reveal the specific interview questions nor the rationale behind each question. Stress the benefits the client can expect from your approach.

Consultants also give away free consulting during diagnostic work. Some consultants perform diagnosis free as a loss leader. They hope that after they identify client needs, the client will hire them to address those needs. For example, a computer consulting company routinely identified its clients' computer needs and designed appropriate systems free of charge. The consultants expected the clients to engage them for implementation. Unfortunately, the clients took this information and hired other firms to install it. The computer consultants soon began charging for this diagnostic work.

Even if you charge for diagnosis, you can inadvertently perform free consulting. Often you will uncover many unrelated problems during diagnosis. The consultant's curiosity investigates these unrelated problems, exploring them and sometimes correcting them. If you are on a fixed-fee contract, time spent on unrelated problems comes out of your budget. Consequently, you perform services for which you did not negotiate payment. To prevent this situation, inform the client immediately of new problem areas. Then renegotiate your contract to include working on them.

Clients sometimes try to add on free consulting work. For example, they will say "While you're looking at X, would you also look at Y?" The catch is that you are doing X for a fixed fee. You should respond as follows: "I will be happy to look at Y. I'm confident that our work in X will aid our efforts in Y. In fact, I believe the combined work will benefit you as follows. . . . By the way, I will send you a letter outlining the new project's scope since Y is beyond our original agreement for X. In that way, you can authorize the additional expenditures." With this response, you acknowledge the client's request and receive just payment for your services.

Finally, consultants give away free consulting after the engagement. Frequently, the client will phone you continually after termination. They will seek your advice on the project or new problems, yet indicate that a visit is unnecessary. In these cases, you have two options. Either bill them for your time spent on the phone or secure a retainer for being at the client's disposal. Do not provide this service free.

This does not mean gouging your clients. Rather, you receive payment for services you provide. If you believe that you receive less than you give, then you develop negative feelings. This will affect your work quality and your client relationship. Avoid the problem by not giving away free consulting.

How to Hunt for Consulting Jobs

Not all consultants are prepared to open their own consulting firms. Perhaps you lack the experience or confidence. Perhaps you don't want an owner's responsibilities. In these cases, you have two options. Work for an external consulting operation or an internal consulting unit. In both situations you will learn consulting skills. External firms will teach you how to attract new clients, sell your services, and run a business. You will gain breadth of experience across many problems and industries. On the other hand, internal units give you depth in one industry and its problems. In addition, you will learn organizational politics intimately.

Before seeking employment, reread Chapter 2, since it outlines the requirements of most consulting positions. Also reread the section in Chapter 1, "Types of Consultants," to identify the various consulting opportunities. Try to match your interests with the firm's. For instance, if you work in a CPA firm, you are surrounded by and are usually a step-child to the accountants. The consulting work tends toward financial problems, except in the large, international CPA firms. If you consult with the Small Business Administration, you will work with ailing small businesses. Thus, although the job's requirements are similar for each consulting unit, the working environment is different.

Most novices wanting to get a foot in the consulting door will find the greatest opportunities in smaller external firms and large internal units. These will hire apprentices, whereas most other consulting units expect fully developed consultants. At the same time, the pay is lower for novices. Yet, you can then work your way up the consulting ladder.

Job hunting in consulting is similar to other fields. You must meet the job requirements, have job contacts, and then sell yourself in the interview. Evidence of consulting experience or potential is important. In many cases, you might have to create your own job. For example, suppose you are an expert in university administration. Very few consulting firms have addressed that market. You could propose to develop that new market for a firm. In fact, if you can demonstrate your ability to cultivate a new market profitably, most firms will hire you. Evidence that you can carry your own weight and add to the firm's coffers powerfully increases your chances of employment.

With consulting's growth, job opportunities are increasing. You should have little trouble either working for someone else or establishing your own firm.

How to Exit Consulting for Other Opportunities

Some consultants choose not to stay in consulting for their entire careers. Some decide to go into industry or academia. Others start their own entrepreneurial ventures. A few choose to recycle through consulting several times throughout their careers. Such people want to gain first-hand experience working in an industry, such as electronics, or perform a certain function, such as finance, before consulting. After consulting for several years, they feel a need to reexperience an industry or function simply for a change of pace or to keep a proper perspective. They find professional and personal value in alternating between the client and consultant role.

No one should feel embarrassed about leaving consulting, just as no one should feel bad about leaving any field. It is a sign neither of failure nor of success. Changing jobs and careers is just that—a change. Some insecure people like to put down others who become consultants by claiming that they did it only because they could not find a job. These same insecure people will use your exit from consulting to claim that you could not succeed there either. Don't let their insecurity interfere with your plans. You know your reasons, and decent, reasonable people will respect them. I know several successful consultants who have left the field for a wide variety of reasons, ranging from having made so much money they no longer needed to work to wanting a job with limited travel.

If you decide to leave consulting, you are generally in a very good job-hunting position. For starters, you will have an active network of colleagues and clients that you can access for your job search. Let people know you are looking for a set of new challenges and responsibilities. Don't be bashful, because 70 percent of all jobs are found through referrals.

Also, you will have a set of project reports that demonstrate your competence in your field of expertise. These can be shown to prospective employers as evidence of the value you will bring to their company. Remember to protect client confidentiality by deleting names and proprietary information.

Use your satisfied clients as references about your skills. Besides your expertise, they will have experienced your selling and marketing abilities, your interpersonal skills, your writing and presentation talents, your work habits, and your ability to perform. All of these are important to prospective employers. Satisfied clients are often more credible references because they do not have the vested interest in you that a former employer might have.

Choosing a new employer is often much easier after having been a consultant. Since you will have seen a variety of work settings, types of managers, and corporate cultures, you will be in a good position to know which fit best with your needs. Do not overlook these experiences as a source of data for your job hunt and job decision.

Once you do leave consulting, make sure you contact your clients and colleagues to inform them where to find you and what you are doing. You never know what interesting opportunities might pop up one month or three years from now. If people do not know your interests or whereabouts, you stand to lose those opportunities.

Additional Sources of Help

Getting Things Done. E. Bliss. New York: Charles Scribner's Sons, 1982.

How to Get Control of Your Time and Life. A. Lakein. New York: Signet, 1974.

The Internal Consultant. A. DeKom. American Management Association, 1967.

"Is the Internal Management Consultant in Your Future?" A. P. Lappas. In *Ideas for Management.* Association for Systems Management, 1979.

The Relaxation Book. G. Rosen. Englewood Cliffs, N.J.: Prentice-Hall, 1977.

The Relaxation Response. H. Benson. New York: Avon Books, 1975.

Stress Power. R. Anderson. New York: Human Science Press, 1978.

Theory in Practice. C. Argyris and D. Schon. San Francisco: Jossey-Bass, 1974.

Type A Behavior and Your Heart. M. Friedman and R. Rosenman. Greenwich, Conn.: Fawcett-Crest, 1974.

Conclusion

The Future of Consulting

This book has equipped you with the knowledge necessary to launch a successful consulting practice and to conduct effective consulting projects. The consultant or would-be consultant can integrate this knowledge with technical expertise. Prior to the publication of this book, prospective consultants may have lacked information that barred them access to consulting careers. Now you have a ready reference to guide your consulting efforts.

For the consumer, you now know how consultants operate. This will make you wiser consumers. Primarily, you now can supplement a consulting project rather than interfere with it. For example, by understanding the organizational conditions necessary for implementing recommendations, you can help the consultant create those conditions. By understanding consultants, you also better protect yourself from inept ones.

Consulting has a future. Its growth has just begun. It is an infant industry tied to our infant information society. In fact, consulting's current growth parallels our transition from an industrial to an information society.

In an information society, information is power. The society values mental, not physical effort. In our agrarian society, land was power. In our industrial society, capital, assets, and products were power. For the future, government, business, and other consumers will seek, pay, and value people with information. Consultants are people with information.

In the information society the distinction between expert, consultant, and decision maker will grow. Initially, the expert will produce the information. Our information is expanding geometrically. For example, computers already perform the work of five trillion people. Experts will increasingly specialize; they will know more and more about less and less. Moreover, "information factories" will regularly produce similar types of information. These will replace our industrial factories.

Consultants will either package the specialized information into useful societal applications or make judgments about it. In turn, the consultants will sell their information to consumers. Consultants also will specialize, being on the leading edge of the information explosion.

Finally, all this specialized information will bombard the decision maker, making the job more complex. He or she will need information to aid the decision-making process. But since no one can master every specialty, the decision maker becomes a generalist, relying on consultants for information. Effective handling of consultants will mark the successful decision maker.

Future changes will simplify consulting. Home computers will allow you to create, package, and sell information from your home. Interactive cable TV will eliminate much travel. Through these two tools, you will have access to clients internationally.

As the growth of consulting continues, the industry will move through its life cycle. During infancy, numerous consulting firms will form to capitalize on the opportunities. In the year 2000, the consulting industry's adolescence will begin. The strongest firms will grow, expanding market share. Consolidation of firms will occur in order to compete. During the early part of the 21st century the industry will mature. In each major consulting specialty, three to ten firms will dominate the market. However, due to the computer and interactive television, small, "cottage" consultants will find and maintain sufficient market niches. Consequently, consulting will offer numerous small business opportunities even though a few firms dominate.

I am frequently asked if we need consultants. My answer is yes. Every wise leader has used consultants. In an information society only the wise will survive. They will heed Andrew Carnegie's epitaph, "Here lies a man who knew how to enlist into his service people better than himself." In fact, due to the consultant's unique position between the expert and the consumer, he or she will increasingly shape how people survive.

Appendix

Sources of Information About Consulting

Professional Associations

AAHC—
   American Ass'n of Hospital Consultants
   2341 Jefferson Davis Highway
   Suite 830
   Arlington, VA 22202

AAMLC—
   American Ass'n of Medico Legal Consultants
   2200 Benjamin Franklin Pkwy.
   Philadelphia, PA 19130

AAPBC—
   American Ass'n of Professional Bridal Consultants
   42 Woodridge Circle
   West Hartford, CT 06107

AAPC—
   American Ass'n of Political Consultants
   Suite 1406
   1101 North Calvert St.
   Baltimore, MD 21202

ACCCE—

>   Ass'n of Consulting Chemists & Chemical Engineers, Inc.
>   50 East 41st St.
>   New York, NY 10017

ACEC—

>   American Consulting Engineers Council
>   Suite 802
>   1015 15th Street, N.W.
>   Washington, D.C. 20005

ACF—

>   Ass'n of Consulting Foresters
>   Box 369
>   Yorktown, VA 23690

ACME—

>   Association of Consulting Management Engineers
>   230 Park Ave.
>   New York, NY 10017

AERC—

>   Ass'n of Executive Recruiting Consultants, Inc.
>   30 Rockefeller Plaza
>   New York, NY 10020

AFCCE—

>   Ass'n of Federal Communications Consulting Engineers
>   525 Woodward Ave.
>   Bloomfield Hills, MI 48013

AHCC—

>   Academy of Health Care Consultants
>   Suite 3342
>   875 North Michigan Ave.
>   Chicago, IL 60611

AICPA-MAS—

>   American Institute of Certified Public Accountants,
>   Management Advisory Services Division
>   1211 Avenue of the Americas
>   New York, NY 10036

AIMC—

>   Association of Internal Management Consultants
>   P.O. Box 304
>   East Bloomfield, NY 14443

AMC—

>   Association of Management Consultants
>   811 East Wisconsin Avenue
>   Milwaukee, WI 53202

APA—

American Psychological Association—Division of Consulting Psychologists
1200 17th Street, N.W.
Washington, D.C. 20036

APEC—

Automated Procedures for Engineering Consultants, Inc.
Miami Valley Tower
Suite M-15
Dayton, OH 45402

APMHC—

Ass'n of Professional Material Handling Consultants
1548 Tower Rd.
Winnetka, IL 60093

APS—

Ass'n of Productivity Specialists
One Illinois Center
Chicago, IL 60601

ASAC—

American Society of Agricultural Consultants
Suite 470, Enterprise Center
8301 Greensboro Drive
McLean, VA 22102

ASCA—

American Soc. of Consulting Arborists
12 Lakeview Ave.
Milltown, NJ 08850

ASEC—

Ass'n of Consulting Engineers of Canada
130 Albert St.
Suite 616
Ottawa, Ontario K1P 5G4

ASCP—

American Society of Consultant Pharmacists
2300 9th St., South
Arlington, VA 22264

ASCP—

American Soc. of Consulting Planners
1717 N. St., N.W.
Washington, D.C. 20036

CABC—

Canadian Ass'n of Broadcast Consultants
2639 Portage Ave.
Winnipeg, Manitoba R3J 0P7

CAMC—
> Canadian Ass'n of Management Consultants
> 1243 Islington Ave. #615
> Toronto, Ontario M8X IY9

FFCS—
> Food Facilities Consultants Soc.
> 135 Glenlawn Ave.
> Sea Cliff, NY 11579

FCSI—
> Foodservice Consultants Soc. Internat'l
> 1400 Pickwick Ave.
> Glenview, IL 60025

IABPC—
> Internat'l Ass'n of Book Publishing Consultants
> 52 Vanderbilt Ave.
> New York, NY 10017

IMC—
> Institute of Management Consultants
> 19 West 44th Street
> Room 810
> New York, NY 10036

NAFC—
> Nat'l Ass'n of Financial Consultants
> Suite 114
> 11059 East Bethany Dr.
> Aurora, CO 80014

NAMAC—
> Nat'l Ass'n of Merger and Acquisitions Consultants
> Suite 282
> 4255 LBJ Freeway
> Dallas, TX 75234

NAPCA—
> Nat'l Ass'n of Pension Consultants & Administration
> Suite 300
> Three Piedmont Center
> Atlanta, GA 30305

NAPENA—
> Nat'l Ass'n of Public Employer Negotiators and
>   Administrators
> 1400 N. State Parkway
> Chicago, IL 60610

NCAC—
> Nat'l Council of Acoustical Consultants, Inc.
> 66 Morris Ave.
> Springfield, NJ 07081

NCPSF—
>   Nat'l Council of Professional Services Firm
>   Suite 1200
>   1730 Pennsylvania Ave., N.W.
>   Washington, D.C. 20006

NICMC—
>   Nat'l Institute of Certified Moving Consultants
>   222 West Adams St.
>   Chicago, IL 60606

NPC—
>   Nat'l Personnel Consultants
>   Suite 1702
>   Pennsylvania Bldg.
>   Philadelphia, PA 19102

MCDAM—
>   Managerial Consultation Division of the Academy of
>   Management
>   College of Business
>   University of Southern Florida
>   Tampa, FL 33620

PMI—
>   Project Management Institute
>   Box 43
>   Drexel Hill, PA 19026

PRSA—
>   Public Relations Soc. of America, Inc.
>   845 Third Ave.
>   New York, NY 10022

RAAA—
>   Relocation Assistance Ass'n of America
>   950 17th St.
>   Denver, CO 80202

SMCAF—
>   Soc. of Medical Consultants to the Armed Forces
>   Box 4033
>   Harrisburg, PA 17111

SPBC—
>   Soc. of Professional Business Consultants
>   221 North LaSalle St.
>   Chicago, IL 60601

SPMC—
>   Soc. of Professional Management Consultants, Inc.
>   205 West 89th St.
>   New York, NY 10024

Index